MELANCHOLIES
OF KNOWLEDGE

SUNY Series, The Margins of Literature
Mihai I. Spariosu, Editor

MELCHANOLIES OF KNOWLEDGE

Literature
in the Age of Science

EDITED BY

Margery Arent Safir

State University of New York Press

Published by
State University of New York Press, Albany

© 1999 State University of New York

For information, address State University of New York
Press, State University Plaza, Albany, N.Y., 12246

Production by Diane Ganeles   1 8 ō 3 5̄ ō b ч 2 ๒
Marketing by Nancy Farrell

Library of Congress Cataloging-in-Publication Data

Mélancolies du savoir. English.
    Melancholies of knowledge : literature in the age of science /
edited by Margery Arent Safir.
        p.   cm. — (SUNY series, the margins of literature)
    Includes bibliographical references and index.
    ISBN 0-7914-3973-9 (alk. paper). — ISBN 0-7914-3974-7 (pbk. :
alk. paper)
    1. Rio, Michel—Criticism and interpretation.   2. Rio, Michel—
Knowledge—Science.   3. Science in literature.   4. Scientists in
literature.   5. Literature and science.   I. Arent Safir, Margery,
1947-   . II. title. III. Series.
PQ2678.I563Z713   1999
843'.914—dc21   98-6224
                                                        CIP

10 9 8 7 6 5 4 3 2 1

CONTENTS

Preface
vii

Acknowledgments
ix

Introduction
Margery Arent Safir
1

Editor's Note
27

1. Out of Time in the Dreaming Jungles
Stephen Jay Gould
33

2. "It is not safe to know"
Margery Arent Safir
47

3. A Disenchanted Enchanter
Michel Pastoureau
77

4. Cosmoses and Metaphor
James Ritter
89

5. Topographies
James Swenson
109

6. The Temptation of the Last Man
Jean-Michel Rabaté
129

7. The Aztec *tlacuilo* and the Other
Joaquín Galarza
149

8. The Mind's *I*
Christian Metz
161

Appendices
181

Contributors
193

Index
197

PREFACE

Literature is the mother of matricidal daughters whose names are "natural sciences" and "social sciences."[1] The work of the human mind, with its meandering and its logical and fantastic inventions, was literature's field of observation until first natural and social philosophy, then, in the last century, specialized scientific disciplines dispossessed literature of them. At the heart of this collection is the question of whether literature can, in a world dominated by the sciences, regain a central place in intellectual discourse. This volume is about reading and cognition and the mutual contagion of disciplines, about the being who knows and the being who feels, in other words, about the primitive dream that was the foundation of literature when that old couple, knowledge and imagination, were one, the explication of the world in an encyclopedic sense. Natural sciences and social sciences join literary studies here in an experiment in interdisciplinary criticism. The experiment was born of matricide, and in inviting a number of the perpetrators of the crime, my modest proposal was to defy the laws of gravity and the arrow of time and to try to put "mother" back together again.

Biologist Stephen Jay Gould, medieval historian Michel Pastoureau, physicist James Ritter, anthropologist Joaquín Galarza, semiologist Christian Metz, literary analysts James Swenson, Jean-Michel Rabaté, and myself speak to one another across a body of fiction. By applying a method to a test case, I am targeting the simple question with which I began: Can literature be resituated at the center of intellectual discourse in the age of science?

M.A.S.

---

[1] Michel Rio, *Mélancolie Nord* (1982; reprint, Paris: Editions du Seuil, Points Roman, 1986), 128.

ACKNOWLEDGMENTS

I would like to say a personal word about the contributors to this volume who, working at the highest levels in their respective disciplines, nonetheless agreed to participate in an experiment. Great minds, however occupied they might be with their own projects, are always open to a new perspective on knowledge. I express my gratitude to them, not only for their essays, but for having demonstrated by their generosity that the world of academia can be exactly what it should be.

My thanks go as well to my colleagues from The American University of Paris, Celeste Schenck, who gave me the benefit of her extensive editorial experience; and Daniel Gunn, who lent me his grammarian's eagle eye; also, to my former students Michael Johnson and Ivy Mills, whose bilingual proofreading was meticulous and invaluable. I am grateful to Catherine Goldstein, of France's Centre National de la Recherche Scientifique (CNRS), who examined the introduction with her unforgiving demands of a mathematician; to Stanley Cavell of Harvard University for his wise counsel on that very particular genre, the essay; and to the French Ministry of Culture, whose grant permitted George Craig's splendid translation of several of the essays in this collection. Finally, I would like to thank Acquisitions Editor James Peltz and Production Editor Diane Ganeles of SUNY Press, and to acknowledge my special appreciation to Mihai I. Spariosu of the University of Georgia; it is due to his resolve that this book, first published in French by Editions du Seuil, came to appear in English in this expanded and revised edition.

For my mother, Frances Feldman Arent (1915–1996)

M.A.S.

INTRODUCTION

Margery Arent Safir

Any alteration in man's physical position in the universe must correspond to an alteration in his intellectual and affective position, thus of literary discourse, which is the sum of all these coordinates.[1]

Michel Rio

Alterations

A generation of writers was born into the world according to Einstein and Bohr, the world of the new physics whose questions and concepts and names, let alone proofs, the old physics never knew or imagined. This world has black holes and antimatter, quasars and neutron stars. At the subatomic level, Heisenberg's uncertainty principle rules, with the resulting absence of absolute predictability, and experiments, thought- or real, from Einstein to Aspect, test theories of quantum "ghosts." This world allows for Schrödinger's reading of quantum measurement, which makes whether a cat exposed to cyanide is dead or alive dependent upon the observer, and for Everett's tree of multiple realities, parallel universes that are physically disconnected but equally real, and for the notion of quantum-mechanical nonlocality, a kind of permanent memory or mysterious imprint and

---

[1] Unless otherwise noted, all translations in the introduction are my own.

instantaneous communication between once-linked particles, even when they are separated far in space.[2] In the old physics, Newtonian theory, every atom moves along a trajectory that is uniquely determined by the forces that act on it, forces that in turn are determined by other atoms in a rigid network of cause and effect. Newtonian mechanics is seen as permitting, in principle, the accurate prediction of everything that will ever happen, from the tiniest jiggle of a molecule to the explosion of a galaxy. As Pierre-Simon Laplace explains it, if a mind could know all the forces of nature in any given instant, the future could be read like the past; before the observer's eyes would be the totality of history.[3]

But where is "history" in a world in which space and time are not absolute and universal but rather elastic, not flat and obeying the usual rules of Euclidean geometry, but rather curved or warped; not fixed but rather dynamic, "stretching, shrinking, even stopping altogether at a singularity";[4] a world where one cannot speak of the past or the future, where time no longer "passes" but is laid out as part of a four-dimensional structure, space-time? What happens to the individual, made of history and of memory? What happens to morality in the absence of predictable cause and effect? Or to such ancient debates as free will versus determinism? On the one hand, through quantum theory, the new physics would seem to prescribe for the individual observer an extraordinary role, one never dreamed of by Newton: *influencing* the very nature of physical reality. On the other hand, there is relativity, banishing the notion of universal time, of an absolute division into past, present, and future, conjuring up an image of a future that in some sense already exists, "and so cuts from under our feet the victory won with the help of the quantum factor. If the future is *there*," physicist Paul Davies asks, "does it not mean that we are powerless to alter it?" (Davies, 135).

Conceptual changes of this magnitude obviously affect, as they were affected by, society at large. A way of thinking, an entire vision of the universe and of the self, is altered; the questions posed, and the language in which they are posed, must be invented or reinvented. "The common

---

[2] Some of the concepts to which I refer are a source of debate among physicists themselves, and "mainstream" physicists are quite disparaging of many of the stranger notions put forth. My intention, obviously, is not to enter into the debate of quantum theory but only to catalog some of the ideas that it has put into circulation.

[3] Pierre-Simon Laplace, *Essai philosophique sur les probabilités*, 5th ed. (1825; reprint, Paris: Christian Bourgois, 1986), 32-33.

[4] Paul Davies, *God and the New Physics* (1983; reprint, London: Penguin, 1990), 121, 123.

division of the world into subject and object, inner world and outer world, body and soul is no longer adequate," Werner Heisenberg insists.[5] In effect, one could claim that the new physics relegates to "antiquity" the very notion of "third person" and "first person." Or as Bertrand Russell observes, "It has begun to seem that matter, like the Cheshire Cat, is becoming gradually diaphanous and nothing is left but the grin, caused, presumably, by amusement at those who still think it is there."[6] And I have not even touched upon the implications of fields such as biotechnology, genetics, cybernetics or, for that matter, computer science that in itself has changed our very notion of an educated person, no longer measured by the books in one's library. French author Michel Rio has rebuked literature and literary critics, urging them "to stop pouring out the kind of specialized stupidity that says 'After Proust, Kafka or Joyce, we can't write the same way,' and sooner say 'After Copernicus, Newton, Darwin, Planck or Einstein, . . .' and by this means establish a new relation between the writer and the world, solitude and the collective, or reawaken an ancient one."[7]

That relation, new or ancient, is suggested by Rio through a hired killer. The protagonist of his 1991 novel *Faux Pas* enters the "safehouse" of his prey and, while waiting for the man he will execute on contract, undertakes an examination of the library. The organization is simple: physics and astronomy, followed by biology and ethology, then history, and, finally, literature; this order, we are told, offers "a fairly representative sample":

> It starts from the broadest discipline, from the point of view of the scope, space and time of its object of study, and finishes in the narrowest, each ensemble containing in principle that which follows: physics, biology, history, literature. . . . For moving back up the chain, one can say that the imaginary is no more than

---

[5] Werner Heisenberg, *Physics and Philosophy* (New York: Harper & Row, 1958), cited in Davies (112). Quantum theorist David Bohm makes further observations along these lines in Bohm, *Wholeness and the Implicate Order* (London: Routledge & Kegan Paul, 1980).

[6] Bertrand Russell, cited in Alastair Rae, *Quantum Physics: Illusion or Reality?* (1986; reprint, Cambridge: Cambridge University Press, Canto, 1995), 67.

[7] Michel Rio, "L'essentiel et l'accessoire," in *Rêve de logique: essais critiques* (Paris: Editions du Seuil, 1992), 88.

one of the cultivated fields of consciousness, consciousness an accident of the animate, and the animate an episode of matter.[8]

The fiction with which I am concerned in this volume climbs that chain. It explores the fields of culture, consciousness, and matter and speculates on the shifting levels of relation among them.

Relation and Residue

The word "relation" is key here, and is implicit in my introducing a kind of fiction through reference to matricide by the natural and social sciences and the impact on thought of the new physics. The question in all of this is the relation between bodies of knowledge and imagination, and this leads me back to a specific moment in contemporary intellectual formation. France in the 1960s and 1970s, a "new" perspective takes hold: structuralist theories and method, the basic tenets of which had been laid out in linguistics by Ferdinand de Saussure a half century before, then by Roman Jakobson in the 1920s, become the central intellectual issues of debate.[9] Two phenomena within the structuralist enterprise particularly color the period: after the schismatic cloistering of disciplines born of scientific specialization in the mid- to late-nineteenth century, the embracing of an interdisciplinary perspective, eloquently illustrated by the varied disciplines of the leading structuralists themselves; and the "sciencing" of the humanities, in reality a subphenomenon of interdisciplinarity and inseparable from structuralism's being a *method*.

"Sciencing" comes now to social anthropology, where G. P. Murdock and Claude Lévi-Strauss insist upon the importance of the "mathematization" of the discipline. Both use the method of models, Murdock with simple statistical models, and Lévi-Strauss with more complex algebraic

---

[8] Rio, *Faux Pas* (1991; reprint, Paris: Editions du Seuil, Points Roman, 1993), 18.

[9] As early as 1907 Saussure had called for the "scientific" study of language based upon its systematic nature and had defined linguistic elements in terms of relation and function. Jakobson was already employing the term *structuralism* and calling for the scientific study of language as a system in 1929. For ease and simplicity, I have limited my general references in these paragraphs to one of the standard texts on structuralism, contemporary to the movement I discuss: *Introduction to Structuralism*, ed. Michael Lane (New York: Basic Books, 1970). The collection includes essays by, among others, Roland Barthes, Claude Lévi-Strauss, Jakobson, and Saussure.

ones. Lévi-Strauss, moreover, will hold that the most important line of future advance in the field, the development of laws of transformation, can come about only if anthropologists are able to formulate their structures algebraically. Similarly, other scholars, Georges Guilbaud and H. Hoffman among them, begin applying logico-mathematical techniques and expressions to complex social phenomena (Lane, 34). In linguistics, Noam Chomsky's generative grammar puts forth the theory of an innate, genetically transmitted and determined mechanism that acts as a structuring force in man, a theory that finds general, if implicit, acceptance among structuralists such as Lévi-Strauss, Jakobson, Jean Piaget and, in biology, François Jacob. Of course, linguistics also provides the impetus for the literary domain, where it manifests itself in an attempt to be treated as a science of language applicable to languages that *use* language, that is, to literature. Criticism does not deal with the world but with discourse. Roland Barthes writes: "criticism is discourse upon a discourse; it is a second language, or a *metalanguage* (as the logicians would say), which operates on a first language (or *language object*)."[10] When Barthes speaks of *jeux de figures*, the conceptual equivalent of Lévi-Strauss's models, and of *combinatoire*, a calculus of combinations, "analogous to laws of transformation" (Lane, 37), literature is being "scienced": "mathematics" comes to literary study. Edgar Allan Poe is proven right: out of mathematics, poetry is born.[11]

The euphoria does not last. Reactions, a number of which structuralism had foreseen, and even accounted for within its own methodological framework, set in. By the 1980s, in academia, poststructuralism, then deconstruction, have taken firm hold. But there are residues, and structuralism's underlying tenets have fallout which, in my view, has been underestimated in the development of a certain kind of fiction produced in the following decades. The fallout takes the form of a number of easily observable cultural events, any discussion of which risks painfully belaboring the obvious. My tour of the terrain will be brief, and determined by my specific concern, the production of fiction.

---

[10] Roland Barthes, "What Is Criticism?," in *Critical Essays*, trans. Richard Howard (Evanston, Ill.: Northwestern University Press, 1972), 258.
[11] See, for example, Edgar Allan Poe, "The Philosophy of Composition," in *Edgar Allan Poe: Essays and Reviews* (New York: The Library of America, 1984), especially 15–16. Originally published in *Graham's Magazine* (April 1846).

History, philosophy, and science dwelled together comfortably, or at least cohabited, before their separation into specialized disciplines in the mid- to late-nineteenth century. In the aftermath of the structuralist debate, the dialogue among them reopens in a different form and finds its welcome not in France but primarily in the Anglo-Saxon world. As an academic discipline, that new dialogue bears the label History and Philosophy of Science, its name evoking a trinity.[12] As a field of study it is interdisciplinary, opening up in a number of directions by bringing together historians, philosophers, and scientists, albeit at times to debate which of them should be working on the history and the philosophy of science. In practice it stresses the relation between general culture and scientific development, the relation between John Stuart Mill or William Whewell's choice of scientific models of the universe and their political philosophy, for example, or the relation between the discovery of electromagnetism and the rise of Romanticism. Of central significance is the fact that this field creates awareness of the total interdependence of cultural phenomena in the development of what for long were taken to be "objective" and exact sciences. Stephen Jay Gould, who in addition to evolutionary biology and geology teaches the history of science—a fact wholly pertinent, I believe, to his success as a popular science writer—insists on this:

> All great theories are expansive, and all notions so rich in scope and implication are underpinned by visions about the nature of things. You may call these visions "philosophy," or "metaphor," or "organizing principle," but one thing they are surely not—they are not simple inductions from observed facts of the natural world.[13]

History and Philosophy of Science also recognizes specifically the importance of language in scientific discovery. Discovery brings with it a need to name, a need for coinage (as a philologist Whewell was regularly consulted by scientists for this purpose); and persuasion, or argumentation, based on the use of written language, can play the critical role in the fate

---

[12] History and Philosophy of Science is the British subject title. In the United States it is often simply called "History of Science."

[13] Stephen Jay Gould, *Time's Arrow, Time's Cycle: Myth and Metaphor in the Discovery of Geological Time* (1987; reprint, London: Penguin, 1988), 9.

of a theory. "Science self-selects for poor writing," Gould notes, and serves up an example in nineteenth-century geology's uniformitarianism-catastrophism debate (Gould, 107). While defending James Hutton, on the one hand, against the unkind charge of being the worst writer in the history of science, Gould notes that the standard exposition of Hutton's theories, both then and now, comes not from Hutton's own book, but from that of his friend John Playfair, a superb writer. Charles Lyell, on the other hand, trained as a barrister, owes his reputation, and the success of his uniformitarianism concept of geology, as much to his mastery of language in brilliantly arguing his theories as to the theories themselves. Rhetoric, textual analysis, questions of style, and modes of expression are recognized in History and Philosophy of Science as crucial to the life of scientific concepts. "Literary" considerations are thus brought to the unfoldment of scientific theory.[14]

Language matters in another direction as well, for contemporary History and Philosophy of Science is largely responsible for making scientific material accessible to nonscientists, not only because of its global perspective, but because it talks about exact science in the languages of both the social sciences and the humanities. This is a form of translation, and translation is a good thing. But its perils are well known: *traduttore, traditore,* and this kind of interdisciplinary "translation" opens up a Pandora's box of questions regarding loss of meaning, or the exactitude of meaning, when concepts are translated from the unambiguous language of mathematical equation into the murkier world of the word. Nonetheless, this translation is a critical feature of the decades that follow the apogee of structuralism, and if History and Philosophy of Science resides in universities, it springs off-campus what I call "upscale popularization," or science as best-seller. A scattering of names suffices to illustrate the phenomenon: in addition to Gould, John D. Barrow, Jean-Pierre Changeux, Paul Davies, Richard Dawkins, Freeman Dyson, Martin Gardner, Stephen W. Hawking, Douglas R. Hofstadter, John H. Holland, François Jacob, Robert Jastrow, Steve Jones, Stuart A. Kauffman, Alan Lightman, Jacques Monod, Roger Penrose, Steven Pinker, Alain Prochiantz, Hubert Reeves, Carl Sagan, Isabelle Stengers, Lewis Thomas, Jean-Didier Vincent, Steven Weinberg, Edward O. Wilson. All are scientists writing in nonscientific language and for educated, but not necessarily

---

[14] Gould's own superb science writing is subjected to rhetorical analysis in *Understanding Scientific Prose,* ed. Jack Selzer (Madison: University of Wisconsin Press, 1993).

specialized, publics, opening up to them topics that fifty years ago remained in the closed domain of experts. They are published by commercial presses as opposed to university presses or journals (where they publish their scholarly work). Their topics range from the earth and life sciences to physics and cosmology to history of science to sociopolitical essays, and their book titles are illuminating: *Late Night Thoughts on Listening to Mahler's Ninth Symphony* or *The Enchanted Loom* or *La Chair et le Diable* (Flesh and the Devil).[15]

Within this upscale popularization, a subcategory should be reserved for a new class of speculator scientists. To the question "What do you believe?" Molière's free-thinking Dom Juan answers: "I believe that two and two make four."[16] These speculator scientists, usually found in quantum physics or cosmology, that is, in disciplines where large quantities of observational data are less available than in others, cannot offer such a reply today, and for some, the frontiers between logic and reverie begin to blur. Cosmologists, faced with the unimaginably immense, pushed back to the origin of the material universe, cannot answer the question of original cause, and are reduced to repeating that time and space being born with the "Big Bang," physicists do not speak of "before." Yet the question cannot be escaped so easily, and some make leaps of faith, sound like poets moving toward the cosmological, and, together with philosophers, muse in print as well as in private about the existence of God, in works such as *God and the Astronomers*, *God and the New Physics*, *Dieu et la science* (God and Science); *The Tao of Physics*, *Beyond the Cosmos*, *La Mélodie secrète* (The Secret Melody); or *Quarks, Chaos and Christianity*.[17] Quantum physicists, partaking of the bizarre subatomic world that I evoked at the

---

[15] Lewis Thomas, *Late Night Thoughts on Listening to Mahler's Ninth Symphony* (New York: Bantam Books, 1984); Robert Jastrow, *The Enchanted Loom: The Mind in the Universe* (New York: Simon & Schuster, 1981); Jean-Didier Vincent, *La Chair et le Diable* (Paris: Odile Jacob, 1996).

[16] Molière, *Dom Juan*, in *Oeuvres complètes*, ed. Georges Mongrédien (Paris: Flammarion, GF, 1965), 2:382.

[17] Robert Jastrow, *God and the Astronomers* (New York: Norton, 1978); Davies, *God and the New Physics*; Jean Guitton, Grichka Bogdanov and Igor Bogdanov, *Dieu et la science* (Paris: Grasset, 1991); Fritjof Capra, *The Tao of Physics* (Boston: Shambhala, 1975); Hugh Ross, *Beyond the Cosmos: What Recent Discoveries in Astronomy and Physics Reveal About the Nature of God* (Colorado Springs: Navpress, 1996); Xuan Thuan Trinh, *La Mélodie secrète* (Paris: Fayard, 1988); John C. Polkinghorne, *Quarks, Chaos and Christianity: Questions to Science and Religion* (New York: Crossroad, 1995).

beginning of this introduction, observe and accept events that in another century would have been taken as the equivalent of declaring that 2+2≠4; for instance, that something can be both a wave and a particle, or at least sometimes behave like each. Forced to deal with such facts, faced with the unimaginably minute, deprived of total predictability, or freed from it, some sound as if they were speaking from through the looking-glass (Lewis Carroll himself, of course, was a man of science, a mathematician, a professor of symbolic logic). "Da Vinci was both a prodigious scientist and an artistic genius!" affirms the artist Laurence Richardson in a contemporary French novel. "Da Vinci, like all his contemporaries, did not know very much. At the very least, his knowledge allowed a considerable dose of imagination," responds the scientist Henry Sterne.[18] Today, for a section of modern physicists, what they *do* know, as much as what they do not know, opens up an enormous field for imagination. Again, language is informative, and when coinage is necessary, where the new physicists have not formed neologisms based on Latin or Greek (*muons, hadrons, mesons, pions, baryons*), they have had recourse to terms such as *quark, charm, beauty, truth*, appellations that sound almost fanciful.

Whether informative or speculative, the upscale popularization of science has today assumed functions once belonging to other disciplines, not the least among them a central function previously held by literature, that of holding the "true" keys to the world and its mysteries.[19] Contemporary science has become a veritable mythology of knowledge, and this mythified science is today looked to for clear answers that were once sought in ancient elucidating fictions. The authors of these scientific works have never made claims to such clarity. On the contrary, they as often multiply as resolve fundamental philosophical questions, working with a kind of knowledge which, built upon its own ruins, flaunts the instability of theory and accepts the paradoxes, at times the contradictions, of experimental evidence. But it matters little that the legend is contradicted by its own actors. Scientific publication has become the preeminent space for discovery, possesses the strongest hold on denotation, and constitutes the core of modern philosophy by reason of the epistemological and

---

[18] Rio, *Les Jungles pensives* (1985; reprint, Paris: Editions du Seuil, Points Roman, 1989), 53. Cited from *Dreaming Jungles*, trans. William R. Carlson (New York: Pantheon Books, 1987), 47–48.

[19] The ideas expressed in this paragraph follow Rio, "L'essentiel et l'accessoire," in *Rêve de logique*, especially 83–84.

metaphysical questions which, wittingly or not, it raises. Without hesitation I state my conviction that the literature that is discussed in this volume's collected essays would not have been the same had this upscale popularization not made of scientific publication the privileged space of discovery.

But there is also downscale popularization, finding its element not in universities and bookstores but in the mass media, and here too there is high and low. On the high end are daily press reports of advances and discoveries in science and medicine; weekly health and science pages in the general written press; educational television where David Attenborough introduces life on earth, Jacques Cousteau life underwater, Carl Sagan walks through a larger-than-life model of the brain, and cartoon characters initiate young children into the mysteries of science. On the low end, the downside of downscale, is the unbridled mediazation of science, not science as best-seller but the selling of science, or science for selling, its habitat the readily for-profit mass media and T-shirts. Popularization becomes utter commercialization: consumer products, from medicine and laundry detergents to cosmetics, sold with the "guarantee" of a science created piece by piece in the laboratories of advertising agencies, or "genius hype," the sale of a scientific image having symbolic value (Einstein, packaged in gift shops and malls, sticking out his tongue on posters or metamorphosed into a cuddly "Al*bear*t Einstein" teddy bear, complete with cardigan sweater boasting the inscription "E = mc²").[20] Undoubtedly the height of current "genius" exploitation today, resembling more a sideshow than a physics show, is Stephen W. Hawking, and on occasion it becomes difficult to distinguish the scientist from the object of radical mediazation: *A Brief History of Time*, the upscale popularization by an important physicist, from its multimillion-volume sales or from *A Brief History of Time*, the movie; or the selling of Hawking, whose computerized voice hails British Telecom over the airwaves.[21]

---

[20] I can only applaud turning a great scientist into a popular hero, for once favoring intellect over beauty, muscle, or military might; nonetheless, much of this smacks of what one could call, paraphrasing Gould on dinosaurs, "the Einstein rip-off" ("The Dinosaur Rip-off," in *Bully for Brontosaurus: Reflections in Natural History* [New York: Norton, 1991]).

[21] Stephen W. Hawking, *A brief history of time: from the big bang to black holes* (London: Bantam Books, 1988).

If I have gone through this list of items that we all know and see in our daily lives, it is to make this point: Despite (or perhaps because of) specialization and the sheer complexity of late-twentieth-century science, despite the emergence of scientific laboratories centered upon astronomically costly instruments of research, which places certain kinds of knowledge not only beyond the reach of the layman but beyond that of scientists outside of their own specialized domains, there is a concurrent and opposite movement, an integration of science and the general public. Formed intellectually at the emergence of interdisciplinarity, a generation of authors today writes in a world where science, whether scholarly, popularized or vulgarized, is everywhere present. The proliferation and promulgation of intelligent and intelligible scientific publications, and public interest in them, have allowed for the return if not of the early-nineteenth century's amateur natural philosopher, at least of the eighteenth-century's *honnête homme*, in the fashion of Buffon, naturalist and poet, who urged before the French Academy the simple proposition that man make use of all of his faculties; and today's "canon," that prescribed number of things that *Homo sapiens, faber,* and *ludens* must possess, once again embraces knowledge of the functioning of the physical universe in which he lives, while with the return of speculation to science, the object of inquiry into the unknown is not merely a *how to* in the applied sense, but a simple, and deeper, *how* and *what,* and for the most speculative, *why.*

The Sum of the Coordinates

Where is literary discourse in all of this?

"Welcome to the twentieth century, Mr. Wilmot; we all have some catching up to do. Amazing things are coming out of European physics. Time is the fourth dimension, it turns out, and slows down when the observer speeds up. The other three dimensions don't form a rigid grid; space is more like a net that sags when you put something in it, and that sagging is what we call gravity. Also, light isn't an indivisible, static presence; it has speed, and it comes in packets—irreducible amounts called quanta. . . ."[22]

---

[22] John Updike, *In the Beauty of the Lilies* (1996; reprint, London: Hamish Hamilton, 1996), 78–79.

"All these strainings of our common sense are facts," the clergyman Thomas Dreaver concludes. "We don't any more merely investigate reality . . . We *make* it, . . ." (ibid.). Dreaver is the moderator of the presbytery in John Updike's 1996 novel *In the Beauty of the Lilies*; his remarks are directed to the newly faithless minister Clarence Wilmot. In the earlier *Roger's Version* (1986), Divinity Professor Roger Lambert, a man comfortable with the theological assertion that "*The god who stood at the end of some human way would not be God*,"[23] faces an upstart computer-whiz-cum-cosmologist who insists that physicists, having "pared things down to the ultimate details," now find that the "last thing they ever expected to happen is happening. God is showing through" (9). Facts are facts, he sums up, the case of "people in the religion business . . . at last is being *proven*." "What kind of God is showing through, exactly?" Lambert questions (ibid.); and therein begins the sparring match, with jabs of biochemistry, paleontology, biology, biophysics, quantum physics, "Big Bang" theory, astronomy, mathematics, theology, and, this is after all John Updike, sex.

In Tlalpan, Mexico, Ernest Rutherford, Max Planck, Niels Bohr, Wolfgang Pauli, Albert Einstein, and Werner Heisenberg stare out from a rogue's gallery of Nobel physicists in Carlos Fuentes's tumultuous novel *Cristóbal Nonato* (1987; Christopher Unborn).[24] Oppenheimer, Fermi, Watson, Crick, de Broglie, and Pauling join them later. Cristóbal's (Christopher's) grandparent-scientists, the "Curies of Tlalpan," work with applied science to alter matter; the scientists in their portrait gallery worked with fundamental science whose discoveries relative to matter would alter minds and contemporary man's way of viewing the world. Need it be said? The dimension of the conceptual changes provoked by the new world of the new physics uncovered by these scientific mentors can be likened only to the dimension of that event that constitutes the point of departure of the entire novel: the confrontation between Christopher Columbus and the new world he discovered, or first invented.

In France, Michel Rio publishes a novel with the title *Le Principe d'incertitude* (1993; The Uncertainty Principle).[25] Rio's uncertainty starts

---

[23] Updike, *Roger's Version* (1986; reprint, New York: Fawcett Crest, 1987), 42. In a note on the copyright page, Updike acknowledges the role of popularized science writing in the formulation of the ideas in this novel.

[24] Carlos Fuentes, *Cristóbal Nonato* (Mexico City: Fondo de Cultura Económica, 1987).

[25] Rio, *Le Principe d'incertitude* (1993; reprint, Paris: Editions du Seuil, Points Roman, 1995).

where Fuentes's leaves off, looking out over the sea from an old world in the direction of a new. Rio's protagonist is not a Mexican scientist but a French writer, and he is not as optimistic as the Curies of Tlalpan: "I believe that death is not a transformation," he says, "but a complete disappearance of the essential, and that consciousness, along with all its products—identity, memory, invention, feeling, logic, morality, aesthetics—dies with the cell from which it came" (38).

The speaker is Jérôme Avalon. He is sitting in the garden of an aging movie idol, a private domain that he has violated because of its perfect aesthetic of uncertainty, an "exemplary piece of universe" (22–23). The two men, owner and intruder, have begun a conversation.

"So you see no intention, no project, no finality? No motivated universal intelligence?" the aging actor Dan Harrison asks. "In other words, no God?"

"Which God are you speaking of?" replies Avalon, and he proposes several: the God of believers, the God of metaphysicians, the God of physicists, each with His or Her own qualities and limitations (38, 41).

But Harrison's concern is the universal versus precisely the individual. And so he protests:

"Even if history is an 'accident of geometry,' as Hawking says, or matter's attempt to understand itself, as you say, it has scandalous consequences to the extent that I am part of that accident or that attempt . . . and the fact that my atoms will return to a more normal destiny does not console me in the slightest for the loss of their present identity, made up precisely of consciousness and history." (51)

"In your case then I can only think of a fourth God," Avalon says (53). And so this fiction writer offers up the God of mathematicians, and with Him the mathematical foundations of the freedom of disorder within constraints, a sort of deterministic chaos well known to physicists. He proposes Bernoulli's distribution, which ends up with a paradox applied to the probabilities of Harrison's own passage from transitory to definitive without loss of consciousness, a paradox in which relative 0 is worked into equaling 1, an ostensible contradiction in terms (ibid.).

"Are you reassured?" Avalon asks the actor (55).

And the reader? How reassured is he when in the seemingly "literary" act of picking up a work of fiction, he finds himself faced with explanations of chaos theory, of the relation among the natural sciences, the social sciences, and artistic creation; when, along with Bernoulli, he sees parade before him Laplace, Newton, Poincaré, Pythagorus from the world of mathematics; Alfvén, Arnold, Einstein, Galileo, Hawking, Heisenberg, Lerner, Moser, Prigogine, Schrödinger from the world of physics; Darwin from biology; Keynes and Marx from economics; Aristotle, Descartes, Heidegger from philosophy; not to mention a movie mogul named Cronk (Australian slang for "crook") who insists that his business is so wildly successful because he has understood something that is neither capitalist, nor communist, but Darwinian. I might add that the players in this mixture of physics and cinema, cosmology and flesh, all appear in the first 99 pages of a novel that in total contains 124, leading some to accuse Rio's work of having the approximate density of a black hole.

Across the Channel, a narrator of Nicholas Mosley's *Hopeful Monsters* (1990) studies physics at Cambridge with Paul Dirac; his girlfriend, later his wife, is an anthropologist.[26] His friend Donald is a student of Ludwig Wittgenstein. The Larmarckian-Darwinian debate, the question of the transmittal of acquired characteristics, the nature of the atom and of atom splitting all enter the novel. Natural science is joined by social science, by anthropology and history. This is Europe between wars and on the brink of war: Stalin's Russia, Rosa Luxemburg's Germany, the rise of the Nazis, the explosion of Spain's Civil War. History meets science directly when the student of physics becomes a physicist working on the Manhattan Project. In this epistolary novel, the protagonists' actions and thoughts, and so their letters, seem to be in relation, to communicate, even when the two writers are far apart in space and the letters do not coincide in time. Having once been together, there is permanent relation and memory. Otherwise put, the theory of quantum-mechanical nonlocality, just being developed at the time, and discussed by the characters, serves as a fundamental metaphor for the movement at all levels of the text, from the romantic bond between the two protagonists to the novel's very structure.

Elsewhere in the British Isles, Graham Swift's *Waterland* (1983) is narrated by history teacher Tom Crick, not a forebear of the Nobel

---

[26] Nicholas Mosley, *Hopeful Monsters* (London: Martin Secker & Warburg, 1990). Both Max Ackerman, son of a Cambridge biologist specializing in genetic inheritance, and Eleanor Anders, daughter of a Jewish disciple of Rosa Luxemburg, are first-person narrators; until the final chapter, a postscript, the novel is told through their alternating first-person texts.

biophysicist, but the son of simple Henry Crick, whose life he relates through a kind of comprehensive research, a storytelling discourse on *historia* in all its variations, from inquiry to narrative, natural history to the nature of history; world and regional history, social and industrial history, family history, his history; historiography and the teaching of history.[27] At the center of Swift's *Ever After* (1992), the life course of the nineteenth-century surveyor Matthew Pearce is indelibly altered by two events, separate in time but related in thought: He sees an ichthyosaur and he reads Charles Lyell, then Charles Darwin. His twentieth-century descendant reads Pearce's Notebooks, Lyell's *Principles* (and his *Elements*) *of Geology*, the 1853 edition (revised, he specifies), and adds his own appraisal of the author of *On the Origin of Species by Means of Natural Selection*.[28] In Ireland, John Banville writes imaginary but historically-informed biographies: *Kepler* (1981), *The Newton Letter* (1982), *The Book of Evidence* (1989).[29] In Nicaragua, priest, poet, and political figure Ernesto Cardenal writes his *Cántico cósmico* (1989; Cosmic Canticle), treating, among other subjects, cosmology, astrophysics, relativity, quantum mechanics, chaos theory, thermodynamics, biology, evolutionary theory, and paleontology.[30] In Manhattan, Joseph McElroy writes *Women and Men* (1987),[31] and while dealing with the relation explicit in his title, passes through an encyclopedic range of subjects from the economy and space exploration to planetary meteorology, using chaos theory as a model for the relation between big and small, near and far; he is, in the words of Tom Leclair, "the preeminent American artist of the Age of Systems."[32]

On a campus in Illinois, Richard Powers writes *The Gold Bug Variations* (1991).[33] Amid references to Poe's story and Bach's music, four

---

[27] Graham Swift, *Waterland* (London: William Heinemann, 1983).

[28] Swift, *Ever After* (London: Picador, 1992).

[29] John Banville, *Kepler* (London: Martin Secker & Warburg, 1981); *The Newton Letter* (London: Martin Secker & Warburg, 1982); *The Book of Evidence* (London: Martin Secker & Warburg, 1989). Banville's *Doctor Copernicus* was published in 1976 (New York: Norton). This earlier novel first appears in paperback in 1993, and this, along with the fact that all of Banville's novels have been extensively reprinted in the 1990s, perhaps suggests a heightened interest in his subject matter corresponding to the period I discuss.

[30] Ernesto Cardenal, *Cántico cósmico* (Managua: Editorial Nueva Nicaragua, 1989).

[31] Joseph McElroy, *Women and Men* (New York: Knopf, 1987).

[32] Tom Leclair, "Joseph McElroy: expérimentation et technologie," *Magazine littéraire*, no. 281 (October 1990): 104; and, introduction to *Plus*, by Joseph McElroy (New York: Carroll & Graf Publishers, 1977), vii.

[33] Richard Powers, *The Gold Bug Variations* (1991; reprint, London: Abacus, 1993).

characters, all researchers, twist about each other as if in a double helix formation. Paragraphs in this novel read:

	ATTCGAGCCT	ATTCGAGCCT
	:::::::::	:::::::::
ATTCGAGCCT		CAAGCTCGGA
::::::::: →	→	
TAAGCTCGGA	:::::::::	ATTCGAGCCT
	TAAGCTCGGA	:::::::::
		TAAGCTCGGA (196)

"Cryptanalysis" (239) is a central activity, as is love. Science and desire mingle. Discussions turn around the target enzyme and codon table and the assignment of CAG to glutamine; the four basic notes of the Goldberg variations are played and replayed, analyzed and reanalyzed in the search for this "self-generating, self-defining system—residing nowhere, unknown by any of its constituent parts" (270–71). What is being sought (coveted) is nothing less than a model for reading the entire genetic code on the basis of the four nucleotides. Fascination with self-generating systems continues in *Galatea 2.2* (1995), where now a (the) writer with a forma-tion in physics, the "humanist-in-residence," spends a year at a "Center for the Study of Advanced Sciences," and between neural physiologists and algorithmic formalists enters into the connectionism debate cen-tering on the work of Dr. Philip Lentz.[34] Neurons, axons, dendrites, synaptic connections, Boolean operators, algorithms and a nonalgorithmic system, and a stimulus vector and a response vector: The vocabulary is from this novel (71), where around a "machine" named Helen, and between networks and poetry, a writer named Richard Powers confronts the question of where consciousness begins.[35]

---

[34] Powers, *Galatea 2.2* (New York: Farrar, 1995).

[35] A name that might have appeared here but for the fact that he is not principally a writer is Nobel Prize chemist and poet Roald Hoffmann. In contrast both to the specu-lator scientists to whom I have referred, who write essays, and to the literary work of scientists such as Fred Hoyle and Isaac Asimov, who write science fiction, Hoffmann works on a literary form that is lyrical, stressing chemical data and emotional response. (Interestingly, Fuentes expresses his gratitude for the help of "Professor Roald Hoffman[n]" at the beginning of the novel I have cited above, *Cristóbal Nonato*). See Hoffmann, espe-cially *The Metamict State* and *Gaps and Verges* (Orlando: University of Central Florida Press, 1987 and 1990; respectively); also, *Chemistry Imagined* (Washington, D.C.: Smithsonian

The Old World and the New. The list supersedes borders and national identity. All are works of fiction by living authors. All are published in the contemporary period, the 1980s and 1990s, as this century of alterations draws to a close.[36] The degree of knowledge among these authors and the use they make of it varies greatly; disparate, they cannot be reduced to their interest in "nonliterary" disciplines. Yet the common ground is evident, and my sampling is only to suggest a fact: A generation after the heyday of structuralism, literature crosses disciplinary borders, brings the social and natural sciences back into the construction of fiction, the direct line drawn by Italo Calvino from Dante to Galileo, "the notion of the literary work as a map of the world and of the knowable, of writing driven on by a thirst for knowledge."[37] These works require a dose of real knowledge beyond knowledge of one's self and beyond the utilitarian "tools" of the trade, the technical knowledge of detective stories, sociological knowledge of a milieu, geographic knowledge of placement, psychological knowledge of character; their "action" in substantial degree is centered around debate.[38] This is not science fiction, not applied knowledge but speculative. Thought is not isolated but has a determining impact on the thinker, on his vision of the world, and on his affective relationship to it. This is literature with an intellectual utility. This is elucidating fiction.

Institution Press, 1993). Another case is physicist Alan Lightman, turned fiction-writer with *Einstein's Dreams* (New York: Pantheon Books, 1993).

[36] A group of authors also knowledgeable about the physical world published in the immediately preceding decades, among them, Italo Calvino, Primo Levi, Luis Martín-Santos, Nicanor Parra, and Raymond Queneau; Jacques Roubaud and Don DiLillo produced major works in the 1970s; Jorge Luis Borges continued exploiting mathematics, Severo Sarduy delved into speculation (although in essay form), Thomas Pynchon into aviation and chaos theory; McElroy's *Plus*, while more science fiction than the works I consider, appeared in 1977, and a number of authors span the decades. Yet in many cases these earlier authors used their knowledge differently, in my view, and if "explication" is the mark of the later fiction, perhaps "questing" marks the earlier works (one can also note the greater abundance of trained scientists among these authors). My interest here is the later literature, in part because it is later and nonconcurrent with structuralism, in part because it defines, necessarily, the "state of the art" as the century ends.

[37] Italo Calvino, "Two Interviews on Science and Literature," in *The Literature Machine*, trans. Patrick Creagh (1987; reprint, London: Picador, 1989), 32.

[38] From this common factor, not surprisingly, spring others. A disproportionate number of these novels, if one were to calculate simple probabilities, are set in universities or research centers, reconsider God, at least as a factor in debate, and, in an almost revised form of Platonic dialogue, make extensive use of argumentation, whether face-to-face or in epistolary or journal form.

It is possibly also power fiction. The question put a generation earlier
to the structuralists can be reformulated today: Are authors of fiction
seeking to share in the power and authority that contemporary society
accords science?[39]

Mythologies of Knowledge

Here is a fiction that opens up the opportunity for a different critical
approach, and a broader one. The methodology that I experiment with in
this volume is of a simplicity bordering on the self-evident: the grouping
of specialists in a wide range of disciplines around a common work. While
fully compatible with other interdisciplinary approaches, it differs from
them by way of a clear shift in direction, a shift that can be expressed as
three divergences. All three have in common my intention to move toward
a more comprehensive and more inclusive interdisciplinary practice.

1) Rather than bilateral this methodology is multilateral, reading a
work of fiction not solely through a second discipline, be it science or
history or philosophy or indeed any other separate discipline. Criticism that
reads a work of fiction through a second discipline or theory brings an
added perspective that can brilliantly illuminate the text; this is the case, for
example, of N. Katherine Hayles's reading of Thomas Pynchon's *Gravity's
Rainbow* in terms of chaos theory.[40] It can also be reductionist, however,
seeing a work in the light of a particular discipline or theory only, without
giving proper weight to the rest of what is, in the end, a total vision; this is
the case of Hayles's reading of Jorge Luis Borges in terms of Cantor set
theory.[41] The methodology that I use here goes in another direction; rather

---

[39] Mihai I. Spariosu discusses the involvement of power with science in *Dionysus Reborn:
Play and the Aesthetic Dimension in Modern Philosophical and Scientific Discourse* (Ithaca:
Cornell University Press, 1989). The issue was also brought to my attention by Professor William Rowe at the University of London during a talk I gave at King's Col-
lege, "Working with Science and Literature," 10 May 1996.
[40] N. Katherine Hayles, *The Cosmic Web: Scientific Field Models & Literary Strategies in the
20th Century* (Ithaca: Cornell University Press, 1984), 168–97.
[41] Ibid., 138–67. My disagreement with Hayles is not with what she says, which can be
extremely interesting, and I applaud her for taking the care to document that Borges was
indeed familiar with Cantor set theory. Rather, I am concerned with what is not said, for
there is the danger, particularly for a reader who cannot himself fill in the gaps, of
reducing Borges to this single concern.

than multiple works of fiction being read or seen through a second discipline, I propose multidisciplinary perspectives on one test body of fiction.

2) A corollary of the first divergence is that this methodology
demands knowledge of multiple disciplines of no *one* reader. Serious interdisciplinary criticism, as differentiated from dabbling, has thus far been
restricted, necessarily, to a certain kind of critic or reader, often one with
a bidisciplinary formation; again, Hayles, with advanced degrees in chemistry and English, can serve as an example. It is not a method for everyone, either in the doing or in the evaluation of the result. I have no argument with this, and to a degree it is the inevitable outcome of in-depth
specialized analysis. But I would rather not leave interdisciplinarity in the
sole hands of the interdisciplinary, so to speak, where it risks becoming
restrictive rather than expansive. There are evident limits, and I think a
few dangers, in a focus that can only be practiced or enjoyed by a certain
eye. I have preferred to return to an earlier, and in some ways more
generous, interdisciplinary methodology and project: the encyclopedic
tradition, which I apply to a kind of contemporary fiction that in many
ways itself is encyclopedic. Inevitably, my methodology shares in the
strengths and weaknesses of that tradition.

3) Inseparable from the previous two is a third divergence. This
methodology calls not for literary critics to invoke another specialized
discipline in the reading of literature, but for literature to be read also by,
and from the perspective of, *specialized scholars in other disciplines*—disciplines well-within and beyond the so-called boundaries of the humanities.

These are the things that I wanted to do. There are others that I did
not want, pitfalls and perils of the frontier that I sought to avoid. I did not
want fusion or the melting down of all disciplinary borders. Nor did I
want unbreachable borders, parallel essays never connecting. I did not
want scientists as amateur literary critics. I did not want reductionism. I
did not want what Richard Powers calls "trend-surfing." I did not want a
little bit of knowledge to be a dangerous thing. And there was one final
thing I did not want. In an oft-quoted essay, Borges recounts finding hints
of Kafka in Zeno, Han Yu, Kierkegaard, and Browning, and concludes
that an author creates his own precursors: Had Kafka never written, or
had Borges never read a line of Kafka, he would likely never have put
those disparate authors together.[42] May Borges forgive me; I did not want

---

[42] Jorge Luis Borges, "Kafka y sus precursores," in *Otras inquisiciones*, 6th ed. (Buenos Aires:
Emecé, 1971), 145–48. Originally published in *La Nación* (19 August 1952).

to contribute to another suspicious list of precursors. I did not want Carlos Fuentes's portrait gallery or Michel Rio's novelistic title to lead to Heisenberg being a precursor of either. I did not want the uncertainty principle itself or definition by wave collapse to become fused with Borges's art of reading.

Today science is influencing not only the writing but the reading of this or any other page, in some cases creating pages of analysis that sound like a Borges story itself. While one can speak of "ideas in the air" that manifest themselves in diverse domains in any given period, caution is needed in attributing a specific theory to a specific author. Lautréamont is now studied with regard to entropy; Julio Cortázar, and almost everybody else, is studied with regard to chaos theory and fractals; certain authors of fiction are credited with scientific theories that mere scientists arrived at only belatedly, if at all. In this atmosphere my questions risk being iconoclastic. Superimpositions of this kind make a clear contribution to the art of reading, but are they a contribution to knowledge? Does a coincidence between a certain vision of the world and certain scientific theories alone suffice for linkage? For the moment at least my personal answer is that I would not have discussed any of the works I have cited in terms of a specific discipline or theory had the author not explicitly introduced that discipline or theory into the work of fiction. This is not a retrogressive bow to authorial intention. Rather, it is the humble suggestion that not every work of art that moves from order to disorder is doing so necessarily in recognition of the second law of thermodynamics.

The universal laws of physics are called "universal" because they are universal, which means that applying them anywhere and reading them everywhere brings us indeed very close to Borges's contention that all books are the same book. The play in a literary work between the universal and the individual is perhaps Leibnitz's combinatory art, but a work of art cannot be reduced to universal laws precisely because the individual at the center of artistic creation cannot be reduced to a mathematical formula. In other words, beware if not the Jabberwocky at least the Ettelson effect—that Hassidic doctor cited by French critic Jean-Jacques Lecercle, who uses Humpty-Dumpty's very own methods in the questionable enterprise of proving that *Through the Looking-Glass* is nothing other than a secret Talmudic text.[43]

---

[43] Jean-Jacques Lecercle, "Lewis Carroll et le Talmud," in *Epistémocritique et cognition 1, Théorie, Littérature, Enseignement* 10, ed. Noëlle Batt (fall 1992): 169–87.

All of my divergences from established interdisciplinary practice grow from the initial difference of purpose I stated: My question is not the influence of any one discipline or theory on a work of fiction, but rather the intellectual utility of fiction in a contemporary context. What happens when literature is exposed to different systems and mythologies of knowledge? At issue in this volume, at the base of this experiment, always, is that question: Can literature hold a place at the center of intellectual debate in the age of science?

That, quite simply, is why I brought natural scientists and social scientists to literature. I invited biologist Stephen Jay Gould, historian Michel Pastoureau, physicist James Ritter, anthropologist Joaquín Galarza, semiologist Christian Metz to join literary analysts James Swenson, Jean-Michel Rabaté; and myself in explicating the novels of one of the authors of fiction I have quoted, the French writer Michel Rio.

Why Michel Rio? A conjuncture of content and circumstance, both practical and historical, determined the choice. The practical considerations are matters of common sense. Rio's novels are short and dense. They are "classical" in structure and language, as opposed to postmodern or experimental (the Fuentes novel, both in length and language, would appear at the other end of the spectrum). Their difficulty resides in the density of their intellectual debate, in content not form. This is not a negligible consideration when asking nonliterary specialists to turn from their own discipline and area of research to a work of fiction. Another circumstance is that Rio, who is translated into some twenty languages and who has lectured at universities from Boston to Tokyo, adds multi-nationality to multidisciplinarity in his work. There is also the very important fact that Rio is extremely aware of the issues that concern me here and has written eloquently on them, forming a veritable theory of the novel, the application of which is his literary work. I quote from him liberally in this introduction.

The final circumstance is the one I call "historical." By chronology and geography, Michel Rio is a product of many of the cultural phenomena I have discussed. Nor can he be seen as a pure and simple spectator. On the contrary, he was in the fray. After two years of study in economics at Rouen and five years of modern languages and literature at the University of Caen, in 1972, amid full structuralist agitation, he entered the bastion, the virtual citadel of structuralist activity: the sixth section of the Ecole pratique des hautes études, later to become the Ecole des hautes études en sciences sociales (EHESS). Its faculty reads like a *Who's Who* in structuralist thought: A. Greimas and Christian Metz, both of whom were Rio's directors of research; Roland Barthes, Gérard Genette, Charles Morazé, Tzvetan Todorov, Oswald Ducrot, and Jean-Pierre Vernant (Lucien Goldmann had been at the sixth section until his death in 1970; Jacques Derrida, structuralism's *enfant terrible* and later nemesis, would arrive years later).[44] Rio's early essays bear full witness: the jargon is telltale, the subjects as well, the titles "Cadre, plan, lecture" (1976; Frame, Shot, Reading) or "Le dit et le vu" (1978; The Said and the Seen) suffice to make the point and to place him in a specific time and critical context.[45] Both Rio and French intellectual discourse subsequently evolve, of course.[46] And yet I venture that Rio's novels maintain elements of the essential, while abandoning the accessory, of that central intellectual current. Interdisciplinary concerns and the introduction of logic and scientific discussion into the realm of fiction are notions fundamental to the underlying enterprise of his opus. As is building. The etymological basis of the word "structure" is the Latin *struere*, "to build,"[47] and "structure" originally entered other fields precisely as a metaphor derived from building (Lane, 19). Building, constructing, making, *doing*, on levels figurative, literary, and manual, are central to every Rio novel. Moreover, a number of concepts specific, although not exclusive, to structuralism are notably and consistently present in the literature that Michel Rio produces. Among them: the central role of binary opposition, the notion of structure as a syntax of transformations, synchronic perspectives, the importance of metalanguage, the interest in a calculus of combinations. Two areas of attack on structuralism also seem particularly relevant: the accusations that structuralism ignores history, and that it eliminates cause as a prime consideration. Whether as reaction or not, the relation to time and to causality is integral to Rio's fiction. The question is not: Is Rio, or any of the other authors I have

---

[44] Todorov was officially associated with the Centre National de la Recherche Scientifique (CNRS) but gave courses at the EHESS. Derrida was named Director of Studies there in 1984.

[45] Rio, "Cadre, plan, lecture," *Communications* 24, EHESS (1976); "Le dit et le vu," *Communications* 29, EHESS (1978). Both reprinted in *Rêve de logique*, 7–30 and 31–54.

[46] One has only to compare the treatment of object and frame in the 1976 essay and in Rio's 1983 novel *Le Perchoir du perroquet*; or the 1978 essay with his description in that same novel of Taddeo di Bartolo's fresco of hell (*Le Perchoir du perroquet* [1983; reprint, Paris: Editions du Seuil, Points Roman, 1987], 29–30 and 63–68).

[47] *The Oxford English Dictionary* (Oxford: Oxford University Press, 1971), compact edition, 2: 3104.

quoted, a structuralist? I am hardly suggesting that his or their novels are the literary transposition of structuralist method or concerns. But I am claiming for structuralism a deep impact. In the case of Rio, his work is both *about* the relation of binary opposites, and is itself a product of, and demonstration of, that kind of relation. Rio's intellectual trajectory, from the study of literature to the scientific analysis of language to the creation of literature, as well as the novels considered individually and collectively that come of it, embody absolutely the movement between knowledge and poetics that is at issue.

This brings me to content. Michel Rio's novels are obsessed with the effect of exact, universal knowledge on the individual, affective being; with questions of the relation between knowledge and imagination, between what he calls the "logician" and the "dreamer." He defines the novel as the melding of three founding conditions: a well-informed worldview, action, and poetics. The task of a writer "having some degree of pride and an 'honorable' ambition" is

> nothing other than to describe a sensitive, unique being reacting to a new disposition of his surroundings, without restriction, not only as regards social mores or landscapes, but also, and perhaps above all, as regards knowledge, the state of man's theoretical conception of the world.[48]

This means that the writer has to know something. He must master the explanatory myths of man and the universe and draw from what his age has to offer. What this century offers up, among other curiosities, "is what a character in [Rio's novel] *Archipel* [1987; Archipelago] calls 'the trinity that founds our vision of the world' [*sic*]: History, biology, physics, in other terms what we know of man, of living things, of matter"; or, in more literary terms, of consciousness, of sex and of death, of Nature (72). In this interplay of elements, knowledge is not opposed to but is a source of poetics:

> Three writers above all have impressed me as outstanding com-posers in the French language: Gautier, Hugo and Flaubert. As if by chance, all three happen to have a disproportionately large vocabulary, which prompts the thought that knowledge is no

---

[48] Rio, "Le rêveur et le logicien," in *Rêve de logique*, 71–72.

stranger to poetics, for the simple reason that the combinatory possibilities of one hundred thousand words are in principle broader and richer [in sound and in sense] than those of the usual one thousand words. From that one can postulate the musicality of specialized vocabularies and the poetic aptitude of the encyclopedic mind, . . . all of which is reassuringly interconnected. (75–76)

Yet there is a hierarchy. Poetics is at the service of meaning, must be its slave. Poetics is the particularity of literature but cannot be its objective.[49]

The novel that Rio theorizes aims at elucidation but belongs neither to pure knowledge nor to the pure ramblings of the imagination. It is an in-between space whose subject is not a restitution of knowledge but knowledge's affective impact, not the "freedom of dream but its limits."[50] In his 1989 novel *Merlin*, the future king's half sister and incestuous-lover-to-be dreams a solar system. Morgan's dream deduces the weakness of the geocentric model and advances in great detail the principles of a heliocentric model. The scientific discussion is real, not adornment; but Rio is an author of fiction. What matters in the end is not that Morgan has come to heliocentrism at the age of seven and some nine centuries before the monk and astronomer Nicholas Copernicus, but the tension between the logician who insists on knowing at all cost, and the dreamer who finds intolerable what knowledge brings. And all of Morgan's geometrical calculations, all of her precocious knowledge, will come down to one question asked by this seven-year-old child: "Why must we die, Merlin?"[51]

There are twelve novels in all. Each is built around a thesis. The whole constitutes a coherent opus that is a veritable interdisciplinary playing field. From the jungle of the Ivory Coast to an imaginary island off the coast of modern Mexico to Manhattan's "Usher Building"; from the fifth century to the present; through shipwrecks, sentimental journeys, and Aztec codices; peopled with monks, naturalists, a librarian, the contract killer who reads the historian Marc Bloch, women of intellect and beauty and libidinous particularities, and narrators from age fifteen to

---

[49] Rio, "L'essentiel et l'accessoire," in ibid., 26.
[50] Rio, "Le rêveur et le logicien," in ibid., 73.
[51] Rio, *Merlin* (1989; reprint, Paris: Editions du Seuil, Points Roman, 1991), 65.

one hundred, Rio's concerns remain the same: the logician and the dreamer, and the trinity that founds our vision of the world, history, biology, physics, what we know of man, of living things, of matter.

"All literature worthy of the name is useful by nature because it aims at elucidation," affirms the protagonist of Rio's 1995 novel *Manhattan Terminus*.[52] He is a fiction writer with a notable intellectual resemblance to the author, and he is responding to an attack that his novels have no social utility. "Elucidation," he explains, "not some lesson":

> "And in this I see it [literature] as closer to science than to morality. . . . When I say 'elucidation,' I am thinking 'evolution' in the Darwinian sense, since the evolution of man is now a function not of nature but of culture, therefore of the knowledge that shapes his environment." (48)

In response to the attack that his dialogues are too literary and that "Nobody talks like that" (54), Rio's narrator, as if constructing his own unified theory, concludes:

> "Dialogue is contaminated by the language of description, which is poetic, and that of reasoning, which is mathematical, to become an integral and harmonious part of a *rhetorique d'ensemble*. That's right. Nobody talks like that, the way I write. And so what? . . . Poetry and mathematics in no way preclude flesh and blood, suffering and desire, humor and fear." (55)

This is the literature that I submitted to the scientists. What does an evolutionary biologist derive from seeing a theory he himself has written about as a scientist "translated" by an author of fiction? How is the perception of this scientific and mathematical knowledge changed by its insertion into a work of fiction, where it itself becomes fiction? How do different bodies of knowledge operate on the same body of fiction? What is the reaction of a specialist in a discipline when he sees cold fact acting on an individual who feels, when knowledge weighs on a life? What is the effect of man's knowledge of the world on man, where knowledge not only does not preclude but operates on flesh and blood, suffering and

---

[52] Rio, *Manhattan Terminus* (1995; reprint, Paris: Editions du Seuil, Points Roman, 1997), 48.

desire, humor and fear? Like Michel Rio's fiction, this volume aims at a comprehensive grammar, a unified rhetoric of logic and human sensibility, of the mythologies and melancholies of knowledge.

Editor's Note

For ease of reference, Michel Rio's major works are listed here in their order of publication. Each work is preceded by the abbreviation that is used for it in the essays. All titles are given here in the original French, with the English translation, if different, in parentheses. The date of original publication is indicated below the title, followed by the date of the paperback edition; where applicable, the translated titles are followed by the date of publication in English.

A complete bibliography of Rio's work, including foreign editions, is provided at the end of the essays, as is a catalog of proper names that appear in his novels, classified by discipline and identified as to the work(s) in which they appear.

Novels

MN   *Mélancolie Nord* (Melancholy North)
(Prize of the French Society of Letters)
1982, 1986

PP   *Le Perchoir du perroquet* (Parrot's Perch, 1985)
(Grand Prize of the French Society of Letters)
1983, 1987

TW   *Alizés* (Trade Winds)
(Creators' Prize)
1984, 1987

DJ   *Les Jungles pensives* (Dreaming Jungles, 1987)
1985, 1989

Ar   *Archipel* (Archipelago, 1989)
1987, 1989

M   *Merlin*
       1989, 1991
FP   *Faux Pas*
       (C.E. Renault First Prize)
       1991, 1993
Tl   *Tlacuilo*
       (Medicis Prize)
       1992, 1994
UP   *Le Principe d'incertitude* (The Uncertainty Principle)
       1993, 1995
MT   *Manhattan Terminus*
       1995, 1997
SL   *La Statue de la liberté* (The Statue of Liberty)
       1997
D   *La Mort: une enquête de Francis Malone* (The Death: An Investi-
       gation by Francis Malone)
       1998

Theater

O   *L'Ouroboros* (The Ouroboros)
       1985
HW   *Baleine pied-de-poule* (Hound's-tooth Whale)
       1990

Critical Essays

DL   *Rêve de logique: essais critiques* (Dreams of Logic: Critical Essays)
       1992
       Contents: "Cadre, plan, lecture" (Frame, Shot, Reading); "Le dit et le vu"
(The Said and the Seen); "Signe et figure" (Sign and Figure); "Le rêveur et le
logicien" (The Dreamer and the Logician); "L'essentiel et l'accessoire" (The
Essential and the Accessory)

The essays that follow all use the same editions of these works for
page citations: for the three novels published in English, *Parrot's Perch*,

Dreaming Jungles, and *Archipelago*, the U.S. edition;[1] for the other novels, the French paperback edition; for the theater and critical essays, the French first edition. To facilitate reading, the essays use italicized English titles for all of Michel Rio's works. Where no published English version exists, all translations of quoted passages are by Professor George Craig of the University of Sussex and myself.

I have added to the essays a series of cross-referencing footnotes, commenting on, and sending the reader to, other essays that deal with the same work or concerns; in these notes, essays are listed always in their order of publication in this volume. My notes are indicated by letters (*a, b,* etc.), in order to distinguish them from the authors' footnotes, which are designated by numbers. The essays are grouped according to the novels they consider, so that, for example, *Merlin* viewed by a medieval historian is juxtaposed to *Merlin* viewed by a physicist specialized in twentieth-century relativity theory and the history of science.

Rio's tenth, eleventh, and twelfth novels were not available to the contributors when they were writing their essays for this volume. *Manhattan Terminus* became available to me in manuscript form shortly before publication; *The Statue of Liberty* was published well after; its sequel, *The Death: An Investigation by Francis Malone*, arrived too late for any consideration here beyond a bibliographical mention. Any new publication necessarily alters the way in which one reads the work of an author; it is the risk of working on a living author. *The Statue of Liberty*, a detective story centered on the debate between global free enterprise and the French notion of public service, has little to do with the elucidating literature that is the focus of this collection; *Manhattan Terminus*, on the other hand, is entirely pertinent to it. Filled with cosmological speculation based on classical and the new physics, this novel occupies an important place precisely in the area that is at the origin of this collection; of all of Rio's novels it offers perhaps the most intense exploitation of scientific knowledge and its effect on human sensibility. A farewell party in Manhattan's 3 Ws Bar (*W*ho are we? *W*hat are we doing here? *W*here are we going?), *Manhattan Terminus* reads like an epilogue to the works that precede it. The informed vocabulary of one of the characters, Alan Stewart, highlights the meaning of the title's second word:

---

[1] Trans. Leigh Hafrey, William R. Carlson, and Margery Arent Safir, respectively.

"I imagine the whole universe, conscious of being, forced to become conscious of the necessity of no longer being, whether it is a question of a hot and violent death by collapse or a cold death, an almost eternal agony by dilution of matter and energy. . . . To return to my companion's question, if consciousness is finality, why must it die? And if, all in all, it's no more than the consciousness of death, isn't it useless, and even harmful?" (*MT*, 115)

Or, in the words of his companion, the narrator, are we but "a kind of Tantalus condemned to death with eternity right under his nose?" (116). In the end, and despite centuries of accumulation of knowledge and scientific data about the origins of matter and the universe, the question in this tenth novel remains the same as that asked by the seven-year-old Morgan in *Merlin*: Why must we die? Because in so many ways questions that are raised in earlier novels and characters who appear in them come together in this later novel, I have added to my footnotes throughout the essays references to that mixture of metaphysics and striptease that is *Manhattan Terminus*.

All eight of the essays in this volume are concerned with the relation between knowledge and imagination. Each contributor was selected not only as a representative of a discipline, but because something specific in his own research touched on the theses of Rio's novels, a specificity that seems to me indispensable in this kind of methodology. Taken together, the eight essays not only shed different lights on the same body of fiction, but reveal recurring issues and themes among themselves. Signaled by the cross-referencing footnotes that send the reader from one essay to another, the dialogue among disciplines goes beyond any single work, and one begins to see natural scientists, social scientists, and literary analysts struggling with similar questions, although framed differently by the objectives and discourse of their disciplines. In this way Stephen Jay Gould's discussion of man's relation to his biological origins and to cultural adaptation, for instance, is put in contact with James Swenson's discussion of aesthetics and the relation of natural and man-made landscapes, and with Jean-Michel Rabaté's reflections on psychological anthropomorphism. History, its displacement and rewriting, interests Gould for the scientific truth revealed by informed fictional invention. In my own essay history becomes a matter of pedagogy and its perversities, displacement the dynamic in a literary corpus of incest and knowledge, rewriting a matter of intertextuality. For Michel Pastoureau the object of study is not a species but a legend, yet it too is seen in a context of evolution, history, and anachronism. Similarly, James Ritter sees the universe as a whole rewritten with each new stage of cosmology and the metaphors on which it depends. In Joaquín Galarza, the question of historical displacement turns tragic in the context of the lost history, the inevitable anachronism, of the Aztec *tlacuilo* after the conquest and the search for his lost language, while for Christian Metz it involves the intertextual histories among characters who move from one novel to another. Order and disorder, creation and "de-creation," the concept of difference, material exactitude and the precision of language and specialized vocabularies, the relation between nature and culture, art and science, and the insertion of the one into the other, are among the topics on which these eight essays converge and converse. Another dimension emerges here, an integral, and integrating, part of this project, a second level of interdisciplinary dialogue, independent of, but nonetheless provoked by, a work of fiction.

M.A.S.

1

Out of Time in the Dreaming Jungles

Stephen Jay Gould[a]

The arrow of time provides our primary sense of order in an otherwise confusing and chaotic world. Consequently anachronism has special power as a literary device because nothing can be quite so disorienting as a mistimed person or idea. When Shakespeare talks about chiming clocks in *Julius Caesar*, we are jolted from imperial Rome into modernity, and Caesar and Brutus might as well be Lincoln and Booth, or Louis XVI and the Jacobins.

I have long been intrigued by one particular form of studied anachronism, the most intellectual of all modes: the use of later knowledge to grant "prophetic" insight to characters in historical fiction. Hans Sachs, for example, in the last scene of Wagner's *Die Meistersinger*, can speak with great prescience about the dangers of imposed cultural standardization, and the need to preserve local traditions, languages, and diversities, because Wagner knew, as the historical Hans Sachs (1494–1576) could not, that indigenous German music and literature would suffer eclipse,

---

[a] Stephen Jay Gould is named by Michel Rio in a number of essays and interviews, as well as in his novel *Manhattan Terminus*. In his own essays, Gould has often written about the theory of kin selection that is put forth in *Dreaming Jungles*, and that he discusses here. See "Biological Potentiality vs. Biological Determinism," and particularly "So Cleverly Kind an Animal," in *Ever Since Darwin: Reflections in Natural History* (1977; reprint, London: Penguin, 1982), 251–59 and 260–67, especially 255 and 262; also, "Caring Groups and Selfish Genes," in *The Panda's Thumb: More Reflections in Natural History* (1980; reprint, London: Penguin, 1983), 72–78.

and that Frederick the Great, regarding German as a language of boors, would conduct court business in French.

Michel Rio's *Dreaming Jungles* draws its primary intellectual strength[1b] and being from the same brand of anachronism. I suspect that most literary readers will miss this central brilliance of Rio's remarkable novella simply because the history of twentieth-century evolutionary theory, and particularly the study of altruism in behavioral biology, has not permeated into general intellectual culture, and is therefore not well known to scholars and general readers who are not professional biologists. I therefore felt that I could best serve the purposes of this volume, and could best honor Rio's work, by presenting, in this essay, a primer for this issue and a commentary on Rio's thoroughly accurate and expansive use of a central theme in my own field.

I am not a literary critic and shall resist most temptations at amateur commentary in this area. But I do wish to note that Rio quite explicitly informs us, at two pivotal places in his text—both at the very beginning and at the very end—that anachronism, or the more general phenomenon of things in the wrong place or time, provides the glue for his narrative.[c] *Dreaming Jungles* opens with our hero, a young and well-bred French scientist, aboard a ship about to land in Africa. He asks the first lieutenant, "Do you happen to know . . . whether there are any sea crocodiles in these parts?" (*DJ*, 4). The lieutenant, clearly fearing for our hero's mental state in the tropical sun, questions the existence of such incongruous creatures, but the hero assures him: "*Crocodylus porosus*, Lieutenant. It is not a naturalist's joke. I saw some off the coast of Sumatra two years ago, near a mangrove swamp identical to this" (ibid.).

---

[1] Rio's *Les Jungles pensives* has been translated into English as *Dreaming Jungles*. Although I understand the translator's intent in this choice, I should also point out how badly this English title records the major intellectual import of Rio's book. In English, "dreaming" is almost opposite to thinking. Dreaming is unconscious, wandering, intuitive, romantic. But Rio's jungle is "pensive," or thinking—in the sense of challenging, rational, provocative, logical, and expansive. Since Rio uses the jungle as a source for important revision within evolutionary theory, leading to insights about human nature and a partial resolution of the old dichotomy between humans as apart from, or entwined with, nature, I assume that the intellectual character of the jungle is even more central to his novella than the stereotyped notion of jungles as holistic and romantic.

[b] On *Dreaming Jungles*, see Arent Safir and Metz.

[c] On anachronism and the rewriting of history, see Pastoureau for the historical personage and Ritter for Copernican astronomy in *Merlin*. There is also, in another sense, the inevitable anachronism of the postconquest *tlacuilo* of which Galarza speaks.

The hero then speaks of mangrove swamps as breeding grounds for creatures out of time in mixing environments of earth and water: "It was, at the dawn of the twentieth century, a living relic of the first biological era, the anachronistic manifestation of an unfinished world where the walking fish was still struggling to climb from the water to the earth" (5). And the lieutenant, returning to the original query about marine crocodiles then adds incongruity (out of place) to this theme of anachronism (out of time): ". . . I have never seen a crocodile swimming in the sea. It seems so . . . out of place. I would have remembered it." "Do you think, Lieutenant," the hero responds, "that a crocodile venturing out to sea is any more out of place than we are right now in this primeval hell—or paradise, depending on your taste?" (ibid.). Rio then leaves this subject and we might think that he used all this space (in such a spare work of a mere 100 pages or so) just to stress the rather banal theme that an aristocratic Westerner in the Third-World tropics (or "darkest Africa" as the protagonists might have said at the time) would feel both out of place and time. But Rio's intentions are much deeper and far more subtle, as we shall see.

Lest we should lose sight of anachronism and incongruity as a central theme, Rio returns explicitly to it at the very end. The protagonists, fresh from a year with timeless nature in the field, are wrenched into contemporary life and sent forth to do their various duties in the First World War. Our hero, once more on a boat, and now en route to his wartime posting, again meets the lieutenant, who inquires: "Did you end up finding your sea crocodile? You remember, the one that was so out of place?" "Not in the flesh, Lieutenant," the hero replies, "but I believe I have made some progress in understanding its mentality" (113).[d]

What then has the hero grasped, and why had Rio made anachronism and incongruity so central to his novella? When the lieutenant first asks the hero why he has come to Africa, he receives as an answer:

"I have come here to study chimpanzees in their own environment, their behavior with respect to ourselves, and to make my modest contribution to the work of Darwin's successors. Others are doing the same for the gorilla or the orangutan. That would tend to prove, despite my first, traveler's impression, that I do not

---

[d] On history, the war, and this return at the end of *Dreaming Jungles*, see Arent Safir.

feel us to be strangers to this savagery, which must also be in our
genes, to use Mr. Johannson's [*sic* for Johannsen] word." (6)

Already, Rio is teasing us, so early in the novella, with themes of
anachronism. Nothing stated by the hero contradicts what might have
occurred or been conceived in 1913, the novella's actual setting. But the
three-prong study of great apes in their natural habitats has truly been
done by women anthropologists in our own generation—by Jane Goodall
for chimpanzees (the obvious model for Lady Jane Savile, Rio's second
protagonist), Diane Fossey for gorillas, and Biruté Galdikis for orangu-
tans. Similarly, the phrase "in our genes" as a source for human behaviors,
is very much a favored line of current times, although technically, the
word was available, through Johansen's coinage (as Rio correctly notes) in
1913. So Rio has already placed us into temporal ambiguity by translating to 1913 some work and language not really done or much used
until our own days, but logically available (though historically unexploited)
in the years before World War I.

But these examples are just teases. Rio's true intellectual tour de
force centers upon a pivotal issue in the application of evolutionary
theory to human behavior—the problem of altruism. In particular, if
Darwin's theory states that natural selection works to maximize the reproductive success of individuals (and remember that our hero explicitly
states his allegiance to Darwinian theory), then how can altruistic behavior be part of our evolutionary legacy—since actions undertaken for
the benefit of others must entail personal danger and consequent reduc-
tion of the altruist's individual reproductive success. Any genetic tendency
for altruism should therefore be selected against in a Darwinian world
and quickly eliminated from the gene pool of a population. Since, nonetheless, altruistic behavior not only exists in humans, but seems to stand at
the heart of our moral systems, such unselfish behavior would seem to
require either an evolutionary principle directly contrary to Darwinian
natural selection, or a claim that culture has freed humans from our biological past to a point where our genealogical continuity with the rest of
nature offers no insight into those central behaviors that we call "human
nature." Even worse, if altruism can only be built and sustained by culture, and must be construed as directly contrary to Darwinian processes,
then nature and culture are at war and biology cannot enlighten human
behavior at all.

Our hero and his English counterpart, Lady Jane Savile, can accept neither of these alternatives—for both are Darwinians and both are committed to the idea that extensive study of chimpanzees in their natural habitat may help to unravel the basic biology of human behavior. How, then, can they proceed—both to save Darwinism in the study of human nature, and to make the behavior of chimpanzees relevant to our own evolution? How can they carry forward the great Darwinian program of human continuity with nature and fight the age-old prejudice of our godlike separation?

Lady Jane Savile expresses this central argument with eloquence in her major conversation with the hero:

> "Here is my hypothesis: according to Darwin's model of evolution and natural selection, organisms can act only in their own self-interest and struggle to increase their offspring, that is to say the representation of their genes, to the detriment of their congeners. No higher principle exists in nature. Personal advantage is the sole criterion of success. . . . But the theory runs up against serious obstacles, which, incidentally, did not escape Darwin himself. . . . [I]n a number of species that live in collective societies, altruistic behavior has been observed. Further, if we admit that altruism is the highest moral value and the bond of human society, it would mean, if we were to respect the letter of Darwinian theory, that human society is fundamentally foreign to nature and that the fruits of consciousness are absolutely independent of biology, which I, personally, cannot accept. It would amount to postulating the unique origin, if not the divine essence of our species, in spite of everything we know about evolution. How then can one reconcile altruism and biology, or, in Darwinian terms, altruism and natural selection?" (69)

Evolutionary biology solved this problem, at least with a sound theoretical argument (for empirical validation can only arise later, after much hard work), in the 1960s, with an important extension of Darwinism now generally called the theory of "kin selection." The logical and mathematical bases for kin selection were developed by the British biologist W. D. Hamilton in the 1960s, but hints abound in earlier literature and anecdote—particularly in a famous story, perhaps apocryphal, that J.B.S.

Haldane, probably the most brilliant evolutionist since Darwin, once did a back-of-the-envelope calculation in a pub and proclaimed: "I will lay down my life for more than two brothers or more than eight first cousins."

In this cryptic remark, Haldane had broken through conventional thinking to a new formulation that might solve the problem of altruism. True, Darwinian theory speaks only of a struggle (metaphorical to be sure) for personal reproductive success. "No higher principle exists in nature," as Lady Savile states (ibid.). But what constitutes such "reproductive success"? We cannot measure it in terms of personal survival, for all flesh is mortal. Traditional calculations had only included lineal descendants—children, grandchildren, and so forth. But Darwin's true criterion should be expressed as passage of one's own genes (or faithful copies thereof) into future generations (for one cannot pass one's body along into posterity!). And relatives share copies of one's genes to an extent that can easily be calculated. For example, a person shares as high a percentage of genes with his siblings as with his children—50 percent in each case. For first cousins, percentage of genes held in common works out to 12.5 percent or $\frac{1}{8}$. Thus, an "altruistic" act done to save three siblings would not, in the proper Darwinian calculus, be self-denying at all, but would rather be quite properly selfish and in the interest of one's own genes—for each sibling is 50 percent of you, and three siblings are therefore 1 $\frac{1}{2}$ of you. In other words, if you (100 percent of your genes) die to save three brothers (150 percent of your genes), you have actually increased your personal Darwinian fitness through your act of self-immolation. (Haldane's remark about dying for more than two sibs or more than eight first cousins now makes perfect sense.)[e]

Darwinian selection for copies of your genes held by relatives is called "kin selection," and the "altruistic" actor is said to be working in favor of his "inclusive fitness"—that is, for copies of his genes held not only by himself but also including his relatives. The extension to a general theory of altruism follows directly from the foregoing argument. How do we recognize who is kin, and who is unrelated? Humans, with maximal

---

[e] In February 1993, the Harvard geneticist Richard Lewontin presented before a group of his sociobiologist colleagues Marcel Blanc's demonstration that, within a family, an altruist who aids his brothers finds in fact the number of his genes transmitted to the following generation diminished. To be theoretically sound, Blanc concludes, kin selection theory must take into consideration conditions other than the mere observation of the degree of correlation among relatives. *Translator's note added to the French edition of Gould's essay.*

cognitive power among animals, may know by linguistic report, but other animals must use clues of appearance, odor, or simple proximity during early life. In fact, the following biological rule might work well: "treat as kin worthy of altruistic acts the members of your species who share your den or home." As humans became more social and began to include large numbers of nonkin in their domiciles, cities, and workplace, this rule, once so effective when our ancestors lived in small kin groups, might begin to go awry (in purely Darwinian terms of maximizing genetic passage, not in terms of our preferred moral standards)—and we might systematically perform acts of altruism to nonkin. We might even be led, from this original biological core of Darwinian utility, to establish a general theory of altruism, whose moral value would then compensate for the superseded criterion of raw Darwinian fitness.

This theory of kin selection did not arise within evolutionary biology until the 1960s but—and now we come to the key point—absolutely nothing would have prevented its origin in 1913, if only someone (like Haldane in the pub) had reasoned the matter through. All the necessary pieces were available within Darwinian theory as it existed in 1913—but, as a matter of contingent historical fact, no one happened to put them together. Michel Rio has understood this curiosity and has therefore, like Wagner placing future German history into the mouth of Hans Sachs, given to his hero and to Lady Savile the enviable role of putative inventors for the theory of kin selection. And why not? It could well have happened this way. This form of "iffy history" can be so fascinating as a source of conjecture about alternative plausible pathways for our cultural lives. But this important intellectual exercise must be, and has traditionally fallen into, the domain of novelists—and Rio has risen brilliantly to a superb opportunity.

As they discuss their plans for joint research, the hero asks Lady Jane if altruism will require an abandonment or overturn of Darwinism, and she replies:

> "I have rather sought a solution within the theory, and I have arrived at a mathematical extrapolation of the most recent genetic data. . . . [T]here exists a great number of cases where an individual, governed purely by instinct, would find it in its interest to sacrifice itself for its close relatives, if they are sufficiently numerous, because all of them together would have a greater capacity than it alone to propagate its own genes. This is

what I would call family selection, . . . which makes altruism a sophisticated form of egoism." (*DJ*, 70)

The hero, filled with admiration, gets the point and even (if anachronistically) uses Haldane's example of sibs and cousins:

"Do you mean that in order to favor its own reproductive success, it is in the interest of an individual to sacrifice itself for a given number of siblings, or a greater number of cousins?" (ibid.)

Lady Jane then makes the extension to altruism as a general human behavior to nonkin as well, and ends with a brilliant commentary on the deepest issue of human unity with, or separation from, nature:*f*

"And that would make human morality and biology compatible, insofar as our consciousness would have simply seized upon this instinct to make of it an absolute, positive value, altruism, by extending it to larger units, such as social class, nation, culture, or, more rarely, alas, the entire species and even the whole of all living things. I really do not understand why we insist on systematically attributing to the mind what we consider noble in ourselves and to instinct what we consider base. It recalls the foolishness of dualist philosophies which postulate a radical difference of essence between the soul and the body." (*DJ*, 70–71)

Rio's excellent understanding of the biological issues also extends to his denouement. The hero goes into the jungle to spend the better part of a year trying to test Lady Jane Savile's hypothesis by observing chimps in the wild, without interference. (Note that this is the method used in our generation by Jane Goodall in her monumental work, extending over more than a quarter century, on the chimps of Gombé.) In their earlier conversation, the hero had recognized that three kinds of data would be needed to test the hypothesis: degrees of kinship ("Possible," he correctly

---

f On this issue Rio is consistent in refusing to separate man from nature while, at the same time, making clear his rejection of anthropomorphism. See Rabaté's discussion of *Parrot's Perch* and *Faux Pas*.

argues, "if the study of a population is sufficiently long and detailed"), costs and benefits of relevant behaviors, and reproductive success itself (71–72).

During his many months, the hero observes much that is consistent with kin selection and nothing clearly contrary, but he cannot adequately measure either the costs and benefits of behavior or overt reproductive success in so short a time—as would indeed have been the case then, and would still be now, for Goodall has been working for twenty-five years and has only slowly built such a base of data:

> As I had foreseen, I managed more or less to establish the degrees of kinship, which required long and difficult observation; but it was impossible for me to measure the costs and benefits of all the monkeys' behaviors or real reproductive success. Nonetheless, the prime importance of kinship imposed itself on me. . . . Nothing allowed me to prove Jane's theory, but neither did anything invalidate it absolutely. (98)

If Rio's invocation of evolutionary theory had ended here, my praise would still be warm for his novelistic use of my profession. But, in a final twist that ties together all the disparate parts of his novella, and with a further virtuosic nod to anachronism as a literary device, Rio then criticizes the naive version of kin selection theory within evolutionary biology and gives (in my view) the right and balanced solution that also, as a consequence much to be welcomed, links art and science in a richer view of human nature.

The theory of kin selection has too often been used, both in journalistic accounts of pop sociobiology and also in many professional publications on the adaptive value of behavior, to propagate a naive and unsupported biological determinism. This literature tries to identify a Darwinian and genetic inevitability (or at least a nearly unchangeable predisposition) for human behaviors. After all, if our valued traits of altruism have a genetic basis in Darwinian utility, then why not attribute all our less happy commonalities—our aggressivity, our racism and sexism, our xenophobia, our prevarication and duplicity—to our genes as well. For these traits are even easier to construe as beneficial to our reproductive success, because old-fashioned and overt Darwinian struggle, rather than more subtle kin selection, can be invoked as the motor. Biological determinism is dubious enough as a moral philosophy (blaming inborn genes for our undesirable attributes), but becomes more pernicious as an unsupported political boost for conservative causes (why fight for racial or sexual equality of opportunity if people are biologically predisposed to the unequal roles now adopted; why sink public moneys into better education for the poor if poverty reflects inherent intellectual inability).[8]

The fallacy behind all biological determinisms in evolutionary theory lies in the assumption of pervasive adaptation—the idea that all important behaviors must be viewed as explicitly evolved for benefits thereby conferred to individuals in their Darwinian struggles for reproductive success. If altruism, or any other crucial human behavior, must be seen as a Darwinian adaptation, then we are determined products of our biology, and human choice and free will (beyond trivial incidents of no concern to the Darwinian overseer) are illusions. But if many important human behaviors are not adaptive, and not even explicitly genetic (but rather products of cultural flexibility and choice within an uncontrolling biological substrate), then nature and nurture are equal partners, and human uniqueness can be affirmed as an outcome of our unusual biology of unparalleled mental power and flexibility, and not by such antiquated arguments as divine sparks or special somethings contrary to nature.

The hero of *Dreaming Jungles*, speaking from eighty years past, also presents a trenchant critique of biological determinism properly rooted in the central fallacy of adaptationism. Here, Rio has used anachronism in another remarkably clever way that will only be clear to professional evolutionists who know the history of terminology in their field—and I wish to distribute his insight more widely by presenting this explication.

The hero criticizes a view that he calls "neo-Darwinism." Now modern evolutionary theory also goes by the name of "neo-Darwinism,"

---

[8] In *Manhattan Terminus*, where the noncorrelation of evolution and progress is a central question, Gould is cited by name and his ideas on the subject win approval. In a clear wink to Gould, Rio ridicules precisely the racist utilization of biological theory. The parody comes in the form of a song interpreted by the black jazz pianist "Scipio Africanus," comparing the opposing theories of the Dutch anatomist Louis Bolk and the German biologist Ernst Haeckel, the "kind Mr. Bolk" and the "mean Mr. Haeckel," whose diametrically opposed reasoning arrives at the same racist conclusion: black is inferior. See *MT*, 71–77, and Gould, "Racism and Recapitulation," in *Ever Since Darwin*, 214–21; also (on Bolk), "The Child as Man's Real Father," 63–69.

but the two uses are quite separate. The hero, in 1913, is criticizing August Weismann's version of Darwinian thought, called "neo-Darwinism" at the time. Modern neo-Darwinism refers to the suite of ideas that converged in the 1940s and 1950s as the "modern synthetic theory" of evolution. The two neo-Darwinisms are quite distinct in their beliefs, and do not have historical continuity. But they do share one attitude in common—pervasive adaptationism. Thus, by criticizing neo-Darwinism in 1913 for its overreliance on adaptation, Rio's character can also be viewed as commenting upon modern neo-Darwinism and its own overcommitment to the doctrine of utility. I applaud Rio for this ingenious and unifying ploy of rhetoric.

The hero writes of his disenchantment with one aspect—the bio-determinist implications—of Lady Jane Savile's theory of kin selection:

> These contradictions led me to formulate a criticism of what seemed to me the greatest danger of neo-Darwinism and its totalitarian spirit. Just as, in my view, all the characteristics of an organism did not necessarily correspond to a narrow and utilitarian principle of adaptation, so experience tended to show me that an organism was not the simple support, the slave of its own genes, subject only to their will to propagate themselves. Rather, it represented an inseparable entity with, according to the degree of its evolution, its perplexities and even, ultimately, its choices. I saw in this a kind of hesitation in instinct, and even more in learning, something decisive among the chimpanzees, for whom the competence necessary for survival seemed to depend more on the acquired than the innate. . . . I thus forged, obviously without being able to prove that it was real, a chain between nature and culture, animality and humanity, whose links connected instinct to learning, learning to innovation, innovation to consciousness, consciousness to morality. (DJ, 98-99)

The hero has found the right solution—right for 1913, just as right today. He has found the exit from a false and stultifying reductionism that would link nature to culture by viewing our institutions and behaviors as determined epiphenomena of Darwinian biology and the struggle of our genes for future representation. In so doing, Rio has rightly balanced the independent, mutually reinforcing, and equally enlightening realms of our

biological heritage and our cultural uniqueness.[h] He has therefore spoken
for humanism in its truest, most liberal, and most desperately needed
form—not as a counterpart at war with an alien biology of determination, but as an ally in our struggle to understand human uniqueness in
the context of our genealogical connection with all other living beings.

During the many months that our hero works alone in the thinking
jungles, he contemplates life and meaning, and he muses upon a dichotomy
in viewing nature: on the one hand as a locus of integration and fundamental rightness:

> I felt myself filled with the power and the clarity of this natural
> world, linked organically with the totality of a universe that had
> no other justification to offer than its existence alone, and in
> which the loss of any part was but an episode, quickly healed.
> (*DJ*, 96)

But on the other hand as a locus of senseless cruelty, from which
humans had been able to escape by using the fruits of consciousness:

> At times, on the other hand, I felt full of terror and indignation at
> the brutality of the aggression, at the pangs of anguish and phy-
> sical suffering around me. I began to hate this world, occupied
> solely with destroying itself better to endure, with regenerating
> itself by a continual baptism of blood. The whole blind and
> ferocious mechanism seemed to me an absurdity. . . . and I
> wished only to return to my fellow men, to their capacity for
> intelligence and kindness. (ibid.)

Yet just as free will and complete biological determinism are incor-
rect extremes in the study of human nature, so our hero eventually realizes
that earthly nature cannot be dichotomized as romantic oneness versus
senseless cruelty—for these "extreme states, quite rare, were only the
critical moments of an excess of solitude" (ibid.). We need the integration

---

[h] This is much the same spirit as Rio's insistence on the necessary interaction between
dreamer and logician, poetry and calculation, art and science (the last evoked by the
narrator of *Dreaming Jungles* and by Gould in these pages), or on an aesthetics that
demands mutual reinforcing between nature and culture. See the introduction in this
volume, Arent Safir, Pastoureau, Ritter (especially the end), and, on aesthetics, Swenson.

of our disciplines, the end to false and extreme dichotomizations, the recognition that we cannot grasp human uniqueness unless we both practice art and understand science.[i] We must celebrate a novelist who can teach scientists so much about evolution with a literary ploy rooted in anachronism—and we must tolerate a scientist who chooses to pay his respects by writing for a book of literary criticism. Please do not view either of us as a crocodile in the wrong place!

---

[i] On the encounter of art and science, and Rio's use of scientific method, see the introduction in this volume, Pastoureau, and Ritter. On the incorporation of scientific hypothesis in a work of fiction, see also Galarza.

2

"It is not safe to know"[1]

Margery Arent Safir

Incest stalks Michel Rio's work. His novels are furnished with immense libraries and theoretical discussions of encyclopedic diversity. One of these libraries is presided over by the encyclopedic Leonard Wilde, *Archipelago's* resident misanthrope, later the unwitting hero of *Tlacuilo*.[a] Studying his file of checkout cards documenting the books that each student and teacher has over the years borrowed from the Hamilton School library, his way of knowing individuals without having to frequent them, Wilde concludes of the novel's young narrator:

> "All of this expresses a good deal of irony and pessimism and a melancholy attraction for the solitary freedom of the heights, or the abysses. Dreams of logic and the logic of dreams. You are not far from obsession, indispensable for doing something." (*Ar*, 67–68)

The observation applies equally to the protagonists of Rio's other novels. Irony, pessimism, and melancholy are known to them all, as is the attraction of extremes, "the heights, or the abysses." All know solitude. In each, that fundamental couple, the dreamer and the logician, plays out its

---

[1] "It is not safe to know," a verse from D'Avenant that serves as the epigraph to *Trade Winds*: "But ask not Bodies doom'd to die, / To what abode they go; / Since knowledge is but sorrow's spy, / It is not safe to know."

[a] On *Archipelago*, see Swenson and Metz. On *Tlacuilo*, see Galarza and Metz.

role. For each, "doing something" is obsessive, and indispensable. And "All of this" in all of them is born of an ultimate obsession: the knowledge of death. The seduction of death inhabits Rio's novels. Action—building, doing, producing—is a way of putting off its pull, of keeping it at bay and the mind occupied so as not to fall into the inevitable melancholy that lies in wait. Action encompasses, is dependent on, the dreamer and the logician:

> The logician lays out the law of nature and reason, which lead ineluctably to death. The dreamer refuses, protests, searches vainly elsewhere. Together they form a couple that confronts each other, enriches one another, at times is reconciled to one another, and in any event that cannot be wholly dissociated. (*DL*, 72)[2][b]

The dreamer represents affective capacity and imagination; the logician, knowledge and the possibility of "doing." Alone, each is incomplete. The dreamer is incapable of action. The logician is sterile, without purpose or invention. Only in their encounter is real action possible: "Dreams of logic and the logic of dreams." In the meeting of extremes action is born.

All of this, by odd twists and turns, points back to my initial two sentences: There are many incests and there are many libraries in Rio's novels. What interests me is "why?": not why incest, nor why libraries, but why incest *and* libraries; what, if any, is the relation between the two? Taken individually, each of my two opening sentences is indisputable. My hypothesis is that the two are inherently related. Libraries lead Rio's characters to incest. Otherwise put, personal relationships for Rio are not founded on sentiment, not even primarily on lust, but on an encounter between logician and dreamer, a category of *action* within this larger system of binary opposition, and as such never far from the question of death. The nature of action that constitutes personal relationships is singular and invariable, and is pedagogy. Likeness and difference: pedagogy presupposes a dialogue between unequals; it presupposes on the part of the one the possession of knowledge, on the part of the other the desire of possessing knowledge. Its dynamic is a movement between extremes, pre-

---

[2] See also *Dreaming Jungles*, 57.
[b] On *Dreams of Logic*, see the introduction in this volume, Galarza, and Metz. On *Dreaming Jungles*, see Gould and Metz.

cisely the movement from difference to likeness in the realm of knowledge. From this dynamic perverseness is born, not psychoanalytic but "kinetic" perverseness, much as Poe speaks of it, a turning back on oneself in an irresistible dynamic of simultaneous doing and undoing.[3c] My argument is limited to what I consider a closed cycle, Rio's first six novels: *Melancholy North, Parrot's Perch, Trade Winds, Dreaming Jungles, Archipelago,* and *Merlin.*[d] It is limited of necessity by the very dynamic that I postulate.

What follows is a personal reading, an alloying of essay and study, mythologies, speculation, and demonstration, composed of two rapid parts that overview a number of novels; one slower part focused on the reading of a single novel, *Dreaming Jungles,* with a kind of Q.E.D. tone that feels appropriate to me for Rio's universe in which synthetic argumentation is at the very base of imagination; one final part, the pure pleasure of going beyond the text toward what I believe Rio has been talking about from his very first novel: pedagogy brings us to mother. Sexual possession and the possession of knowledge are inseparable. Mother is woman and the prime pedagogical figure, and the perverseness of incest derives less from the fact that mother is a forbidden woman than from the reasons at the base of that interdiction. The beauty of knowledge. Seduction and knowledge. Sin and knowledge. We are back not only with all mothers but with the mother of all mothers, Eve, and her apple.

From *Mentor* to *Mater*

But first was Mentor, the loyal friend of a sea voyager, and tutor to his son Telemachus. Olaf Borgström and Brieuc de Goulven are both older than the seafaring narrator of Rio's first novel, and specifically identified by him as "father" figures and "mentors" (*MN*, 35–37). One could easily insert *Melancholy North* (1982) into the long tradition of Western literature wherein knowledge is transferred from man to man, from Mentor to Telemachus, Socrates to Plato, king to prince, father to son.

---

[3] See the three perverse stories: "The Tell-Tale Heart," "The Imp of the Perverse," and "The Black Cat."

[c] On this dynamic, see Rabaté's discussion of making and unmaking.

[d] On *Melancholy North,* see Rabaté and Metz. On *Parrot's Perch,* see Ritter, Rabaté, and Metz. On *Trade Winds,* see Metz. On *Dreaming Jungles,* see Gould and Metz. On *Archipelago,* see Swenson and Metz. On *Merlin,* see Pastoureau, Ritter, and Metz.

But the gods are tricky, and Rio too begins slyly, or shyly. At the seashore following the assembly of Ithaca, Mentor appears to Telemachus but it is not Mentor; it is Athena, the goddess of knowledge. She sails with the son of Odysseus on the first leg of the voyage to Pylos. This throws us into the heart of the matter: that the mentors in *Melancholy North* are men is but an accident of physiology, a misunderstanding of sorts, I would speculate an initial fright on Rio's part, and Olaf Borgström and Brieuc de Goulven do not partake of that male to male tradition but of another, that of *Mater Sapientae*. Like Athena dressed up in Mentor's clothing, these mentors are quite simply disguised mothers, possessing exactly the same characteristics that will define the women/mother figures when Rio gets closer to the point in the novels that follow. They are solitary and geographically isolated, physically superb (albeit somewhat disembodied as far as description goes, undoubtedly a result of their mistaken gender), seductive, sexually active, and linked to death (34–36); they possess magnificent libraries and encyclopedic knowledge. There is a triangle, a geometric form to which Rio seems particularly attracted: mentor-narrator-mentor. The narrator voyages from one (mentor) to the other, a voyage characterized by a life-death struggle at sea. In Norway, death awaits. He has crossed the sea to find "father," Borgström, dead, and a letter in which literature is identified as "mother": from the French *mer* (sea) to *mère* (mother), a fundamental homophone to which I shall return.[e]

Athena removes a glove in Rio's next novel, revealing gender adaptation, a *woman* of significance. Although she appears in the most abstract, minimal way, this woman will be the prototype, or rather the embryo of prototype, for all the women of substance to follow. This is somewhat surprising, for the novel in question is *Parrot's Perch* (1983), a novel set in a monastery, another novel that appears almost exclusively male. In fact there are two women. The first, a peasant-woman, is a sort of pedagogical failure, looking to Joachim, the protagonist, as a mentor, seeking from the tormented Latin American priest a guidance he can no longer give. The second woman is the one to whom I refer above. She is solitary. She is depicted reading a book. She awakens feelings of desire and disquiet in her son. She is Joachim's mother. This is the very first time that this portrait, now assigned sexually to a woman, appears. It is fleeting but sets the standard irrevocably: the conjunction of solitude, knowledge, and uneasy desire.

---

[e] On Borgström's death, a suicide, see Rabaté; also, note *l*, p. 142, relating this death and that of Leonard Wilde in *Manhattan Terminus*.

Trade Winds (1984) goes further, putting forth a woman who is not only solitary, isolated by reason of knowledge, and beautiful, but the first woman of palpable flesh. Veils fall. Sexual scenes appear in a Rio novel for the first time (the narrator's masturbation at sea in *Melancholy North* being more hygienic than erotic), and even they are pedagogical: the narrator initiates Suzanne into the knowledge of sex. But sex education is only one course in this novel of universal knowledge. Suzanne learns French, almost as fundamental as sex for Rio, and, lest we forget, the mother tongue. She learns the entirety of Western culture. In all cases, the action between Suzanne and the narrator is pedagogical. She is his pupil and in turn becomes his tutor. She is not the narrator's chronological superior but she is on the island before he is, and therefore, in her realm, the possessor of a knowledge, practical, historical, and cultural, which is superior to his. She possesses a manuscript to be deciphered, which holds the value of myth; he possesses a bilingual, bicultural encyclopedia, which represents European knowledge. Metaphorically one could say that the action of the novel is the dialogue between these two books. In the end it is Suzanne who instructs the narrator, and Suzanne who determines his departure. Sea, death (or risk of death), pedagogy; a triangle of cultures Anglo–French–pagan. A dynamic that repeats itself: a coming together of difference, action that is pedagogy, and, when what was to be learned has been learned, the impossibility of further action, with the inevitable consequence. They separate.

In a kind of slow striptease, with each succeeding novel the prime pedagogue, initially masked and disguised, is being disrobed and progressively revealed. In *Archipelago* (1987), she almost comes forth in the unadorned flesh. "Mother. Mother. . . ." cries Prince John sucking his thumb in the Disney epigraph that introduces the novel.^{f} The work is an island of pedagogues, mother substitutes, mother lovers (or dreamed as such by their sons), and multiple variations, beginning with Alexandra Hamilton, a school friend and perhaps wishful lover, of the young narrator's mother. She is the first protagonist who is both female and of parental age. Madame Hamilton is beautiful, solitary, isolated because of superior knowledge, and she owns a school, making her the possessor not only of knowledge but of

---

^{f} The quotation is from the 1973 Disney film *Robin Hood*. This cry of "Mother" is taken up again in *Manhattan Terminus*, but how mother has changed: "Oh! Mother! . . . Poor hateful Mommy dear! Not only was she an atrocious educator, but on top of that, was she spiteful and nasty!" (*MT*, 80)

pedagogy. The narrator's mother has sent her son to Alexandra Hamilton to be educated, and asks Madame Hamilton to stand in for her on the occasion of nothing less than that most mother-related of all holidays, her son's *birth*day. Alan Stewart, the narrator's friend, and mentor in certain regards, also has plans for the narrator on the occasion of his sixteenth birthday: *his* mother (Alan's), offered sexually. Here too there is substitution, since Alan confesses his passionate love for his mother, a confession that in turn troubles the narrator as regards both his own mother and her stand-in, Madame Hamilton. And, of course, all of this is pedagogical. The setting is the celebrated Hamilton School, and the narrator to be educated, unlike his diverse "teachers," is a virgin. Still another caretaker and willing instructor appears in the form of the school nurse, Miss Atkins, under the direction of Alan Stewart; *in loco matris*, she initiates the narrator, she and Alan. But she is a pale surrogate. She in no way resembles mother, and precisely because of her willingness, lacks that essential element held by mother, the knowledge of taboo, and in consequence a sense of fault, what gives meaning to transgression. Alan explains:

"[The sense of fault] fascinates me in a woman insofar as it contributes inevitably to an increase in her pleasure, and thus my own. It exists in her in proportion to the disparity between her public propriety and her secret desire for corruption. A disparity that counts above all else, for it is a multiplier that exploits the energy born from the meeting of extremes; . . ." (*Ar*, 43)

Naturally, Alan puts forth mother as the summit in this proportionality of disparity, but beyond their testimony as to the delights of incest, his words count for the dynamic they define, "the energy born from the meeting of extremes." Still one more tutor must be added to Hamilton School's pedagogical roster: the selfsame Leonard Wilde, the librarian, Alexandra Hamilton's childhood tutor, her adult lover-from-afar, her voyeur.[8] In the end, completing or complementing the curriculum of her already extra-

---

[4] With so many preceptors, here too triangles abound: Alexandra Hamilton-narrator-Leonard Wilde; Alan Stewart-narrator-Miss Atkins; Alan Stewart-narrator-Lady Stewart; Alexandra Hamilton-narrator-narrator's mother; and my list does not include the governess nor exhaust the possible combinations.
[8] It is the male trio narrator-Alan Stewart-Leonard Wilde that reappears in *Tlacuilo* and then again in *Manhattan Terminus*.

ordinary institution of learning, Madame Hamilton offers the narrator
the "sentimental education" he both seeks and fears. The sexual acts, oral
and manual, fall short of penetration, but the intention is clear: Alexandra
Hamilton *does* resemble mother, and this is the first real and affirmed act
of incest-by-surrogate in a Rio novel. I repeat that it occurs with a
woman who, beyond her traits shared with the previous women and her
closeness to the narrator's mother, is first pictured seated in a magnificent
library,[h] almost invisible among the tomes that dwarf her, a woman who
possesses not only knowledge but a pedagogical institution that bears her
name. At the end of the novel they separate. The narrator, his "education"
accomplished, is left alone and melancholy on the isle of Jersey. He takes
to the *mer*, contemplates death, but returns.

Lastly, for triangles and educators and variations on incest only
Merlin (1989) outdoes *Archipelago*, and so confirms the logic of chronological progression. Merlin is tutored by his grandfather who is also his
father, having impregnated his mother while in the guise of Satan. He is
tutored also by Blaise, in the service of his grandfather/father, and the
tutor of his mother. Of all the employees of the grandfather/father, who
happens to be king, only the tutor is introduced; not a warrior, not a
page, not a buffoon but a preceptor.[i] Merlin is the son (and lover?) of a
mother who is beautiful and solitary, isolated by knowledge and love of
learning, and Merlin in turn is the tutor of Arthur, the teacher of kings, of
the new order, the Round Table, the preceptor of Morgan, his most
brilliant student, his most spectacular success, and failure. Morgan is the
mother and tutor of Mordred, born of incest. Vivian comes to Merlin
seeking knowledge and offering her body. Vivian in her turn is the
adoptive mother of Bohort, Lionel, and Lancelot, lover of the adulterous
Guinevere, and she "herself took charge of their education" (*M*, 127).

Let there be no mistake. There is another sine qua non, beauty, and,
improving on legend, in Rio's world, Athena takes the form not only of
Mentor but of Venus. No ugly pupils browse in Rio's libraries, and
among the women at least, no ugly tutors are found (among the men,
Leonard Wilde once more holds the honor of exception). Nonetheless,
action remains the interplay between the logician *and* the dreamer, and so
like intellect, physical attraction falls into the category of necessary but

---

[h] On the description of this library and others, see Swenson.
[i] This choice of the preceptor Blaise joins what Pastoureau says regarding Rio's choice of
Merlin himself as the central figure of the book. See Pastoureau.

insufficient. It suffices for an engineer's wife or a school nurse, even for a queen, Guinevere (Rio cannot be faulted for class prejudice here), but not for a significant relationship. Beauty arouses the dreamer, intellect calls to the logician, and only where both are engaged can pedagogy, and so passion, begin.[5]

But I have left out a book, *Dreaming Jungles* (1985), the novel that constitutes the chronological midpoint of the others. It alone appears problematic in the schema I have put forth. The novel's narrator is a young man of good family, handsome, intellectually strong, articulate, ironic, a naturalist by profession, and the leader of a scientific expedition; he encounters and loves a woman who is young, of good family, beautiful, intellectually strong, articulate, ironic, a biologist by profession, and the leader of a scientific expedition. And, she loves him. Not only does equality rather than difference seem to be the rule here, but mirror images. The likeness between the two is stated the very evening that they meet, not once but twice: "Are you of the same breed as Lady Savile?" Henry Sterne inquires of the narrator (*DJ*, 55). Nor does he leave any doubt as to the answer to his rhetorical question: "You seem to me a double of Lady Savile. My God! Two Jane Sheldons! That's a great deal of honor for an encampment of mere mortals" (62). Sterne's irony serves a double master: not only to equate the two exceptional beings, but to remind us that they are indeed exceptional.[j] They are doubles also in gender confusion (we remember *Melancholy North*): the feminine traits attributed to the perfectly masculine narrator, and the masculine traits attributed to the perfectly feminine English woman. Twice the narrator is compared to women, first as being the "living image" of his mother (*DJ*, 16–17), a remark reinforced by his own reflection of reproducing, in the governor's eyes, and in the "most striking fashion," the "maternal phenotype" (26); as for Lady Savile, her camp is "methodical" and "warlike," a kind of scientific "fortress," reminiscent of a "military camp" (41), while her sexual explicitness bears evidence, according to Mr. Sterne, of

---

[5] It is telling in this regard that Rio uses versions of the same Gautier phrase to define beauty both in Alexandra Hamilton and in Guinevere, but in inverse order, the difference being precisely the degree to which the logician is or is not seduced: Madame Hamilton had that particular quality of seduction that "did not attract the eye but held it" (*Ar*, 12); the queen's perfect face "fascinated at first glance more than its seduction lasted" (*M*, 103).
[j] On Rio's taste for "exceptional" characters, see Metz on juvenile fantasies; also, notes *o*, p. 166, and *bb*, p. 172, on *Manhattan Terminus*.

"the very masculine freedom of her temperament and mind" (61). To this might be added that Lady Savile's very first direct intervention in the novel is a demonstration of this temperament and spirit which, stereotypically, Sterne has defined as masculine: She intervenes on the side of logic, defining scientific meaning as the only "real meaning," intellectual activity, that is to say logic, as the "true and essential attribute of mankind," and openly opposing "real meaning" to "affective meaning" (50). The narrator and this woman appear so deserving of one another that it sounds like a fairy tale.

A pedagogical relationship demands, as a first condition, difference. Can one speak of pedagogy where two protagonists and lovers are portrayed as doubles? If pedagogy, and pedagogy that aims at mother, is the fundamental dynamic of the personal relationship in this novel, it does not jump forth the way it does in the others. For this reason I have held *Dreaming Jungles* apart. Unlike the other five novels, *Dreaming Jungles* demands not summary but demonstration.

Tutors and Lovers

Fairy tales too have their perverseness, or disguise our own, and the one I have just recounted is no exception. That the lovers in *Dreaming Jungles* are virtual doubles is factual, and the conclusion to which it leads is false. The two protagonists are "likes" but not equals. Nor is Lady Savile merely Lady Savile. Rather, Lady Savile shares traits with two other figures in the novel, and it is in their shared traits that the true nature of the relationship between her and the narrator is found.

"She was remarkably beautiful, and with a mind so brilliant that it heightened her beauty" (17): such is the first woman described in the novel. This sounds like but is not Lady Savile. It is the narrator's mother, considerably thickening the plot. Solitary, intellectual, the object of her son's troubled feelings, she is the prototypical mother of *Parrot's Perch*, both repeated and magnified. And Lady Savile is the image of the narrator's mother. *They* are doubles, *word for word* doubles: Rio employs for both the same specific vocabulary and mechanisms of description. The same character, the governor, introduces both, and both are spoken about before (or instead of) being seen, a distance advisable for myths. Both are immediately situated as to intellect, and temperature: the mother's is "that of a cold light"; Lady Savile is a "cold perfection" (17, 45). If the mother has an "irony full of grace," Lady Savile has a "gracious and detached superiority" (17, 44).[6] If the mother is a sort of goddess or Greek statue, Lady Savile is an *angelus* of marble, the object of Richardson's "cult" and Richardson a lover of "statues" *(DJ*, 19, 44, 61). Clairvoyant, the narrator sees beyond marble to the contrasts that characterize both women: the goddess is of flesh; the angel suggests her opposite (19, 45). The mother stands apart, as Lady Savile is set apart, logistically (her tent is "set apart from the others" [40]), socially (her aristocratic title), racially and sexually (as a white European in black Africa and a woman in a camp of men). Each woman is portrayed first by her effect on others, how she is looked at, then by the narrator's effect on her, how she looks at the narrator. To each of these women, the narrator is compared (see the preceding section), and each comparison employs a structure of likeness, followed by a trait of humor on gender-confusion, which reintroduces difference (26, 62). We are well beyond the realm of general type. So specific, in fact, is the identification, that most often when a character speaks of one of the ladies he might as well be speaking of the other. "We were all in love with her," the governor says of the mother (17); "that touchy sentimentality she has the art of arousing wherever she goes" (55), Sterne says of Lady Savile. The mother is loved by a man who can imagine only studies as her passion, and whom she does not love; Lady Savile is loved by a man who "takes comfort in the thought that the object of his worship is by definition too highly placed to feel love" (17, 61). The governor's love for the mother will remain "until his death a splendid sketch, richer, more beautiful, and more intact than any finished work that exhausts its subject" (18); Richardson's love for Lady Savile would doubtless make him "suffer far more if he achieved his aims" (61). The mother confers, or withholds, a sense of existence from men (17); Lady Savile, indifferent to Richardson's passion, accords a kind of existence to the narrator when she ceases to consider him "a scientific expedition" and takes into account that he is "a human being" (55). For both of these women, married or widowed, portrayed without husbands, the narrator is singular, the "chosen."

The narrator meets Lady Savile, a woman defined by extremes, a European, in an enclave of Europe in Africa, and the tumult she awakens

---

[6] The published English translation here reads "her charming irony." I have translated the French *pleine de grâce* literally to make the point that the author actually uses the same vocabulary in describing the two women (Rio, *Les Jungles pensives*, 23).

in him he likens to the African jungle;[7] the image of Lady Savile standing alone, juxtaposed to the African jungle, closes the novel's second chapter. The narrator's mother, a European, is evoked in Africa by the governor, and is defined by him: "She was a mystery, a kind of Africa before its time" (*DJ*, 18).

This moves us to the other figure involved in these likenesses. The African jungle is a botanical *mer* ("sea of graminae" [34]), and a place of extremes.[8] Birth images, sexual images, and images of pedagogy are attached to the jungle.[9] Both the mother and Lady Savile are identified with it. The narrator enters the heart, or the womb, of the jungle because of Jane, for reasons of learning related to reasons of love, and he is reborn. The jungle is his second mother (*DJ*, 102).

If nouns define the triangle mother/Jane/jungle, in other terms Europe/Europe-in-Africa/Africa, verbs define the dynamic of relations and the nature of action. Backing up and starting over we can replay the initial encounter between the narrator and Lady Savile from the beginning, viewing it now from a different angle than that of the initial fairy tale of "likes" I first proposed. Focusing on verbs, the question changes from *who* or *what* each character is to *how* each is introduced in the novel.

Lady Savile is introduced by reputation, in a context of influence, power, and professional renown, while the narrator is introduced as a son. He first appears within the context of *family*. He is only three or four years older than the young lieutenant who accompanies him to Grand-Bassam, and who looks as if he had just left his mother's arms (3); the two young men's families know each other. Upon arriving on the

---

[7] For pairs of opposites used to describe Lady Savile, see, for example, 53–54 and 65, and especially 80 ("the mixture in this woman. . . ."). As for the effect she produces on the narrator being compared to the African jungle, see 56 ("This mixture of peace close at hand and turmoil taking shape in the distance . . . the canvas screen").

[8] Here we find the weighty homophone to which I referred in the preceeding section: the word for "sea" in French and the word for "mother" differ in only one letter, and are pronounced *exactly the same* (*mer, mère*). This opens up all sorts of associations that are lost in translation. Rio's use of the two words is significant, and fundamentally so, as I show further on. For this reason I am retaining the original French in my discussion of the text. As regards the jungle being a place of extremes, examples are everywhere, but see especially 94–97 ("this permanence of opposites. . . ."), and 102.

[9] See especially the abundance of pedagogical vocabulary, 90–92 (". . . initiation . . . apprenticeship . . . studied . . . learned. . . ."), as well as the association of the jungle and mother, each an "initiator," 102.

African continent, the narrator is received with fanfare because he is his mother's son, and in consequence, and much to his annoyance, the governor's "protégé" (27). More significant still, he is, everywhere, the newcomer, the one who must be initiated to Africa, to the English base camp, to the jungle, a status that is underscored by the nature of the initial discourse in the novel. Without exception it is—yes, that word again—pedagogical, with the narrator on the receiving end. Blanchot, the knowledgeable and frustrated bureaucrat, gives him lessons on geography and ethnology, the boat captain on the ins and outs of navigating the lagoon, the governor, beyond unwelcome sentimental information, offers him a dinner that proves "if not pleasant, at least instructive" (20). Lefèvre, the guide, then takes up the narrator's education. In a word, between his arrival on the African shore and his setting out toward the African interior, the narrator not only offends most everyone whom he meets but submits to a pedagogical process that starts him on the path from newcomer (initiate) to—the maximum degree of difference— veteran (initiated). His arrival with Lefèvre in the jungle signals a second playing of this same movement, and his arrival at the English base camp signals a third.

For when the narrator arrives at the English base camp, a kind of Europe-in-Africa, repeating in the colony the hierarchy of class and race known in the metropolis (as previously the organization on the train had), he is again the newcomer. This is critical in the dynamic that will be the order of the day between him and Lady Savile. He arrives not only as newcomer, faced with a woman equal to his mother, but he arrives, so to speak, in *her* home, a camp already established, and structured according to her direction. She heads both the table and the expedition. She scolds like children the men who surround her when they step out of line. Each asks her permission to be excused and to retire. She is the authority; all the men present are her subordinates. We can add to this that Lady Savile is not only introduced in the novel as a woman of renown and influence (young, beautiful, and intellectual, of course), but as a widow. The detail is charming, and could pass for a coquetry on the part of an author who, one suspects, might well have applauded Celimène, were it not that it also corresponds to a factor in the equation I am setting forth. Widowhood places Lady Savile on a different level from the narrator in terms of life, of rites of passage, of stages marked by marriage, "official" knowledge of sex, and above all by the knowledge of death, the terrain of the logician and the dreamer.

In the twenty-four hours that follow their encounter, Lady Savile shows her authority.

As to sex, she makes the overtures. Her actions are deliberate, calculated, unhesitant, and in perfect contrast to the narrator's own inebriated perplexity and indecision. She leaves the door of her tent open, he crosses the threshold only gingerly; she lounges on her camp bed, he is unable to determine if she is waiting for him or not; he decides to flee, she commands him to close the door (64). In short, lest there be any doubt as to the holder of authority, consider first the narrator's words, and then Lady Savile's response to them:

> "Forgive, madam, my confusion, and one final lack of tact, which could not make an already hopeless case any worse, but I do not know which side of this door I am to be on after closing it."

> . . . she lay down again, slid her long dress up over her legs, and began to caress herself slowly and skillfully until she reached orgasm. Not for an instant, not even at the very peak of pleasure and abandon, did she stop staring at me. (64)

As to intellectual discourse, Lady Savile initiates the dialogue. Like her sexual attitudes, Lady Savile's scientific projects are more deliberate, calculated, and defined than those of her chosen interlocutor. She articulates the scientific problem that will constitute the theoretical center of the novel, the question of altruism and egoism in evolutionary doctrine, and with her hypothesis of kin selection, advances by some twenty years J.B.S. Haldane.[10][k] I have said that the two protagonists share a profession, *naturalist* and *biologist* at the turn of the century being virtually synonymous terms. Yet Rio consistently refers to Lady Savile as a "biologist" and to the narrator as a "naturalist." If one were to search for a distinction between the terms, it would be that *naturalist* refers back to a general tradition of natural philosophy, open to an *honnête homme*, while *biologist*, looks forward to the specificity of modern science and to its division into disciplines, requiring specific training and methodology. This difference

---

[10] The English biologist J.B.S. Haldane is the real originator of the theory of kin selection attributed in the novel to Jane Sheldon. Haldane's intuition was later developed formally in the early 1960s by the theoretical biologist W. D. Hamilton.

[k] On the theory of kin selection, see Gould; also, the list of essays by him in note *a*, p. 33.

will not always be true of the two protagonists, but in their first scientific exchange, each emerges true to his or her appellation.[1] The previous evening Lady Savile's "cold perfection" had left the narrator a "dazzled spectator" (*DJ*, 45); the view from below, looking up at the pedestal, holds intellectually as well, and faced with Lady Savile's brilliant hypothesis, the narrator avows: "I looked at her with undisguised admiration" (70).

As to sentiment, it is she who defines the boundaries. Moved "to the point of worry" by the "simple fact of seeing and hearing" Lady Savile, the narrator dutifully patterns his behavior on hers (68). When he does not, he fares ill, and is quickly called back to order: "'Let us please stop speculating on the improbable,' she said, 'whether it be scientific, philosophical, or personal, and whether suggested allusively or not. Instead, tell me what you think of my hypothesis within the more concrete perspective of our work'" (71). The young Richardson comes to mind, or *Archipelago, avant la lettre*. Only when she determines the moment, immediately upon the admiring narrator's offering his gratitude, "madam, for your splendid theory" (72), does Lady Savile herself, in almost authoritarian fashion, turn to personal matters: "I would like us to make love. . . . Now," she commands (ibid.).

I do not intend to prolong the demonstration, nor to claim total innocence of caricature in my rendering. But about the essential point's validity I have no doubt. That point can perhaps be summed up in one image, a measure of the gap between the two protagonists at the moment of their initial meeting. I turn back again to the immediate aftermath of their first sexual relations. As if he were "at the seaside in Harwich during the bathing season," the narrator plunges into the Sassandra (66). Lost in erotic images of Lady Savile, he enters a reverie that in the circumstances reflects imprudence and irresponsibility, reminding us once more that he is a novice in the jungle. He comes face-to-face with a crocodile. He must be rescued by others, like a child, pulled out of the water by one of the nightwatchmen from the Gold Coast, while Fielding shoots the beast. There is a simultaneous, and instructive, image: While the narrator emerges from the water "embarrassed to be the cause of this disturbance and to be making such a spectacle of myself" (ibid.), Lady Savile is standing apart, observing him. Illuminated by the "cold white glow of a bolt of

---

[1] The personal evolution of the two in this regard is demonstrated clearly in Gould's essay, which comments on the narrator's scientific conclusions after his sojourn in the jungle. See Gould.

lightning," she is an image of calm and authority, almost of a goddess, absolutely of the mother described by the governor, and the object of all eyes:

> all of us watched in its [the lightning's] intermittent flashes the successive apparitions of this feminine splendor, immobile in the midst of the outburst, impassive in the multiple and gaping maws of savagery. (ibid.)

The apparent equality of the protagonists in *Dreaming Jungles* is only apparent, for it is limited to exactly that, to appearances: decor, class, profession, beauty. And as Lefèvre says, "Appearances don't count in the jungle" (23).

Difference is the true point of departure, and the novel's action, as always, is a movement from difference to its opposite.

Within a set of extreme limits (beginning and end of the story), a geographic separation from Europe and a political return to Europe via war, occurs a series of departures and returns, of separations and reunions, which are played out multiple times. These "departure-return" pairs, identical to the larger departure-return pair that contains and frames them, almost geometrically structure the degrees by which difference is reduced through pedagogy and the novel's point of departure is left behind. A look at two of these pairs seems to me necessary, and sufficient, to demonstrate this structure and its dynamic as a measure of progressive distancing from the initial encounter between the child/newcomer and the mother/ authority.[11]

---

[11] It is possible to tally the arrivals and departures in various ways, but one counts at least the following: departure from Europe; arrival at/departure from Grand-Bassam; arrival at/departure from Abidjan; with Lefèvre, arrival in the jungle, then arrival at/first departure from the English base camp; arrival at/departure from the provisional jungle camp, one month later; arrival at/departure from deeper jungle with Fielding, one month later; return to/departure from the provisional camp; first return to/second departure from the English base camp; arrival at/departure from the heart of the jungle, ten months later; second return to/final departure from the English base camp; return to/final departure from Grand-Bassam; return to/final departure from Abidjan; return to European boat, the young lieutenant, the marine crocodile, and European affairs, that is, war.

First departure from the base camp and first return to the base camp. At the moment of this departure, the degree of difference between Lady Savile and the narrator, under the appearance of likeness, is at its greatest. The interval between departure and return will be two months, divided into two equal periods. The first is the group expedition, the second that of the narrator alone with Fielding.

The group expedition (devoid of Richardson, who has remained at the base camp) moves deeper into the jungle for a collective study of chimpanzee behavior. We are one month after the initial encounter between Lady Savile and the narrator. Learning, of course, has taken place, with the result that the narrator no longer stands out as green in the jungle or newcomer in the group. But the expedition has not met with success, and the relationship between the protagonists has suffered as a result. Lady Savile's position of absolute command also shows the strain, and if her "theoretical genius" continues to be evoked, for the first time her "philosophical weakness when confronted by failure" is remarked (*DJ*, 80). More grave, no doubt, this woman of authority is suspected of betraying her "masculine spirit," of harmonizing mind and body, and of harboring romantic sentiments more "true" to her gender: Might Jane Sheldon be all woman? (77) In any event, the deference of her subordinates gives way to another tone, even to a touch of paternalism. When she gives her orders and announces her intention to remain alone at the provisional camp, Lefèvre dares pose a condition: that his best man stay at her side to protect madam (78); and Fielding, with humor but with a surprising familiarity, warns this experienced biologist who is the head of the expedition, of the taste that African leopards have for the flesh of the English aristocracy (78). In all of this there is a germ of reversal, as if Lady Savile were in the novice role earlier held by the narrator. This first atrophy of difference between the two is followed by their first separation. Still, as the narrator moves deeper into the jungle, accompanied only by Fielding, he does so under Lady Savile's orders.

The second period is more decisive. We are now two months since the initial encounter between Lady Savile and the narrator. Reentering the provisional camp after a month of observing the chimpanzees, the narrator and Fielding learn that Lady Savile, devoured by fever, has been transported to the base camp. Illness may not be a metaphor, as Susan Sontag has written,[12] but it is an expedient equalizer, an excellent acceler-

---

[12] Susan Sontag, *Illness as Metaphor* (New York: Farrar, 1978), 3.

ator of a process already· underway. The narrator, returning to the base camp, the place of their initial encounter, finds a Lady Savile bathed in sweat, unconscious, reduced to the throes of her body, robbed of the strength of her intellect and the firmness of her will. Richardson, the lovesick secretary for whom this woman was unapproachable, attends to her like a nanny, passing a humid cloth over her forehead. Without conscious will, cared for and watched over by others, without use of language or reason, subject only to the instincts of body, Lady Savile is quite simply the portrait of an infant. And the narrator picks her up like a child. He carries her like a babe in arms to the river and plunges her into the cool water, a well-known remedy for high fever, prescribed above all by pediatricians for infants. "The others had followed me and were watching, silently, planted on the shore like statues of salt," the narrator recounts (*DJ*, 82). Compare this image with the previous bathing scene in this same English base camp: The narrator, with childish irresponsibility, plunging into the Sassandra, threatened with death, paralyzed with terror for himself, is saved by a nightwatchman, while the others, planted on shore, silent, observe the scene; and alone, apart, also observing, stands the distant perfection of Lady Savile, a "statue," at the same time goddess and mother (66). A statue now transformed into a child in his arms; decidedly, reversal is playing more strongly.

This narrator, in any event, has a real vocation, at the very least a marked taste, for plunging into bodies of water, or plunging bodies into water, as the case may be, a predilection admittedly not wholly surprising in the work of an author whose every novel includes a shipwreck, drowning (suicide), or near-drowning. This is the novel's third immersion or "rite by water": a plunge on the initial march into the jungle with Lefèvre avoids possible death; a plunge after the initial sexual relations with Lady Savile puts the narrator face-to-face with possible death; the plunging of Lady Savile saves her from the clutches of death. Not only is there a tendency to plunge into water, but the plunge is uniformly linked to life-death or death-rebirth situations. Water; the homophone will not go away: *mère/mer*, "mother"/"sea." The narrator leaves the one and arrives in Africa via the other, will find a second *mère* (jungle/Jane) and leave definitively by *mer*. Add to this, Freud *oblige*, that both *mère* and *mer* wear double signs, both desired and dangerous, both givers of life and in both one can drown. The addition can be done *ad libertum* but leads to a specific tradition of initiation that is linked both to water and to the ambiguity death-rebirth: baptism. Let me be clear. Not for a moment do

I believe, nor could anyone who has read *Parrot's Perch*, that Michel Rio consciously constructs initiatory water scenes in *Dreaming Jungles* or any other novel as a baptismal image.[13] The absence of intention, however, does not remove the text, nor the interest of the image. Nor can it be argued that the author of *Parrot's Perch* ignores the slightest nuance of Catholic symbolism, whatever the force of his rejection of it. That baptism comes to mind where there are repeated immersions into water, all the more so in *Dreaming Jungles* where each immersion has witnesses, would not win any prize for original insight. However, it is not only the *religio aquae* (the denomination is Tertullian) that provokes the thought, but the innate ambivalence of baptism as well. Like that of the *mère/mer* signs, this ambivalence may begin with baptism's tie to water ("In the element that drowned Pharaoh, Christ—the Fish, *Ichthus*—thrives," Alexander Murray writes[14]) but is not limited to it. For beyond the liquid itself, whether amniotic, maternal, fontal, sexual, oceanic, or other, and once more like the homophone *mère/mer*, baptism wears a dual symbolic sign as regards life and death. Ambivalent also as regards *time*, baptism draws past and future into a single event, proposes a "mysterious conjunction of moment and continuity," and not only for the individual (Murray, 3). Augustine speaks of harvesting "the fullness of time from the transience of history," of mortising "the isolated, individual consciousness into the vast, living structures of world-history" (ibid.). These questions are hardly foreign to the play, in *Dreaming Jungles*, among global history, geological time (biological evolution), and personal history, all marked by "rites by water."

When Lady Savile emerges from the water, her fever subsides. She is reborn to consciousness. She is "other." Her beauty is no longer haughty but touching (*DJ*, 83); she is weak and, more radical an alteration, she is perplexed: "Everything is rebelling. . . . The body, things, feelings. . . ." she says to the narrator. "You make me vulnerable and scattered. . . . You are an unwelcome emotion for me, a pleasure that drives me to despair" (83–84). *Un plaisir désespérant* (a despairing pleasure) in the original French formulation,[15] suggesting a reversal even in rhetorical devices.

---

[13] He does employ the word once, in the jungle, and precisely with reference to the tension and alliance between life and death: ". . . occupied solely with destroying itself better to endure, with regenerating itself by a continual baptism of blood" (*DJ*, 96).

[14] Alexander Murray, "Resurrection at the font: The ambiguous mysteries of baptism," *TLS* (25 March 1994), 3. Murray's article discusses Peter Cramer's *Baptism and Change in the Early Middle Ages, c. 200–c. 1150* (Cambridge: Cambridge University Press, 1993).

[15] Rio, *Les Jungles pensives*, 89.

Oxymoron, so present in the narrator's earlier depictions of Lady Savile, is here used by her.

Illness entered the novel as a deus ex machina of acceleration, but offers a second advantage. Being circumstance and not inherent condition, illness can be discarded, can disappear, quickly if necessary, which it proves to be. The narrator, left with the choice between "surrendering myself to her definitively or backing off, offended" (*DJ*, 84), proves that while the relationship between the two has evolved greatly, he is still the lesser scientist. He refuses empirical evidence. Childishly, he holds to, even flaunts, an earlier image:

> "You slander yourself, madam. I believe your heart and mind too well organized to yield to such a vulgar affection, in all senses of the term. No proximal [kin] selection impels you to show any altruism whatsoever on my behalf." (ibid.)

Illness is no match for such derision, and evaporates into thin air: " 'Precisely,' she said icily. 'From now on, we are going to apply ourselves to respecting the [natural] law' " (ibid.).

The last images of this chapter recall once more through repetition and contrast the last image of the preceding chapter. If earlier light flashed on the splendid and solitary figure of Lady Savile, "impassive in the multiple and gaping maws of savagery" (66), here, "crushed by solitude," the narrator heads toward the "heart of darkness": "The jaws of the jungle closed on me" (86).

Second departure from the base camp and second return to the base camp. Difference and separation act in inverse proportions: this time the narrator will not return for ten months.

Having traveled from Europe to a Europe-in-Africa, the narrator arrives in the heart of Africa, the birthplace of the species, the heart of the jungle, his own heart of darkness. Once more he is the newcomer. He travels back in time for *Homo sapiens* and for himself as an individual. He voyages in space toward the interior, geographically moving in an evolution from the collective to the individual as well. Language evolves in parallel: from the metaphor of mother-Europe—her culture and tongue, reason and acquired knowledge, vehicle of society and appearance—to the social repartee of the governor's dinner table, a colonial reproduction and distortion of the metropolis; to the English base camp, and to a metacultural and metalinguistic dialogue on Western civilization, the relative value of art and science, of literature and mathematics looked at as languages, and the theoretical discourse of Lady Savile's kin selection hypothesis; to the provisional camp deeper in the jungle and to minimum dialogue; then to the language devoid of artifice spoken by a Lady Savile disoriented by illness, a language for which the narrator is not yet prepared; then to the permanent silence of the jungle. There, the narrator must "unlearn" language as he has known it. He is reborn in the heart-womb of the jungle, without language and must learn one, like all newborns. The jungle is a second mother and a pedagogical encounter.[16] It finishes what Jane started to do, break down barriers. Lady Savile, called Jane only once before in the novel (*DJ*, 73), will now be known only as Jane, a simple appellation, bared of decor, of her husband or father's name, and of social title (but not of humor in the choice of this first name for a white woman in the African jungle).[m] When the narrator next speaks to her, it will be in the language of simple truth. Numbers evolve also: from the collectivity of European society in Abidjan to the English base camp of six Europeans, to the reduced expedition of five, to the two-person foray into chimpanzee territory with Fielding, to absolute solitude in the heart of the jungle. Law evolves from state and societal to natural law. Knowledge too evolves. Theoretical knowledge forms a midpoint between practical and affective knowledge, and it is for reasons of affect that the narrator undertakes the practical experimentation of theory. In the heart of the jungle, and of the novel, he moves toward the center of a scale of knowledge that I have synthesized in Rio's terms *logician* and *dreamer*, and this means a complete knowledge of death. Lady Savile's widowhood remains a final chasm between the protagonists. In stages this chasm is closed. Starting from his initial innocence of death, the narrator passes through the risk of death ("rites by water"), to the witnessing of unceasing death (natural law) and of one individual death (the chimpanzee),[n] to become himself an agent of death, an actor in the jungle's perpetual spectacle. In his slaughter of the leopard and his response to it, all difference is eradicated:

---

[16] See note 9, p. 57.
[m] Gould is correct, of course, in evoking the name and work of Jane Goodall (see Gould); but the name also recalls Tarzan's Jane.
[n] This is the critical moment in his observations regarding the theory of kin selection proposed by Lady Savile. See Gould.

I let myself sink down next to the feline and buried my face in its fur. Overcome with trembling, I felt my tears flow. And I did not know whether I was crying for the monkey, the leopard, or myself, my love, my fear, and my solitude, controlled so long and now in a crisis overflowing. Perhaps, out of anguish and pity, I was crying simply for the world. (*DJ*, 101)

The logician's theoretical knowledge of death as natural law and the dreamer's affective knowledge of death fuse here. This is the ultimate lesson the jungle has to teach him. Learning is at an end, and he leaves this second mother. When the narrator emerges from her, he is forever marked with melancholy.[o]

Not as novice but as veteran he returns to the English base camp. To Jane, as if he were bringing a bouquet of roses, he hands a ream of paper. To his tutor and lover he offers knowledge, the fruit of his ten months in the jungle. Without artifice or defense he can say that he loves. For the first time he is Jane's equal.

This is, of course, what condemns their relationship, condemns it in the act of its optimal fulfillment, for Rio does not write fairy tales,[p] and these protagonists cannot live happily ever after. In his world likeness means stasis, and stasis is on the side of melancholy and death. The lovers are now the "likes" I originally described, which means that their relationship is no longer pedagogy, no longer an encounter of difference, can no longer be action, hence for Rio can no longer *be*.[17] No reason beyond the compulsion of this mechanism condemns the lovers to separate, and so their separation, to be accomplished, depends on a second deus ex machina. This time the external device is not a mere expediency, but a force woven intimately and necessarily with all the questions developed throughout the novel: history.

---

[o] On melancholy, see the introduction in this volume, Pastoureau, Ritter, Rabaté, and Metz.

[p] He does write children's stories, but of a different nature. See Metz.

[17] Within this context of "likeness" one might think back to the "rites by water"; baptism as an initiatory rite is a step toward likeness, whose intent is to make of the initiate "one of us." See Murray, 3.

"Ritual is a history lesson," Peter Cramer writes, and in this novel history is the final arbiter.[18] Numbers return from the singular to the plural, from solitude to society, and the individual is now caught up in the collective: war. It is 1914. Law moves back out to the meeting ground of state law and natural law: the battlefield, where order breaks down, where man appropriates natural law, where killing becomes massive and "official," the "law" of war. Civilization (metropolis, coast) versus "barbarity" (colony, jungle) becomes barbarity in the name of civilization, natural law perverted in the name of the State. In Jane Sheldon's hypothesis of kin selection, "altruism," an instinctive and more subtle form of egoism that only has the appearance of paradox, can determine the death of an individual for the greater propagation of his genes, his likeness. This is natural history, or its theory. But in the history of nations, "altruism" becomes war, not an interspecies but an *intra*species affirmation of likeness against difference,[q] an ideological application of kin selection wherein one goes off to die, says the State, now magistrate of natural law, so that his likes might live.

The schema of pedagogy is that of *mater* and child, of *mater patria*, metropolis and colony, of *materia*, the element of life itself, carrying the same inherent perverseness of annihilation being contained in the seed of conception. For species likeness may mean survival, but for the individual personal relationships in this novel likeness brings annihilation. Self-knowledge is the knowledge of one's own perpetual foreignness. This is the very image that opens and ends the novel: the marine crocodile approaching one bank only to go in the opposite direction toward the high seas, the movement repeating itself like the novel's departures and returns, like history, like natural law, a kind of Vico spiral in which circular and linear time meet. The marine crocodile lives in perpetual motion between extremes, forever strange, forever foreign, forever different.[r] Because in Rio's universe life is difference; difference is action, unceasing movement, whose only alternative is melancholy and the immobility of death.[s]

Not a *deus*, finally, but an unrelenting *machina*, history enters this *historia* to end it. The narrator who has before left his biological mother

---

[18] Cited in ibid.
[q] On difference, see Gould on racism and Galarza on "the Other."
[r] On Rio's use of this image, see Gould.
[s] On this melancholy and death, see Rabaté.

and the jungle, his second mother, leaves Jane Sheldon to go to war, a wisp in the winds of history: a necessary separation in Rio's system of pedagogy as the action of personal bonds.

Dreaming Jungles is not the exception but the necessary repetition of the rule.

Killing the Trade

The sermon that opens *Parrot's Perch* uses the church's own creed to condemn the church, and in the mouth of Joachim the exposition of doctrine perversely constructs a discourse of blasphemy (*PP*, 1–11). The abbot in this same novel speaks of the invention of original sin as "a perversion of consciousness—it has turned against itself, negating its own functional principles and thus the legitimacy of its existence" (29). Joachim's loss of faith in words is expressed in words. In his struggle, the logician first combats the dreamer and the memory of suffering, only to emerge on the opposite side, at the end serving not the resistance but the abandon to suffering. With his ultimate loss of faith Joachim arrives at an "ultimate profession of faith" (77), and on the brink of a suicide born of vanished faith in words and prayer he turns to words and prayer, asking "that the God Whom he found guilty of creating pain should also create oblivion" (83).[t] My point is that there is in these novels a process of turning back on oneself and undoing:[u] "I created a world, and it is dead," Merlin says. "Whatever is godlike in that claim is tempered by its outcome, which is a corpse, and the two meanings of the word 'vanity' cancel each other to give an approximation of nothingness, where my end is" (*M*, 9).

Personal relationships partake of this doing and undoing. Not one in any of the novels I have cited endures. This is why it matters that pedagogy is the action, and that lovers are tutors in these novels. Autophagous, pedagogy devours its own substance and disappears in the precise degree of its success, placing personal relationships in that "kinetic" perverseness to which I referred in the beginning, determining that they cannot both be successful and endure. Nor can the dynamic itself that governs them. *Dreaming Jungles* takes its place in a progression that began with *Melancholy*

---

[t] On Joachim's suicide, see Rabaté.
[u] See Rabaté; also, what Metz calls "parody" in Rio's work.

North, being more explicitly pedagogical and mother-oriented than the novel that precedes it, *Trade Winds*, and more indirect still than *Archipelago*, which follows. In *Merlin*, pedagogy and incest become explicit, and logically the dynamic should end here. It does and it does not, an ambiguity due precisely to another. There are three cases of incest in *Merlin*, or rather two and a question, and therein lies the doubt. The two indisputable incests are father-daughter and brother-sister, but the incest that matters to Rio, like nearly all else in his universe, has a precise order: it is necessarily mother-son, and demands penetration. "Why the devil, my boy . . . don't you go to bed with your mother, instead of beating about the bush?" Leonard Wilde inquires of the narrator in *Archipelago* (*Ar*, 85). Merlin certainly tries. But he is five years old and trapped in the physiology of a child, and Rio leads us to understand that the enchanter's prodigious precocity of mind is not equaled by a similar precocity of body. Age is a final mask, and because of it *Merlin*, the final novel in this progression, is not the final work.

Hound's-tooth Whale is. Perhaps significantly, the work is a play, published one year after *Merlin*. The son, François, is pubescent and "operational," and the mother, Anne, in the end, is accommodating. There is no mask and no bush to beat around:

> *Anne.* The confusion is not in my mind, François. You're my son, and I love you as such. That's a great deal, but it is nothing more.

> *François.* Come on, mother, be generous. . . . It's a question of transforming a neurotic child into a normal adult. Pedagogues and doctors cannot permit themselves moods. They mustn't allow desire or repugnance to stand in the way of duty. And your duty is to carry your endeavor through to the end. (*HW*, 122–23)

The endeavor, naturally, is pedagogical. Finish your duty as a mother. Teach me to be a man.

> *Anne.* Where is there a bed?

> (Silence)

> *François.* In the next room. (125)

The mother enters the bedroom, followed by her son. This is the end of the play. This act on stage heralds the end of the dynamic.[19v]

Incest disappears from Rio's work, and so does the mythical woman/ mother/pedagogue of these novels.[w] Merlin's Morgan is the ultimate, the most brilliant, the most isolated by knowledge, the most perverse, and the last. Guinevere is nonexistent and a passion only for someone who interests Rio as little as Lancelot. The Lady of the Lake, Vivian, and after her, Anne Solon of Hound's-tooth Whale, are hybrid, transitional women containing elements of the women who precede them and announcing the new kind of woman who will follow. The new women are not unattainable, not found in libraries, nor isolated by knowledge. They may be mothers but they are not tutors, and they do not play a maternal or pedagogical role vis-à-vis the narrator. They are women who are in the novels but around whom the novels no longer turn. The Marie Bréments, the Lauras, the Eves of the later novels are integrated into society.[20] Unlike Morgan and like Vivian, they are women with whom one can live for half a century, and who despite their names (Marie, Eve), belong to history not to legend.[x]

---

[19] There is textual "incest" in this play as well. A number of works by Rio introduce the question of intertextuality in the form of rewriting. Trade Winds rewrites Defoe's Robinson Crusoe (or rather employs the general framework with a certain humor); Merlin rewrites the Arthurian legend; and Rio's later works introduce "family" intertextuality, making reference to and reutilizing characters from earlier Rio works (Tlacuilo, The Uncertainty Principle, Manhattan Terminus). In these family exchanges, Hound's-tooth Whale holds a special place, since it goes so far as to reproduce entire portions of previous works by Rio: the discourse on adjectives is taken from Trade Winds; the discussion on art reutilizes passages from Dreaming Jungles; the play within the play, put on by two of the characters for their friends, repeats, with very little modification, the entire first part of The Ouroboros, Rio's first play, published in 1985, integrating it in a perfectly coherent fashion, although the new context modifies, by making more relevant, what was in the original text a rather abstract aim at universal absurdity.

[v] On "family" intertextuality, see Metz; also, note m, p. 165. On rewriting, see Pastoureau, Rabaté, Galarza, and Metz.

[w] Tlacuilo and, in a more significant fashion, Manhattan Terminus make reference to Alan Stewart's passion for his mother, and the physical consummation of it, followed four years later by her death, when Alan is twenty-two years old. Nonetheless, these references in no way constitute a continuation of the theme and refer without exception to a distant past.

[20] Faux Pas (1991), Tlacuilo (1992), The Uncertainty Principle (1993), respectively.

[x] One could say the same of Mary-Olivia Milton Ambrose in Manhattan Terminus. While her name evokes images of the Virgin, of the branch of peace, of epic poetry, and of the

In *Melancholy North* Rio speaks of literature as a "mother" and of the splitting off of knowledge from that mother as a matricide (*MN*, 128).*ʸ* Eight years later he himself is the author of matricide in his works. When mother has no more to teach, when she finishes what she began, pedagogy as the action of personal relationships disappears from Rio's work. Indeed the dynamic of each novel is repeated with the novels as a group, closing a cycle. Perversely, doing is undoing, and attainment is a dangerous activity. As Sterne so wisely warns in *Dreaming Jungles*, "It kills the trade" (*DJ*, 61).

Incest as Hubris

But what, precisely, is the "trade"? Arrows have been pointing to it from that first book-laden, gender-disguised novel. *Melancholy North*'s mentors had libraries, Joachim's mother a book, *Trade Winds* a manuscript and an encyclopedia, *Dreaming Jungles* a theory and a "bouquet" of scientific pages, *Archipelago* two libraries and a school, *Merlin* a kingdom built on knowledge. With Rio, Faustus precedes Oedipus, and at the origin of incest lies hubris, overreaching in the domain of knowledge.

The final novel in the cycle makes explicit the true order of things, and the nature of transgression. Merlin the enchanter is born of the transgression of knowledge, and incest is a simple consequence of this initial sin. The sin is the woman's. Merlin's mother determines "to consecrate my life to knowledge" (*M*, 25). Already the vocabulary is suggestive of excess, "to consecrate" implying deification, making sacred or holy; in a word, Merlin's mother fashions of knowledge a kind of religion, an object of adoration, placing it above all else. Excessive thirst for knowledge is the initial sin out of which all the others are born: social "sins," the neglect of her duty as a woman and as a royal princess to marry and procreate, disobedience of her father and her king; pride, the arrogance of intellectual superiority, viewing all mortal men as insipid; heresy and incest, sin accepted because the sole mate worthy of a woman of knowledge is the prince of intelligence, Satan himself. The incest committed by

---

nectar of the gods, she is not placed on a pedestal but on a stage, and is remarkable above all for her beauty and provocations; under no circumstances can she be taken as a pedagogical figure or a mother. For a different view of Laura Savile, see Metz.

ʸ See the preface in this volume. Ritter also makes reference to this passage.

Merlin's grandfather with his daughter is committed in the name of the mating of the prince of intelligence with a woman who worships knowledge: hubris, not sexual desire, prompts incest here, and heresy, a sexual sin plotted by men of knowledge, a conspiracy of the mother's tutors, who seduce her through the temptation of knowledge. This is the Christian era. No longer Athena disguised as Mentor but a mentor who delivers a worshiper of knowledge unto incest with her father/mentor, appearing to her as the prince of intelligence.

When Merlin is taken from his mother at birth, it is in the name of his education, when at age five he is taken to her it is to *learn* about his origins, and it is again Blaise, his tutor and his mother's before him, who delivers him to her. When he meets this mother, a kind of Alexandra Hamilton raised to motherhood, he takes her for "mother and for wife," mixing "the purest love" and "a violent desire to fuse with her, pour myself into her, for my mind, too early ripened in the body of a child, could understand the nature of these things" (29). He runs freely over her body: ". . . I touched and caressed her flesh rapturously" (30). He spends all his nights with her, "with the mind of a son and a lover" (ibid.). Ambiguous as to consummation but clear as to desire, the image in this novel of iconography is not only of incest but of sacrilege. The pictorial representation is a standard topos: a child's body with the head of an adult, a male child's body, naked, with free reign over the breasts of a young and beautiful mother, the epitome of the inaccessible woman, untouched even by her husband, impregnated by no mortal man, mother with child to the exclusion of all others. This is not the Bronzino painting of the pagan Cupid with his hand happily placed on the naked breasts of the adult Venus used on the cover of *Archipelago*, but something more Christian and so more scandalous: Silent night, Madonna and child. Blaise himself, the tutor of both, makes the comparison between divine inceptions: the tutor as blaspheme and heretic. A variation of the image is "The Virgin and Child with Book," the Virgin as *Mater Sapientiae*, the Mother of Wisdom, to which I have referred.[21]

Merlin becomes *Pater Sapientiae*. The cycle of novels began with mothers disguised as "fathers" and mentors and ends with a true father, *but not a biological father*. Knowledge, not sexual intercourse, determines paternity. Merlin creates, via two mortals, Uther Pendragon/Ygerne, a

---

[21] James Hall, *Dictionary of Subjects and Symbols in Art* (1974; reprint, London: John Murray Publishers, 1991), 329.

child in order to create a universe ("Let there be Arthur"), separates that
child from his mother at birth in the name of his education, holds power
in the realm on the basis not of supernatural gifts, as legend would have
it, but of superior intelligence.[z]

Morgan, who forms the true trinity of passion in this book along
with mother and Merlin and who alone is Merlin's intellectual equal, is
banished from the earthly paradise of Logres and the Round Table. At the
base of all her sins also lies knowledge. Her first words are of knowledge
and of death: "Why must we die, Merlin?" (*M*, 65) As with Merlin's
mother, so with this child of his spirit, knowledge is at the base of transgression. Morgan's evil is born of knowledge. If Jane Sheldon anticipates
Haldane by several decades, Morgan confirms Rio's taste for advanced
women, anticipating Copernicus's heliocentric theories by several hundred
years:[aa]

> "I imagined all this in accordance with your teaching . . . for the
> mind calculates and wants to know, whatever the cost, while the
> spirit dreams and is horror-struck at the discoveries of the mind,
> which wreck its ideal of pleasure and eternity. . . . And so I see
> clearly that God, if he exists, author of all this, is a thousand times
> more cruel and perverse than Satan. And I, Morgan, victim of
> this cruelty, hating this Monster-God and this stupid or lying
> man that you defend, I want to be cruel in my turn, and answer
> universal evil by personal evil, because I am condemned to
> knowledge, fear, suffering, and death." (*M*, 69–70)

The victim of knowledge, Morgan is as well, perhaps is above all, the
apogee of pedagogy, as pupil and as teacher. Like her tutor's mother, she
transgresses sexually in order to transgress intellectually; her incest is not
the result of desire for her brother Arthur but for a child to educate. Like
her tutor she determines the birth of a child in order to teach a child. She
does what Merlin has done, and she educates a child with her vision of
the universe. She uses the tools of knowledge to destroy Merlin's universe
based on knowledge. The dangers of attainment: Merlin says of Morgan's
son and pupil, "Mordred, . . . the perfect product of the world that I had
created and that he destroyed by reason of that very perfection" (134).

---

[z] On Merlin as a character, see Pastoureau.
[aa] On Morgan's cosmology, see Ritter.

Utopia is like infinity in that arrival is nonarrival. The garden of Eden is a utopia, and so is mother. The primal woman, the source of life and of knowledge, is unattainable or ceases to be utopia by definition if reached. Pedagogy, knowledge as transgression, as action of personal relationships and lasting only as long as its ends are *not* met, partakes of this perverseness; it defines these early works and disappears with the last of them, exhausted through fulfillment, through the repetition of its own dynamic.

Sexual knowledge is the ultimate knowledge withheld by mother: the knowledge of creation, the knowledge that *differentiates* man from the gods, the Author's knowledge. But "It is not safe to know." To seek it is hubris (and incest and transgression), and brings banishment from paradise. God does not want you to eat the apple of the Tree of Knowledge for then you would know as much as He: "Be *like* Him," the serpent insinuates in Eve's ear. For Michel Rio, as for the mother of us all, knowledge is well worth an Eden.

3

A Disenchanted Enchanter

Michel Pastoureau

Passengers are not allowed to talk to the driver.

No. 27 Paris bus

"Perhaps the finest; beyond question the least finished, the most uneven," writes Michel Rio of the Arthurian legend in an engaging, narcissistic page that comes in an "Annex" to the text of his *Merlin* (155).[1][a] The adverbs are pointless. Yes, the Arthurian legend *is* the finest that the Western imagination has produced. There is nothing to touch it, not even the most admired episodes of Greek or Norse mythology. Yes, the legend is also dense, disconnected, unreliable; sometimes odd, never fantastic, always coherent.

Michel Rio would no doubt dislike this string of epithets. His aversion to words of this kind—"aesthetic or moral fraud," their only function to conceal the absence of thought—has several times been proclaimed in his fictional work, especially in *Trade Winds* (83–87).[b] But some such string is needed in order to underscore the polymorphous nature of a legend not easily pinned down. It is moreover wholly legitimate, the medieval Arthurian romances having always taken inordinate pleasure in adjectives.

---

[1] The paperback edition, like the original (1989), has a pen-and-ink drawing by Maxime Préaud on the cover.

[a] On *Merlin*, see Arent Safir, Ritter, and Metz.

[b] On *Trade Winds*, see Arent Safir and Metz.

For the polymorphous nature, several reasons. The main one has to do with the sheer number of authors, firsthand accounts, traditions, and transmissions.[2] More than half a millennium lies between the little Celto-Roman warlord Artorius, fighting against Picts and Saxons on the northern marches of island Britain at the start of the sixth century, and his definitive transformation into the literary King Arthur, as he is presented in the great classic texts of the twelfth and thirteenth centuries. Oral tradition, Latin chronicles, and political and literary subterfuges heralding the return of this messianic hero, all came well before its "fictionalizing"; that is, its being written in the vernacular. It is no easy task to say where and how we might place the real Arthur, and what his real history was. Arthurian literature, as we read it today from the pen of Chrétien de Troyes and from his successors and imitators, is unquestionably a learned and militant literature. It can be precise enough to impose its vision of the world and of society. But that in no way prevents it from contradicting itself; nor from locating itself on either side of the Channel in a shifting geography; still less from forming itself round a chronology that bears little trace of the linear. And it is also and above all an ironic literature, which often mocks itself, its public, and the characters it presents.[c] King Arthur appears often (but not always, and that is what makes the enduring characteristic of this literature) as a puppet ruler: hesitant, the plaything of his retinue and his circumstances. Lancelot, "the best knight in the world," is a hero compounded of courage and pride; he is a winner, that is, in the Arthurian system of values, a fool: sometimes ridiculous, sometimes baleful. As for Merlin . . .

The fact that a twentieth-century novelist has fallen under the spell of this legend, has wanted to propose his own reading of it, to work up this episode, leave out that, has its place in the sane logic of literary

---

[2] The best introduction to the Arthurian legend and the literature it has inspired is still, in my view, the work edited by Roger Sherman Loomis, *Arthurian Literature in the Middle Ages* (Oxford: Oxford University Press, 1959). In French, among a rapidly expanding bibliography, we might note a recent survey by Danielle Regnier-Bohler that forms the introduction to the work that she edited: *La Légende arthurienne, le Graal et la Table Ronde* (Paris: Robert Laffont, 1989), I-LII.

[c] On this kind of irony in Rio, see Metz.

history. The Arthurian legend belongs to no man, and not to Chrétien de Troyes any more than to the writers, anonymous or not, who preceded and carried on from him. Michel Rio is a son of this long line, and will be, whether he likes it or not, the father (or rather the uncle, which will be still more Arthurian), of a prolific posterity.[d] Two of his attitudes, however, do seem markedly original. On the one hand, there is his choosing, from within this royal and chivalrous world, of a hero—Merlin—who is neither king nor knight, something to which I shall return in a moment. On the other hand, a constant striving to bring about order in matter that has never had any, and that has been none the worse for it. Legitimate concern of a narrator of our own day? Constraint brought about by writing in a French that is modern, deprived of the Gyrovagan music of Anglo-Norman, Picard, and Old French? Personal choice of Rio, the reader, who has always claimed to be a "dreamer and logician"?[e]

In any event our author, in the "Annex" to his novel, hands over "to the curiosity of the common reader and the savagery of the learned" his "own chronology," and his "own geography of the Arthurian cycle, or rather the cycle of Merlin."[f] In actual fact, a twofold, extremely precise table of the chronology of events, spanning the years from 406 (departure from Great Britain of the Roman legions) to 545 (Merlin's solitary days in Bois-en-Val, in our own Britain, Armorican Brittany); and two maps showing the location of the main pre-Arthurian and Arthurian peoples, places, and territories.

I am not clear what the curiosity of the common reader may be like in these areas, but I am well acquainted with the savagery of the learned. It is boundless, and their bad faith, still more infinite. I shall make no criticism whatever of Rio for wanting to ground his Merlin cycle in space and time, or for making an attempt to pinpoint, on a map of Little and Great Britain, places for which we have only the vaguest of indications; still less for distinguishing, with a biologist's scalpel,[g] between the

---

[d] On intertextuality and the rewriting of stories, see Rabaté and Galarza. There is also Rio's taste for rewriting his own stories. See Arent Safir (note 19, p. 71) and Metz.

[e] On the dreamer and logician, see the introduction in this volume and Arent Safir. On Rio's concern for order and method, see Gould, Swenson, Galarza, and Metz; on order and disorder, see Ritter (especially the final lines); also, note *v*, p. 107.

[f] The pages in the "Annex" are not numbered, but correspond to 155–59.

[g] The reference to Rio's "biologist's scalpel" takes us back to *Dreaming Jungles*, and so to the essay by Gould. But perhaps the real link between this essay and Gould's is the

different generations of characters, choosing the same year—that of the death of Uther Pendragon—for the birth of Gawain, Guinevere, and Vivian, while Lancelot must wait another twenty years before coming into the world. I shall even say that this positivistic endeavor, far from stripping the poetry from the legend, seems to endow it with a new poetic dimension.

Thus, to my mind, the Latinizing form chosen by Michel Rio for the names of peoples and places subtly revitalizes the onomastic music of Arthurian society: Deva, Demetae, Dumnomia, Durotriges, Silures, Brigantes, Moridunum, Venta Belgarum. Moreover it emphasizes the end-of-Late-Empire atmosphere that enfolds the whole genesis of the Merlin cycle. Here is another invitation to dream. Is there, anywhere in the history of the West, a moment more thoroughly dream-charged than the eve or near-eve of the fall of the Roman Empire? Arguably not. In addition, the act of placing the major part of the cycle in the fifth and sixth centuries, and not in the twelfth and thirteenth as literary tradition has it, has allowed the author to change not only the music of names but the color of things.

It is perhaps this that has most struck me as a historian in the work of Michel Rio. The classic tales of the Round Table, put together in the twelfth and thirteenth centuries, even if they are set in a shifting, uncertain temporal scheme, are bathed in an atmosphere of color that is exactly that of the twelfth and thirteenth centuries: two centuries of profound mutations that cover the emergence in Europe of a new order of colors linked to a new search for light, to the sudden promotion of blue, to the endless speculations on the rainbow, and to the massive reappearance of gold in paintings.[3] These luminously bright romances belong to what could be called a "blue and gold library." Nothing like this in the fifth and sixth centuries. At that time we have moved into the "Dark Ages" so beloved of English and American historiography. Not everything is dark yet, but everything is built up around the three primitive colors of European culture: white, red, and black. Something caught perfectly by the opaque and bloody atmosphere of Rio's *Merlin*. Blood and fire impregnate a drenched, cloud-thick world that has not taken on the colors of

---

question of art and science. In the case of *Dreaming Jungles*, the issue is carrying art to science, and science to art; in the case of *Merlin*, carrying science to art, that is, history to legend. See Gould.

[3] On these matters may I refer readers to my book *Figures et couleurs. Etudes sur la symbolique et la sensibilité médiévales* (Paris: Le Léopard d'Or, 1986), 13-57.

the rainbow: "I stood there gazing at the night, soaking in this nature drawn in black and white by the lights in the sky. . . ." (*M*, 122). Only the green of the forest—a dark, gleaming green, like Morgan's eyes—and "gold of the setting sun"—an unexpectedly precious figure from the pen of Rio, but there perhaps to remind us that we are at "the mysterious bounds of the Western world"[4]—appear occasionally to go against this archaistic palette; archaistic in a way that is both legitimate and effective.[h]

Contrary to popular belief, Merlin is not a character that fascinated the medieval public. There are, of course, quite a number of texts that include him; some indeed centrally concerned with him. But as soon as we move outside the textual domain, and start to examine the nonliterary evidence of the spread of the Arthurian legend and its peripheral practices (iconography, name-giving, heraldry, rituals), Merlin disappears. His iconography is meager. His name does not become a baptismal name, like those of Gawain, Lancelot, Percival, and a few others; a nickname just about, later a patronymic. As for his arms, (*gyronné d'or et de sinople*), created by the fertile imagination of Robert de Boron, they go no further, unlike those of the other heroes of the kingdom of Logres. Much more important, in the many jousts, festivities, and performances in which, from the thirteenth to the sixteenth century, princes and their retinue play at King Arthur and his companions, no one makes any attempt to act or even to bring in the soothsayer-magician.[5] Why?

Fear of Merlin? No doubt. In many ways, starting with his birth, he is a disturbing, ambiguous, dangerous character; at once too wise and too mad. Whether in the theater or at court, people hesitate to take on the role of Merlin as they hesitate to take on those of the Devil's creatures, or of creatures of indeterminate or exceptional status: Cain, Judas, Delilah,

---

[4] José-Maria de Heredia, "Les Conquérants," line 8, *Les Trophées* (Paris: A. Lemerre, 1893).

[h] On Rio's taste for the "archaistic," the "out of time," or his choice of historical moments, see Gould and Ritter. To be linked also no doubt to the character of the Aztec *tlacuilo*, on the cusp of two historical moments and two cultures, a kind of cultural relative to the marine crocodile evoked in *Dreaming Jungles* and by Gould. See Galarza.

[5] On all these questions see Michel Pastoureau, "L'enromancement du nom. Etude sur la diffusion des noms de héros arthuriens à la fin du Moyen Age," in *Couleurs, images, symboles. Etudes d'histoire et d'anthropologie* (Paris: Le Léopard d'Or, 1989), 111–24.

Salome, Ganelon, and a few others, of course, but also Virgil, Ovid, St. Anne, St. John the Baptist, and St. Joseph.

But beyond fear, even a certain repulsion, what we have is more probably indifference to Merlin. For he touches neither the sensibility nor the curiosity of the medieval public. To the members of the lower and middle nobility, the main consumers of the Arthurian legend, our enchanter is distinctly unattractive. He is neither king, nor noble lord, nor knight. He does not fight; he does not hunt; he does not fire the dreams of the ladies, even though he is acquainted with love and the pleasures of the flesh. To be a fatherless child, to interpret dreams, to reveal the truth, to work wonder upon wonders, to mock others and oneself, to know the circumstances of one's own end: for the warrior aristocracy of the feudal period, none of this is particularly seductive, noteworthy, or affecting. On the contrary, it is more or less vulgar, more or less artificial, above all completely pointless. Why tell the future? Why try to know the truth? Why work wonders? Why want to be wiser or more learned than other people? For Arthurian literature as for its public, the main thing is to believe, not to understand. What matters is the dream, not the explanation of the dream. What matters is the quest, not the goal (still less the fulfillment) of the quest. Knowing, predicting, revealing: these are clerics' work—or devils'. Noble lords and knights they concern not at all. Given this, Merlin, in their eyes, appears not at all as an enchanter; just possibly a philosopher; rather more, a buffoon: pedantic, impious, and given to moralizing. For them, *Merlin* rhymes with *vilain* (villain, but also ugly, nasty).

In fact it was the literature of the Romantic period that transformed Merlin the Soothsayer into Merlin the Enchanter, thus helping to give him once and for all the outward appearance of an Oriental magician, and to confer on him immense powers over men, animals, and matter; powers that he is never, or hardly ever given in the great texts of the Middle Ages. For these, "Merlin is a magician only because he is a prophet."[6] He works wonders—they are in no way miracles—only in order to promote the success of his prophecies.

Nothing of that in the modern and contemporary Merlin, who, over the decades, moves away from the model of Elijah—probably the Old Testament prophet who most struck the men of the Middle Ages—and closer to the figure of Panoramix, the Gaulish Druid presented in the

---

[6] Paul Zumthor, *Merlin le Prophète* (Lausanne: Slatkine, 1943), 216.

cartoon strip *Astérix*.[7] Elijah was a prophet dressed in dark robes; Panoramix is a Druid dressed entirely in white. Between these two colors lies
the whole historical evolution of the character of Merlin.

Toward the end of the eighteenth century, then, poets and novelists
fasten on the medieval Merlin. As early as 1777, Wieland, the mighty
Wieland, brings out, in German of crystalline purity, a very short text,
Merlin der Zauberer (Merlin the Magician),[8] which has a decisive influence
on the whole German Romantic movement. In turn F. Schlegel, Brentano,
Tieck, Lenau, Uhland, and Heine devote prose or verse to him. Merlin
becomes a compulsory star of Romantic literature, not only in Germany
but in France, and above all in Scotland and England, where a link is
made between his legend and that of Ossian.[9] The poems of Tennyson
carry this vogue on to the end of the nineteenth century. A few years
later, Apollinaire too produces a substantial text on Merlin, this time in
prose: *L'Enchanteur pourrissant* (The Rotting Magician).[10] In it he presents
the eternal drama of man, destined, in spite of his knowledge of the
world and of himself, never to win mastery of anything, and to go on
being, again and always, the victim of his own fate. He also speaks out in
it against the loneliness of the poet, misunderstood and rejected.

Alongside the men of letters, scholars too take an interest in the
character. They it is who, in the first half of the nineteenth century, carry
out the chimerical fusion between our hero, a pure product of learned
medieval literature, and Myrddin, a Welsh (or Scottish) bard (so-called), a
poet and visionary who had made his way into folklore. This assimilation
of the two characters, which for more than a century now the majority
of philologists has argued against, still has a few supporters today. Their
bad faith is patent, but their Celto-militant romanticism, consumed with

---

[7] The idea of linking Merlin and the Druid Panoramix was suggested to me by one of my
students, Dominique Cottard, author of a Masters' dissertation on the myth of Merlin in
modern times.

[8] Christoph Martin Wieland, *Merlin der Zauberer*, in *Sämtliche Werke* (Leipzig: Verlag
Göschen, 1893), XXXV, 364-67.

[9] Which explains the special interest of the Scottish poets and novelists in the figure of
Merlin. As early as 1803, Walter Scott himself devotes a study to him in *The Minstrelsy of
the Scottish Border* (Edinburgh: Longman & Reece, 1803), 2:198 et seq. Scott calls him
"Merlin the Wild."

[10] Guillaume Apollinaire, *L'Enchanteur pourrissant* (Paris: Hachette, 1909). The prose text is
interlarded with passages in verse. This first edition is adorned with splendid woodcuts by
André Derain.

"the savagery of the learned," sometimes has about it, in its perverse ingenuousness, something slyly Arthurian.[11]

Michel Rio's Merlin has nothing of the enchanter about him. Or the Oriental magician. Still less the Welsh bard (fortunately!). He is an obstinate, grumpy demiurge, like Rio himself. Not Rio the novelist so much as Rio the Breton, learned and misanthropic; the one who maintains a close connection with the old melancholy and with the desire for elucidation.[i] Moreover, the book itself is an autobiography. Merlin speaks in the first person; Rio holds the pen for him, and blends his own voice with his.[j] Both appropriate the Arthurian legend, and rightly invite the reader to do the same. Their pen is a quill from a crow—corvus corax; the Devil seems to have supplied the inkwell.

For this fictional Merlin is a black Merlin. Or at least a dark one. This demon's son knows nothing of Christ, practices magic, shows himself as unjust and heartless, flees the town and the company of men, prefers the forest, the cave, and wild animals. Yet he is too wise, or too disabused, too dignified also, to feel hatred for the human species. Morgan on the other hand, younger, wilder, more fanatic, knows this feeling well, and has no hesitation in proclaiming it loud and clear:

> "What is it to me, that man should endure. . . . What matters is I myself, not man. I hate him. He is a slave who resigns himself to his fate, accepting for reassurance all the nonsense about eternal life dished up for him by mad visionaries and charlatans. . . . Do you think that I, Morgan, am satisfied at being perpetuated by this creature whose only permanent feature is his stupidity?" (*M*, 66)

This young woman, half sister to Arthur, with whom she has a sexual relationship from which is born Mordred—that envious, unna-

---

[11] The recent work by Jean Markale, *Merlin l'enchanteur, ou l'éternelle quête magique* (Paris: Retz, 1981), is a good representative of this militant, ecologistic, Celtic, and Druidizing tendency.

[i] See the introduction in this volume.

[j] On autobiography and the *I* of Rio's narrators, see Metz.

tural son whose sedition will bring on the twilight of the kingdom of Logres—is probably the single boldest and most aggressive invention in the novel.[k] As the pages go by, we can feel the author—as indeed Merlin himself—more and more disturbed, if not entranced, by this rebellious child turned untamable woman, "the most beautiful in the West" (*M*, 12, 149). Michel Rio speaks through her voice as much as through that of Merlin. Not only in order to ironize on the fate of men, but also, as in every one of his novels, to hold forth on a number of scientific theories.[l]

> "I have dreamed a theory of the sun. . . . I believe . . . that the earth is round, because the horizon is limited, yet retreats as one tries to reach it, and because on a sphere, even a small one, one can travel a road that never ends. So that our world may be infinite in our eyes and beneath our feet, and insignificant in our minds. It is so in mine. For according to me, it is not the center of the universe. The sun is." (*M*, 67–68)

We are a long way from the Middle Ages, which feel no respect for the sun—the moon is a thousand times worthier of interest—and would never dream of placing it at the center of the universe. But there follows a long discussion between Merlin and Morgan on the Ptolemaic system and on Aristotle's philosophy, which leads the girl to declare:

> "God, if he exists, . . . is a thousand times more cruel and perverse than Satan. And I, Morgan, victim of this cruelty, hating this Monster-God and this stupid or lying man that you defend, I want to be cruel in my turn, and answer universal evil by personal evil, because I am condemned to knowledge, fear, suffering, and death." (70)

Who is talking here? Morgan or Michel? On this sort of ground, Merlin, in any case, comes across as wiser and more merciful. True, he has nothing of the saint, or even the theologian about him, but he does sometimes behave like a Desert Father, learnedly skeptical, and, by that

---

[k] On Morgan, the pride of knowledge and incest, see Arent Safir.
[l] On these scientific theories, see the introduction in this volume, Gould, Ritter (Morgan's cosmology), and Galarza.

very skepticism, somewhat indulgent. Sometimes even, a certain good-naturedness—a typically medieval virtue—sits on him, and gives to two or three of his speeches, especially in the early days of the Round Table, a vaguely Gospel-like tinge:

> "You are instruments of death, and I will make of you instruments of eternity. You are night, and you will be day without end. You are tumult, and you will be the law. You are emptiness, and you will be the substance of the world and its conscience. You are the Iron Age, and you will prepare the coming of a Golden Age which, according to me, has never been, but which, through you, can be. You will be all this because, henceforth, you are the Round Table." (60)

And yet, nothing more alien to Merlin than Christ. He may happen to talk of God; the Savior remains unknown to him. There no doubt lies the great gap that Michel Rio has opened up between himself and his twelfth- and thirteenth-century predecessors.[m] His Merlin is no atheist, but he is no Christian either. The grace of redemption and the breath of the Holy Spirit have touched him not at all. Is it perhaps that the middle of the sixth century is too soon? When we leave him, at the end of the novel, alone in Bois-en-Val, we do not know what will become of him. He has an appointment with Destiny, and Destiny does not love broken appointments. Is he going to die? Is he going to live forever by the common tomb of Arthur and Morgan? Will he, like Elijah, be taken up to Heaven in a chariot of fire, his mantle struck from him? For the moment, he is a hundred years old, and the world that he created has sunk down into death. This death that permeates the whole novel, dropping off a tumbrel-load of corpses in every chapter.[n]

A constantly death-bearing atmosphere neatly caught in the image chosen for the dust jacket of the French edition, a pen-and-ink drawing by Maxime Préaud. In it we see Merlin, leaning on a stick, his back turned to the sea, perched on a heap of skulls, picked clean and grimacing. One of them, picked cleaner still, pushes the irony so far as to wear a crown:

---

[m] On the importance of authorial choice within the context of a discipline and of the history of an idea, see Gould.

[n] On creation and death, always present or imminent, on doing and undoing, see Arent Safir and Rabaté.

this is Arthur's skull. Merlin, alone, bent, melancholic, and black, waits and remembers. He seems to be meditating on the words of Ecclesiastes:

> That which is crooked cannot be made straight: and that which is wanting cannot be numbered. . . . I am come to great estate, and have gotten more wisdom than all they that have been before me. . . . And I gave my heart to know wisdom, and to know madness and folly: I perceived that this also is vexation of spirit. For in much wisdom is much grief: and he that increaseth knowledge increaseth grief.[120]

TRANSLATED FROM THE FRENCH BY GEORGE CRAIG.

---

[12] Eccles. I, 15–18.

[o] See D'Avenant: "Since knowledge is but sorrow's spy, / It is not safe to know": epigraph of *Trade Winds*, recalled in Arent Safir.

4

Cosmoses and Metaphor

James Ritter[1]

What is this particular pleasure that a historian of science takes away from the novels of Michel Rio? That of surprising fictional characters in the midst of informed discussions, often finely critical, on biology and physics, central—in the literal sense—for them as for me?[a] Yes, doubtless. Yet what touches me perhaps more, and what motivates me to write what follows, is the acuity with which Rio captures the social effect of science, in particular that strange science called "cosmology." The exact significance that these scientific ideas have for his protagonists, the ways in which they are moved by them, is what moves me in turn to embark on a voyage from Rio to the history of cosmology and back again. A voyage in the company of Jérôme Avalon, one of the two protagonists of *The Uncertainty Principle*, whose deep and lightly ironic interest for science seems to me to augur a congenial traveling companion.[b]

---

[1] Catherine Goldstein, who translated this article into French for the original publication of this collection, participated in its creation and development in an essential manner. That her name does not appear as coauthor is due only to her reserve with respect to some of its conclusions.

[a] On fictional characters in discussions of biology, see Gould.

[b] On *The Uncertainty Principle*, see the introduction in this volume, Swenson, and Metz. Jérôme Avalon, a writer who has abandoned writing, stops in front of a seascape in the south of France that becomes the point of departure for a dialogue with the aging actor Dan Harrison, a reflection on nature, the cosmos, and death.

Rio's characters are good practitioners of the inducto-deductive method.[c] Observers of external nature or of their own inner states, they mount, through a series of discourses, soliloquies, and dialogues, from the particular to the general, from the psychological to the universal. The sciences are often invited to join in the ascent. And among these, cosmology occupies a special place—the last. From a mythical fifth-century Brittany to an idealized twentieth-century Côte d'Azur, men and women, face-to-face with their inevitable deaths, are confronted with an indifferent and alien cosmos.[d] From this arises the action, often destructive, always disturbing. The almost obligatory eruption of the most intimate emotions whenever cosmology is evoked calls, in its turn, the historian of science to account: how is it that cosmology can play this role so well?

It seems to me that this is due to the peculiar position of cosmology within science itself. In a number of ways, cosmology is a *limit* case and, as such, reveals a great deal, not so much perhaps about the universe, as about the nature of the scientific endeavor itself. Three aspects in particular of cosmology are thrown into relief by such a state of affairs: its object, its arguments, and its relations with both scientists and the general public.

First of all, cosmology is a limit case in terms of its subject matter. The standard definition, current since at least the eighteenth century, is the "study of the universe as a whole." Now this is a particularly seductive definition, conjuring up great expectations—and tenacious misunderstandings. Would not all problems be solved were this program to be carried out? But of course a science so universal as to include all the other sciences or to replace them is clearly out of reach. The cosmologists' "universe as a whole" is not the whole universe. Far from having as its object all the objects of the world, cosmology, uniquely among the sciences, has but one.

Moreover, just what "the universe as a whole" consists of is far from clear. Were cosmology like other sciences, at least in first approximation, one might expect a core of established results, expanding as both observation and theory developed. In fact this is precisely what does not occur. Instead, at different historical moments—generally each time there is a major advance in physical theory—there is a renewed interest in subjects

---

[c] On the scientific methodology of Rio's characters, see Gould, Pastoureau, and Galarza.

[d] On mythical fifth-century Brittany, see Pastoureau; on the individual and nature's indifference, see Swenson. *Manhattan Terminus* continues this confrontation. See the editor's note in this volume.

classed as cosmological. Questions are raised, tentative answers proposed on the basis of the general ideas linked to the new physics, and then, seemingly, interest in the field is abandoned. When the next new theory arises cosmology is rediscovered; the same name, the same vague definition, but with totally new questions, addressing completely new parts of the world or even phenomena. It is not so much that the old answers are found wanting as that the old questions now seem of little interest, even pointless. Each time it is a completely new "universe as a whole": planets in the solar system, local stars, galaxies, galactic clusters. . .

All sciences, of course, change their object of study with time. But the earlier levels retain their interest even if they disappear from center stage. It can happen that the arrival of new objects casts a novel light on the old: the phenomenon of elasticity on the macroscopic level gains from being understood as a product of interatomic forces; some of the chemical properties of the elements can be read off from their electronic structure. Boundary disputes between neighboring sciences, fueled by advances in one or another sister science, also lead to a redefinition of territories, and of their objects of study—chemistry and physics have long had a running feud as to their respective domains of competence. But in the case of cosmology, we have neither a border dispute nor the discovery of new, underlying objects. The very definition of the field of cosmology, so conveniently vague, masks the reality that it has radically changed its objects over the centuries—and with it, the nature of the arguments used within the field. The subject appears to be not so much an autonomous discipline as a permanent outpost of one branch or another of the theoretical physics of the day.

Secondly, cosmology is a limit case in the nature and degree of trustworthiness of its evidence. Even where there is agreement at a given moment on the subject matter of the science, the links between theory and observation remain problematic. Of course, one is faced with the sheer difficulty of obtaining information on "the universe as a whole." Yet in no other science is there so large a gap between the kinds of statements or claims that the theoreticians are led to make and the quantity or precision of the evidence available. Scientific standards vary in time and according to domain; those of cosmology seem always to be the weakest possible at any given time. Today, where—in quantum field theory, optics, solid state physics—huge collections of independent data are considered essential for a true comparison of theory and experiment, cosmological models rely essentially on only four types of data: the expansion of the universe, the distribution of matter, the quantity of light elements, and the background microwave radiation. And only the first and last of this list are currently well established; in the other cases each new measurement seems to place in doubt those previously made. Such coarse-grained and unstable measures, which in other fields would be considered insufficient, are here often all that can be obtained.

And here we rejoin the first point. Paradoxically, it seems that precisely when real, detailed empirical knowledge is gained of some object considered "cosmological" at a given moment (e.g., the physical nature of a distant star), it changes its category (to "astrophysical" in the example given). The real object of cosmology always seems to lie just a bit further on than the limits of licit discussion. The theory of the "universe as a whole," far from being, as might be naively supposed, a synthesis of all current knowledge, is situated always at its outermost limits, constantly in danger of falling off the edge.

Finally, and most importantly for our present interest, cosmology is a limit case in the nature of the relationship between its practitioners and the community of physics as a whole, as well as with the larger public. The nature of its claims has always ensured it a large lay audience; its direct appeal to the interests, hopes, and anxieties of a good part of the population has conferred upon it an appeal it shares in our day only with medicine. Nor are physicists themselves immune from this appeal. There are few among the proponents of a new physical theory who have resisted the challenge of drawing cosmological consequences from their work; yet it is equally true that there are few scientists who have felt it prudent or proper to join these pioneers. Cosmology has never been a "normal science," with a large number of practitioners occupied in solving specific theoretical or observational "puzzles"; there has always been something of the smell of sulfur about it.

As a result, there has rarely been more than a handful of professional cosmologists within the scientific community at any given time. The custom, unfortunately still too widespread, of representing the history of any science as a succession of works by a few geniuses risks masking to what extent this is a bizarre situation. The scarcity of names is here neither historical artifact nor pedagogical simplification: for once it simply reflects the reality of the field.

The bulk of writing on cosmology, commentaries and popularizations of the cosmological models of the professionals, has generally been left to nonscientists: philosophers, theologians, and, since the nineteenth century, journalists. Entry into the domain of cosmology, as for any other mathematized science, for the general public—and the novelist—is reserved for works of popularization.[e] But even here cosmology plays a special role; the competing models and paradigms, which in other sciences have generally been smoothed out by discussion among specialists, confrontations with observation, and creation of a consensus before their presentation to the public, here openly fight it out. Whatever reserves one may hold as to the nature of scientific practice, its imperfections, its mystifications even, cosmology stands out for its transgressions of the most elementary rules of scientific communities. Without any attempt at defining "universal" or "eternal" criteria for scientificity, one is forced to at least this conclusion: that cosmology possesses institutional and intellectual characteristics that distinguish it from, among other things, the vast majority of contemporary fields recognized as sciences.

Let me illustrate this point by taking four crucial moments in the history of cosmology, four moments that coincide, for the reasons indicated, with times of change, both intellectual and sociological, in the domain of physics.

The first great modern synthesis in our physical picture of the world was consecrated by the publication of Isaac Newton's *Principia mathematica* in 1687. In this massive work, he showed that the same physical principles are valid for the movement of terrestrial objects as for celestial objects; in particular he showed how a law of universal attraction, in which any two bodies are drawn to each other, the force depending on their mutual distances and their masses, could mathematically explain and predict the observed movements of the planets.

But though he specifically used the concordance with observation of the predictions of his laws of motion for the planets and the sun to justify his new theory, Newton, in his published work, passed over in absolute silence all questions having to do with any possible cosmological consequences of his theory. With his customary fear of public debate, he preferred presenting his ideas on the subject in the form of private letters, particularly to his friend, Richard Bentley, when the latter questioned him during his preparation of a series of public lectures in 1693.

---

[e] On the phenomenon of popularized scientific works, see the introduction in this volume.

The underlying image for the new physics was that of the hi-tech industry of the time: clockwork—the repetitive, unceasing motion of parts, articulated in a complex but fixed mechanism. The questions considered cosmological were those that could be formulated in terms of this image. Would the clock of the solar system keep good time? What of the Clockmaker? How often need He wind the clock-universe up?

Thus it was that theologians and philosophers like Richard Bentley and Samuel Clarke, friends of Newton and the first popularizers of the new mechanics, were left to draw the cosmological consequences of the new theory—or at least those that Newton had proposed to them in private correspondence: that the universe was necessarily infinite in size and that the natural instability of the solar system required a repeated intervention by God to prevent the planets from falling into the sun. In the second edition of the *Principia* in 1713, Newton added a (nonmathematical) observation in which the second of his two cosmological remarks was outlined, but he refused to be drawn further. Nonetheless, his work inspired a whole industry of publications, public lectures, and sermons in England, elucidating the lessons of the new Newtonian classical mechanics for the nature of the cosmos and the divine governance of the world.

Nor were Continental philosophers far behind; Jean d'Alembert in 1754, in his article "Cosmologie" for that rationalist monument, the *Encyclopédie*, concluded:

> But the principal utility which we may draw from Cosmology is to elevate us, by its general laws of nature, to knowledge of its Author, whose wisdom has established these laws. . . . Thus Cosmology is the science of the World or Universe considered in general, insofar as it is a compound being, and yet simple by the union and harmony of its parts; a whole which is governed by a Supreme Intelligence and whose springs are combined, set in motion and modified by this Intelligence.[2]

---

[2] Jean Le Rond d'Alembert, "Cosmologie," in vol. 4 of *l'Encyclopédie, ou Dictionnaire raisonné des sciences, des arts et des métiers*, ed. Denis Diderot and Jean Le Rond d'Alembert (Paris: Le Breton, 1754) (my translation).

[ʃ] D'Alembert lends his name to a boat transporting an encyclopedia in Rio's *Trade Winds: Le Rond d'Alembert*.

A hundred years later, the French mathematician and physicist, Pierre-Simon Laplace, launched his program of cosmological investigation within the Newtonian framework—a program based, in part, on his desire to show, contra Newton, that God had no need to intervene in the running of His machinery, once He had set it in motion. The results of this research, published under the title *Exposition du système du monde* (The System of the World), unlike everything else from his pen, contains not a single equation. It was also by far the most popular book he ever wrote, running into six editions between 1796 and the last (posthumous) printing of 1835.[8] In this work he summarized the conclusions of his earlier, mathematical, work on the stability of the solar system. Laplace essentially deduced that the universe was indeed a clock, but one so perfectly balanced that the Clockmaker had need of winding it only once and it would run forever. It is interesting to remark that once the stability of planetary orbits became accessible to mathematical formulation and thereby established, the whole question ceased forever to present any properly cosmological interest. It remained however an interesting physical problem, and Laplace's calculations and conclusions have since undergone several waves of critique as a function of later developments in mathematical physics.

My second example jumps a century. By the middle of the nineteenth century a new science was in gestation with very different preoccupations and mathematical techniques from those of classical mechanics: thermodynamics, the study of heat and energy. This was a science quite unlike the Newtonian physics that had been a model for new physical theories up to that point. More concerned with overall balances and exchanges of heat and other forms of energy than with the exact motions of material bodies that had been the focal point of mechanics, the new science not only treated a different subject matter than classical physics had done, it posed quite different questions to its subject. In classical mechanics the motion of bodies, though taking place in time, gives no overall measure of, nor even direction, to it; any motion allowed by the theory is equally possible if time were to be reversed. The founders of thermodynamics felt the inadequacy of this "time" for their purposes. As Jérôme Avalon sums it up:

---

[3] Pierre-Simon Laplace, *Exposition du système du monde*, in *Corpus des oeuvres de philosophie en langue française* (Paris: Fayard, 1984).

[8] On Laplace's interpretation of Newtonian physics, see the introduction in this volume.

"The classical physics of Galileo and Newton implies a symmetry of past and future, a perfect reversibility in time that amounts to neutralizing it or purely and simply denying it." (UP, 44)

Thermodynamics, on the other hand, only works one way; not time but history is now center stage. And, at least in part, that history with its flows of heat and energy can be quantified. In particular, a certain quantity tied to a given system—entropy—can only increase with time if the system is isolated.

The point of departure for the new science had been the analysis of engines that ran on heat. The new thermodynamic universe was no longer a clock but a steam engine. Again, though a number of the early workers shied away from examining possible cosmological consequences of the new theory, the founders themselves, William Thomson (Lord Kelvin), Rudolf Clausius, William Rankine, and Hermann Helmholz, were not shy in so doing; and once again shifted the domain itself.

Thermodynamics had nothing to say about motions or scales of distance; neither did the questions the founders put to the "universe as a whole." However thermodynamics—and its practitioners—did have questions about the history of the universe, its age, and its ultimate fate. By determining the flows of heat energy, its transmission, the work they could do, the inescapable losses they were subject to, one might track down the history of the world.

Thomson concerned himself with the age of the universe and was able to put a limit on it—first one hundred million years, then twenty-four million; in any case sufficiently small, as he thought, to put an end to all that Darwinian nonsense about evolution.[h] But it was especially the results concerning the end of the universe that attracted attention. For the end of the universe was marked not by the end of the motion of the celestial bodies—these were eternal, the domain of clockwork mechanics—but by "heat death," the running down of all energetic processes to a final state of absolute zero.[i]

---

[h] On Darwinian theories (sans "nonsense"), see Gould.

[i] *Manhattan Terminus*, although by way of its characters a sequel to *Archipelago* and *Tlacuilo*, by way of its themes is a continuation of *Parrot's Perch*, *Merlin*, and *The Uncertainty Principle*; its characters ponder the two possible ends of the universe, whether "a hot and violent death by collapse or a cold death, an almost eternal agony, by dilution of matter and energy" (*MT*, 115). See the editor's note in this volume.

Little did it matter now if the planets continued to turn around the sun and if the celestial bodies follow their Newtonian trajectories forever, as Laplace had hoped to show they would. All that counted of life, of warmth, lay dead and wasted, in an eternal sleep. And this elegiac mood permeates the cosmological writings of this period, more marked of course in the popularizations but present even in the colder professional writings. The typical mood is well captured in the closing pages of the standard general popular French text on cosmology, the second edition (1884) of Hervé Faye's *Sur l'origine du monde* (On the Origin of the World):

> Now reduced to the weak radiation coming from the stars, our globe will be invaded by the cold and shadows of space. The continual movement of the atmosphere will yield to a complete calm. The aero-telluric circulation of water which gives life to all will have disappeared. The last clouds will have sprinkled on to the Earth the last of their rains; the brooks and the rivers will have ceased to carry down to the oceans that water which the Sun's radiation had hitherto unremittingly carried away. The seas themselves, entirely frozen, will cease to obey the movements of the tides. . . .

> As for the system itself, the planets, cold and dark, will continue to circle around an extinguished Sun. But for these movements, the last representatives of the primitive nebular vortex which nothing can efface, our world will have spent all the potential energy which the hand of God had accumulated in the primeval Chaos.[4]

The English-speaking world knew similar works; it also—and particularly—found its way into the imagery of some of the most influential English verse of the period:

> Then star nor sun shall waken,
> Nor any change of light:
> Nor sound of waters shaken,
> Nor any sound or sight:
> Nor wintry leaves nor vernal,
> Nor days nor things diurnal;

---

[4] Hervé Faye, *Sur l'origine du monde*, 2d ed. (Paris: Gauthiers-Villars, 1885), 307–08 (my translation).

Only the sleep eternal
In an eternal night.[5]

We might feel the same menace—or respite—ourselves; the scenario remains a possibility. But we do not. Cosmological fashion has changed and it is not the end but the beginning of the universe that arouses our interest. But before turning to the present I want to make a stop at our third example, invoking the name of Albert Einstein.

When, in 1917, Einstein considered publishing his ideas on the application of his new theory of general relativity to cosmological questions, he confided to a friend that to do so "exposes me to the danger of being interned in an insane asylum."[6] Nevertheless, he published a short paper that was to set the agenda for the next half century as to what would constitute cosmology.

His reasons for doing so sprang from essentially philosophical preoccupations: his dislike of an infinite space and his adhesion to views on the nature of space inspired by the writings of the German physicist and philosopher Ernst Mach. The forces behind such considerations were important to Einstein, however; for in order to produce the model of the universe that he felt simply had to be right, he was obliged to modify the equations of general relativity that he had just introduced, a step he was later to call the greatest mistake of his life.

The subject matter of Einstein's foray did not touch on the nature or constitution of celestial bodies—he assumed that they could be adequately represented by smeared-out dust, filling all space. Nor was he concerned with heat, its transmission or its decay—all details of matter and energy were summed up by a single number, the density of the dust, supposed constant. Even motion was banished—the universe was understood to be static and unchanging; indeed it was just this hypothesis that furnished a solution of the desired form to his equations.

The cosmological questions posed were thus very different: How to overcome the problems associated with a boundary to space? What lies

---

[5] Algernon Charles Swinburne, "The Garden of Proserpine," in *Poems and Ballads* (1866), cited in *The Oxford Book of Nineteenth Century English Verse*, ed. John Hayward (Oxford: Clarenton Press, 1964), 805. See in general Greg Myers, "Nineteenth-Century Popularizations of Thermodynamics and the Rhetoric of Social Prophecy," in *Energy & Entropy: Science and Culture in Victorian Britain*, ed. P. Brantlinger (Bloomington: Indiana University Press, 1985), 307–38.

[6] Albert Einstein, unpublished letter to Paul Ehrenfest, 4 February 1917 (my translation).

beyond the boundary? How to understand the fact that with apparently only attractive gravitational forces operating, the universe does not collapse to a single mass?

Einstein felt his new theory could resolve these questions because it operated on the geometry of the universe, on the manner in which the basic structures of time and space were constituted and articulated. He was able in fact to produce a model that reproduced his vision of a static, closed but unbounded universe, somewhat like the surface of a sphere in having no boundary, no "inside" or "outside."

But a new observation came to trouble the debate in the 1920s. Just as the solar system had lost its cosmological interest, an interest transferred to the stars, so the vast majority of visible stars turned out to be only a minor constituent of the universe, making up just one among billions of those huge groups of stars called "galaxies." And these galaxies were in motion; the universe as a whole was expanding at a phenomenal rate.

It turned out that the Einstein theory could handle this new information, paradoxically another indication of the instability of the domain and the fragility of the links between the theory and the objects it is designed to handle. It was sufficient to change the interpretation, so that rather than stars, the dust particles were now to represent the galaxies, and the static models were abandoned, replaced by dynamic, expanding ones. During the next fifty years, this model was modified and generalized in other ways too; the dust was endowed with a few more properties, principally that of pressure; and models other than closed ones were considered. Attempts were made to test by observation the degree of homogeneity of the distribution of matter in the universe, a homogeneity that was assumed in the idealized models used.

There was no real room for detailed studies of stellar (or galactic) dynamics in a theory that represented such things by a practically featureless fluid; their study was relegated from cosmology to astrophysics. Within cosmology one of the major questions was whether the universe would expand forever, whether the sphere-turned-balloon could be infinitely blown up or would eventually deflate. This question sparked off a spate of books concerning the place of God in the new dispensation. Though perhaps less prominently than previously, such speculation found legitimization in the popular writings of such eminent physicists as Sir James Jean and Sir Arthur Eddington.[j]

---

[j] On today's version of such speculation, see the introduction in this volume.

So long as relativity theory remained the dominant theoretical framework within which cosmology was conducted, the questions "natural" to it—or to those who used it—were essentially the only ones posed. With the introduction of a historical dimension to the universe, stemming from both the thermodynamic and the relativistic approaches, there had eventually to be posed the question of the nature of the origins of the universe. The models linked to Einstein's equations had nothing to say about it; the very suppositions of the theory broke down when one approached too near the initial state. Aside from a few figures like Georges Lemaître or George Gamow, the question of origins thus passed practically untouched for a half century.

The situation was to change once again in the 1970s, and this will be my fourth and last example. Two new results in astronomical observation were made in the late 1960s and early 1970s. The first of these, and the most important, was the observation of a diffuse, uniform microwave radiation coming from all parts of the sky. This could be understood as the relic of a very much earlier, very hot phase of the universe. The second was the measurement, difficult and imprecise, of the quantity of deuterium (heavy hydrogen) in the universe; this too could be interpreted as an indicator of conditions obtaining during the early history of the universe.

It was these two new kinds of observations which, offering for the first time some kind of grasp of the early history of the universe, drew into the domain of cosmology in the 1970s a new kind of actor. These were physicists trained primarily in the theories of the quantum field and elementary particles. Their background lay precisely in the theory and experiment of high energies—and thus high temperatures—and they transformed once again the nature of cosmological questions. Of course, it was not a complete change of cast. Some of those who had worked under the old dispensation continued under the new, and those who stayed, like Stephen W. Hawking, were precisely those to whom the new questions were as congenial as the old ones.

Besides the two new types of data, the two classical observations of the older relativistic cosmology—the expansion of the universe and the degree of homogeneity of matter—were still taken into account. But now they were reinterpreted as shedding light on the initial conditions, at the earliest stage of the universe. The interesting part of the "universe as a whole" thus found itself concentrated in its first three minutes; the dominance of the "Big Bang" as the cosmological question had begun. God duly made his reappearance, this time on the front page of newspapers and magazines, no longer the great Clockmaker but now the initial Singularity.[k]

We have seen the recurrent appearance in the formulation of cosmological questions of a series of analogies or metaphors, images that mirror phenomena that are badly understood—or not understood at all—in terms of better-known, more homey situations, where one feels one knows how to get about. And their success is a measure of how close parts of the unknown are reflected in the known.

Metaphors are very important, even essential, in science; they often provide not only the original ideas for the creation of a new theory but also serve as a guiding heuristic for the application and development of ideas within already existing theories. In generalizing an existing theory or in seeking to extend a theory to cover new phenomena, one often asks oneself what worked before; this new phenomenon is like this other (formally, structurally, dynamically, . . .) so perhaps the tools used with success in the one case can be tried in the other.

But metaphor is also dangerous in science, for it is always incomplete, inexact, misleading in one way or another. Of course, the universe, even "as a whole," is neither a clock nor a steam engine nor a balloon nor a creative explosion. Normally these initial metaphors are discarded after a while, when they serve less to advance new ideas than to block, by their inherent limitations, needed innovations. Scientists are generally quite conscious of the complexity of the systems they study and of the necessity for keeping always in mind the eventual impact of their idealizations for the global comprehension of phenomena. In a sense, science only becomes science—or rather "normal science"—by transcending the original metaphors that gave it birth. To paraphrase a certain Austrian philosopher, science is the struggle against the bewitchment of our intelligence by means of metaphor.[7]

Such metaphors are all the more dangerous when it comes time to present a science to a larger public. For a recourse to metaphor is necessary here, particularly in the case of fields like physics and astrophysics where the extreme mathematization of professional work forbids all possibility of a direct access to the concepts themselves. And I must emphasize

---

[k] On God and physicists, see the introduction in this volume. For Rio on Hawking, see *The Uncertainty Principle*, especially 46–47.

[7] Cf. Ludwig Wittgenstein, *Philosophical Investigations* (New York: Macmillan, 1953), 109.

that, at the present time at least, cosmology does not suffer from any lack of a sophisticated mathematical apparatus; certain models, in any event among the most serious, involve quite complex techniques. Its problem comes rather from the lack of sufficient and reliable observational data. There are correspondingly little grounds for deciding between competing models, and the production of new models is limited only by the imagination of the theorist, giving a strong impression that this impressive machinery is turning aimlessly. From a certain point of view one might wish to consider cosmology as a branch of mathematics rather than physics; and this is just the part of the domain which, though representing real work, cannot be transmitted beyond a small circle of specialists.

Normally, metaphors are created—or rather reworked—after the scientific work has been performed; they are a posteriori metaphors, created for ease of communication. They are no longer the original ones that served to create the field; time and technical progress have rendered such once telling images as mechanical clocks and steam engines enlightening more to a handful of historians than to the general public. In cosmology, on the contrary, we seem to see the original metaphors at work—they suggest fundamental questions, and sometimes reply without any scientific work having operated. In the best of cases this work has taken place previously, and the application to cosmology is a by-product that paves the way to the dream; or, if it takes place afterward, the founding images remain intact within the mathematical development. Mathematics may underpin the dream, it cannot validate it.[8] And often there is simply no work done at all; the metaphors follow one another without restraint. This is the aspect that motivates Jérôme Avalon's outburst against the hucksters of popular cosmology:

> ". . . the miracle response to all questions, from which emerges a kind of fast-food metaphysics, cheaply priced, guaranteed by science, and so an ideal consumer product, all of which is a lie that insults the dignity of the author and takes advantage of the reader, or rather the somewhat dull consumer who, seeking proof of God, only finds evidence of his own insufficiency." (UP, 47)

---

[8] The terminology is Rio's, from *Tlacuilo* (158), but I use it here against his own argument.
[1] On *Tlacuilo*, see Galarza and Metz.

Jérôme Avalon, the *homme moyen rationnel* of a particularly lucid variety, comments with intelligence and irony on the usual presentation and actors of cosmology. But there is another door by which the domain enters the life of a number of Rio's characters. If cosmology is a limit case of science it is not astonishing that its metaphorical residue appears in a limit case of human action:

> . . . part of uncontrollable and rich meaning, addressing itself directly to the eye, to buried history, to sensitivity, acting by magnetism or violence, and which gives birth in the mind and nerves to galaxies of dreams escaping the mastery of reason. (*MN*, 38)[m]

Cosmology in *Merlin*[n] and *Parrot's Perch*[o] marks the last stage in a descent into hell, the last stop before the final despair.

Thus Morgan, half sister of the future King Arthur and, with her brother, pupil of Merlin. Aided by some clues from Merlin, she deduces the weaknesses of the Ptolemaic, earth-centered cosmological model and foresees the advantages of placing the sun at the center of the universe, a precocious foreshadowing of the Copernican model, projected back into fifth-century Brittany.

> "How did you come to this conclusion?"

> ". . . I imagine that the heavenly bodies all turn at different distances and speeds around the sun, which is the fixed heart of the universe, just as men gather and move around a central hearth, each according to his own needs of movement, light and heat." (*M*, 68)

What Rio has captured here, of course, is not the real work of the sixteenth-century monk and astronomer Nicholas Copernicus, passing his original neo-Platonic metaphors on the perfection of the sun and its necessary place in the center of the cosmos through the refining fire of

---

[m] The contextual reference here is to the sea, described as offering one part of meaning to be elucidated by intelligence and one "part of uncontrollable. . . ." (*MN*, 37–38). On *Melancholy North*, see Arent Safir, Rabaté, and Metz.

[n] On *Merlin*, see Arent Safir, Pastoureau, and Metz.

[o] On *Parrot's Perch*, see Rabaté and Metz.

long and complex geometric demonstrations and painstaking comparison
with known planetary observations, transforming metaphor into science:

> We will give, in the course of the exposition on the circles them-
> selves, the lengths of the radii of the orbits, from which anyone
> who is not ignorant of mathematics will easily understand how
> such a composition of circles agrees perfectly with the numerical
> data and the observations.[9]

The fact that such knowledge, at the supposed time and place of Camelot,
is quite out of the question historically only underlines the metaphorical
and purely imaginative work of Morgan and Merlin.[p] If they are not really
producing Copernican astronomy but cosmology in its pure state, it is
because metaphor is of its essence. Michel Rio has here evoked what was
truly at stake in the debates around the heliocentric cosmology. And the
final message of the metaphor is precisely that which has been put in by
Morgan from the start, her own horror and despair:

> "What are you afraid of, little Morgan? Of the fact that the hearth
> might have more importance than the beings who come to warm
> themselves around it?"

> "Yes, Merlin. For if the hearth endures and the beings move on
> and die, then the hearth burns for no reason, and the finality
> which man gives to all things that relate to his petty and fleeting
> existence is worthless, a simple snare. And man himself, like
> everything that lives, is nothing more than a passing shadow
> which hot matter projects onto cold matter thus fertilized to
> give birth to an illusion." (*M*, 69–70)

She will make of the indifference of an undying universe in face of the
mortality and finitude of man a reason for her choice of evil, her oppo-

---

[9] Nicholas Copernicus, *De hypothesibus motuum cœlestium a se constitutis commentariolus*
(1514), part II, 187.8-11. This book is a popularization (already!), circulated prior to the
publication of his full treatise *De revolutionibus orbium cœlestium* in 1543. French translation:
Introduction à l'astronomie de Copernic, ed. Hugonnard-Roche, E. Rosen, and J.-P. Verdet
(Paris: A. Blanchard, 1975), 74 (my translation from the French).
[p] The anachronism of a scientific theory is at the heart of *Dreaming Jungles*, but without its
being "out of the question historically." See Gould. On the historical "*displacing*" of
Merlin, in Rio's case a "*replacing*" him into his real historical period, see Pastoureau.

sition, finally triumphant, to the attempts by Merlin to make of King Arthur's court the center of a rational and peaceful future. In the downfall of Camelot is to be found the apotheosis of the scandal that "the conceiving mind is itself subject to time and to death" (*UP*, 48).[q]

Or take Joaquín Fillo, Brother Joachim, twentieth-century Latin American priest, revolutionary, and torture victim, the protagonist in *Parrot's Perch*. Here again, but with a quite different cosmological model, we see the inevitable deception of all those who would take the metaphors of cosmology for anything other than a reflection of their own metaphors of anguish and despair. In Joachim's final soliloquy before his suicide he puts starkly the ultimate, real role of public cosmology:

> And he and the universe might perhaps come together in pain. He reflected on the rending of the primordial explosion, on the stars burning down to the iron limit, on the planets' disappearance, the galaxies' collapse, the protons' and black holes' decay. The totality of that convulsion, that transformation of the identity of matter, reminded him of his own suffering. (*PP*, 88)

The "death of the universe" is in fact his own.[r]

The novelist, like the cosmologist, sets out from an "exemplary piece of universe" (*UP*, 22–23). How then does his work differ from theirs? Michel Rio's work is exemplary in the way in which it sharpens our understanding of the relationship between science and fiction. The writer's job is not to be a purveyor of scientific knowledge to his audience, a middleman between the creative scientist and the literary public. It is rather the impact of this knowledge on the protagonists of his story, the manner in which possession of this knowledge interacts with the inner life of us all, which is part of the subject matter of fiction: not the heliocentric system but the despair at the center of Morgan's life,

---

[q] On Morgan's precocious scientific theory, and its repercussions, see Arent Safir; on this "scandal" as viewed in *Manhattan Terminus*, see the editor's note in this volume.
[r] On this suicide, and the suicide that occurs in *Faux Pas*, see Rabaté; also, note *l*, p. 142 on the death of Leonard Wilde in *Manhattan Terminus*. On suicide in *Melancholy North*, see Arent Safir.

not the death of galaxies but the death of Joachim, not the creation of the world but the end of creative work in the life of Jérôme Avalon.

Nor, on the other hand, is fiction a form of "antiscience," the disjoint complement of rational thought, free to express all that science cannot because it is untrammeled by the demands of logic or reason. This is the position of many scientists themselves. Einstein, taking umbrage at a reader's suggestion that, with relativity theory, scientific discourse could profitably replace the term *concept* by that of *fiction*, replied:

> I must say that the term "fiction" says nothing more to me than the traditional term "concept," and moreover that systems of contradictory concepts, like those that the theory of fiction presents as essential, cannot be considered legitimate.[10]

On the contrary, contradiction is as fatal to a novel as to a scientific theory.

It seems to me that the world of Michel Rio suggests another and more promising reflection on the relation between science and art.[s] The correct level on which to view this question is neither that of content nor of logic, but rather of structure. If the cosmologist and the novelist seem to occupy exactly the same terrain, the novelist, like the ordinary scientist, is also engaged in a struggle against metaphor. For the scientist, the difficult but necessary passage from metaphor to a real understanding of the world is made, as we have seen, through the instrumentality of logical rigor and confrontation with experiment. Part of the force of fiction resides in the emotive power of its imaginative life, the poetry of dreams. But to tame this force, the flow of these metaphors, to make a story tell his truth and not merely evoke reflex reactions in the reader, the author uses style.[t] It is style that permits him to control his fiction, to shape it, to limit its anarchic growth, and to direct it to the end of his own purposes. As Rio himself has put it, "insofar as the meaning of a

---

[10] Albert Einstein, letter to A. Wenzel, 22 November 1924, in Einstein, *Oeuvres choisies*, vol. 5, *Science, Ethique, Philosophie* (Paris: Editions du Seuil, 1991), 129 n. 9 (my translation).

[s] On the relation between science and art, see the introduction in this volume, Gould, Pastoureau, and Galarza.

[t] On style, see Swenson and Metz. On Rio and metaphor, see "Le rêveur et le logicien" (The Dreamer and the Logician), in *Dreams of Logic*, 67–79; also, *Manhattan Terminus*, 92–93, where Miss Milton Ambrose's striptease is a militant act against metaphor.

work of fiction is not the reconstruction of a system of knowledge, but its responsive effect, and nor is it the freedom of dream but its limits" (*DL*, 73).[u]

The feeling that cosmology directly touches certain of our deepest and most intimate hopes and fears is, as I have tried to show, both the source of its attraction and equally the source of its difficulties in transforming the force of its metaphors into a stable but dynamic scientific domain. This same emotive reaction renders the subject difficult to master in the field of fiction. In both cases, our own spontaneous reactions permanently threaten to submerge the arduous construction of both the cosmologist and the novelist:

"If you like," said Avalon, smiling. "There's both: order and disorder, as with all phenomena tied to entropy. There's the order of syntax and of knowledge, which are the stable particles, the protons of literature, and the disorder of free imagination, the residual photons of poetry." (*UP*, 68)[v]

---

[u] On *Dreams of Logic*, and this concept in particular, see the introduction in this volume; also, Galarza and Metz. On the dreamer and the logician, see Arent Safir.

[v] On two separate occasions Rio has called literature the "last discourse of disorder" (*MN*, 128 and *DJ*, 54), and yet his own concern (obsession) with order is present everywhere in his work; see Pastoureau. This question of order and disorder can be related to Gould's observations in biology concerning the interaction of chance or genetic accident and learning, and Swenson's discussion in aesthetics of nature ("disorder") and culture ("order").

5

Topographies

James Swenson

I have forgotten to describe the Tracy drawing-room. Sir Walter
Scott and his imitators would have used that as a point of
departure, but I detest physical descriptions. It is because I find it
such a bore that I am reluctant to write novels.

Stendhal, Memoirs of Egotism[1]

For those who love descriptions, Michel Rio's novels are a true
garden of delights (a French garden, to be sure). My project here, a somewhat curious one, is to describe the topographical descriptions in a few
of Rio's novels, *Archipelago*, *Faux Pas*, and *The Uncertainty Principle*,[a] beginning with architectural topographies and ending with landscapes. I hope
to bring into relief the structures that they share, their function in the
narratives, and the role that they play in Rio's universe. Above all I will
try to focus on the relation that exists between the conspicuous precision
of Rio's descriptive discourse and the generality of these sites, a generality
created by the repetition of certain elementary structures in almost all of
his descriptions. These descriptions, I will argue, play an exemplary role in
the construction of an (im)personal aesthetic.

---

[1] Stendhal, *Memoirs of Egotism*, trans. Hannah Josephson and Matthew Josephson (New
York: McGraw-Hill, 1975), 107.
[a] On *Archipelago*, see Arent Safir and Metz. On *Faux Pas*, see Rabaté and Metz. On *The
Uncertainty Principle*, see the introduction in this volume, Ritter, and Metz.

Loving a description necessarily implies both an appreciation of the aesthetic autonomy it can attain on its own, and an admiration for its thematic and even narrative integration in the unfolding of the text as a whole. The division of fictional discourse into description and narration is thus both unavoidable and entirely relative. The distinctions that could ground such a classification, both on the formal and on the ontological level, cannot be drawn in a rigorously reliable way. If the fundamental ontological distinction separates "representations of actions and events, which constitute the narrative properly speaking" from "representations of objects or people, which make up the act of what we today call 'description,'" we must nonetheless admit that there can be no representation of an action without a subject, and thus without the representation of an object or a character.[2] On the formal side the distinction is usually made, in French, between the static character of the imperfect tense and the punctual character of the preterit (*passé simple*), or, as Gérard Genette puts it, in the fact that

> the narration, by the temporal succession of its discourse, restores the equally temporal succession of the events, while the description must successively modulate the representation of objects simultaneously juxtaposed in space. (Genette, 7)

This semiological opposition between successive signs and juxtaposed signs also constitutes the foundation of the difference between poetry and painting in the aesthetic theory of G. E. Lessing. Just as painting is obliged to select a single moment of an action to represent (which should be as fertile as possible, i.e. suggestive of both the causes and the consequences of the action), poetry must select a single element of the body as a support for its representation, whence the rule of the unique epithet. Lessing's good description—Homeric description—does not enumerate the attributes of an object but recounts the story of its fabrication:

> If Homer wants to show us Juno's chariot, he shows Hebe putting it together piece by piece before our eyes. We see the wheels and axle, the seat, the pole, the traces, and the straps, not

---

[2] Gérard Genette, "Boundaries of Narrative," trans. Ann Levonas, *New Literary History* 8 (1976): 5.

as these parts are when fitted together, but as they are actually being assembled by Hebe.[3]

The poet substitutes temporal succession for spatial coexistence and thereby reestablishes the coincidence between the temporality of the signifier and that of the signified. Description comes to life by being recounted, and thereby reenters the properly narrative dimension of the story. A large part of the success of the classical form of description resides in the various techniques by which this apparent contradiction can be realized. This sort of narration *naturalizes* description, domesticates its opposition with the story proper. And yet descriptions do tend to become autonomous, and seem to aspire to an independent status. The effort of Lessing, as well as of many others who do not like the "length" of descriptions, to exclude description as such from poetry is precisely a reaction to this possibility. The descriptions of Balzac and Zola, as in a past age those of Rousseau and Chateaubriand, are loved (or hated) *for themselves*. They are a privileged site in the text for the magnificent display of personal style, and have always been favored by the compilers of collections of *morceaux choisis*.

Michel Rio's descriptive discourse indeed produces, in a first movement, this effect of independence. A first reading ot almost any of his novels gives the impression of a near-absolute autonomy of the topographic descriptions, which seem to spread out over entire pages and to offer a plethora of details in the midst of an otherwise austere, even parsimonious narrative style. This turns out to be only an effect, for the movement of integration is equally present. But the thematic or even philosophical function of Rio's descriptions still seems to me to depend upon this effect, and to require a substantial degree of autonomy. This is where the aggressive precision of his style (his characters speak frequently of "aggressive rhetoric" to qualify their taste for refined insults, and the word seems entirely appropriate here) is most intensely felt, and thus is where we can interrogate the philosophical as well as narrative signification of this style.[4b]

---

[3] Gotthold Ephraim Lessing, *Laocoön: An Essay on the Limits of Painting and Poetry*, trans. Edward Allen McCormick (Baltimore: Johns Hopkins University Press, 1984), 80.

[4] For Rio himself the absolutely personal character of a true style is one of the surest hallmarks of literary value. "Victor Hugo is one of the rare writers in the world who instituted his own syntax . . . and naturally the more identifiable a syntax, the more forceful it is. . . ." Anne Gillain and Martine Loufti, "Entretien avec Michel Rio," *French Review* 67 (1994): 791.

[b] On style, see the introduction in this volume, Ritter (especially the final paragraphs), and Metz.

Let us take as our first example the description in *The Uncertainty
Principle* of the house belonging to Dan Harrison, an American movie
star who has begun to age and who has withdrawn to this beautiful and
luxurious seaside mansion:

> It was a splendid building in the old style, with two stories, about
> thirty meters of east-west facade by twenty meters of north-south
> gable, which gave it the considerable ground surface of six hun-
> dred square meters, and so double that amount of habitable space.
> The stone walls were thick, the windows numerous, high and
> narrow both to allow in light and maintain coolness. (*UP*, 29)[5]

Rio has reduced the labor of integration of the description into the narrative temporality of the story to a strict minimum here. In two pages of
description, in an ocean of imperfect-tense constructions, there are only
two sentences in the preterit. Harrison's movement through space introduces the passage as a whole—"Harrison reached the house"—and marks
the transition between the exterior and interior descriptions of the house—
"It was by that door, reserved for his use alone, that Harrison entered into
the house" (30). Other than these two references, the enunciation of the
description occurs neither with respect to his movements, nor through his
perceptions and thoughts. Until the end of the description, when Harrison
picks up a book and begins to read, there is only a single verb of perception, *on voyait*, and a single verb of mental action, *faisait penser*. Neither of
these expressions refers to a character, whether explicit or implicit, as a
possible subject of its action (both would have to be translated into English
with passive constructions—"could be seen" and "recalled"). On the other
hand, one finds the verb "to be" in the imperfect tense seven times, com-
plemented by other purely predicative verbs such as "remain," or "give,"
"represent," and "make" used with quantitative expressions. The description
is thus as impersonal as possible. The building is seen, as it were, in blueprint; if the perspective is not angelic it is at least architectural. This purifi-
cation of descriptive discourse allows the discursive armature of the space
to appear with the greatest possible clarity. We can note several general characteristics of this architectural perspective as it functions in this passage:

---

[5] All citations in this and the following six paragraphs, specified or not, are taken from *The
Uncertainty Principle*, 28–32.

1. Orientation is given according to the compass. The words "north," "south," "east," and "west" (as well as their adjectival forms "northern" [*septentrional*], "southern" [*méridional*], "oriental," and "occidental") recur constantly in Rio's prose. In this passage there is no deictic orientation (to the right, to the left, across from, further along, etc.), whether it be with respect to the character's movement or with respect to a previously described site (we will see that when, in other texts, such indications are present, they are given in redundancy with compass-point orientation). The perspective is not that of a character moving through the narrative space but that of one who looks down on that space from above.

2. The house's walls are carefully distinguished into *façades* and *pignons* (a side wall topped with a gable). This use of a technical vocabulary helps to avoid deictic indications and thus to maintain the separation between the description and the character's perspective. Other terms drawn from the vocabularies of architecture and carpentry (here, *embrèvements* [miter joints], but often *perron* [a set of steps terminating in a small, flat landing to form a formal entrance] and *vantaux* [the hinged panels of French or Dutch doors, casement windows, folding screens or shutters, etc.]) appear in their proper places. Rio's work manifests a constant correlation between the delights of the dictionary and a certain superabundance in the described magnificence: the luxury of the decor is echoed by the lexical richness of the discourse.[c]

3. The dimensions are given in figures, often in a great deal of detail. Rio begins by giving the dimensions of the facade and the gable and subsequently calculates the surface. Individual rooms are likewise measured in square meters:

> The library, occupying the western third of the ground floor, taking in the twenty meters of gable in its length and ten meters of facade in its width, was the vastest room of the residence. With its two hundred square meters of area and four-meter high ceilings it represented an enormous volume. . . . (*UP*, 30–31)

This calculation cannot be ascribed to the mental activity of a character; there is no reason to imagine Dan Harrison doing this calculation as he

---

[c] *Manhattan Terminus* is no exception to this. See the description of the 3 Ws Bar, 12–23. On this subject, and for what follows, see also Metz's discussion of Rio's "material precision."

comes back into his home. We can also note here that the library is usually both the largest as well as the most important room of the house in narrative terms, as a privileged site of action.[d]

4. The house is oriented around a grand hall leading from north to south:

> There were only three doors. One, to the north, the main entrance, giving onto the courtyard. . . . Two to the south, the first facing the front door, at the end of a great north-south hall that divided the ground floor into two unequal parts, the second giving direct access to the library from the garden. (*UP*, 30)

We will find this fundamental disposition of interior space in all the houses described by Rio.

5. There are not many rooms, but they are enormous: the library is immense, and the living room and dining room occupy between them yet another two hundred square meters, "which left to each more than a considerable area" (32). The immensity of these spaces is rendered even greater by their near emptiness.[e] The library is "almost empty in its center furnished only by a large desk and chair" (*UP*, 31). But the few pieces of furniture that occupy this nearly empty space are comfortable, even luxurious. The house's "furniture was reduced to the strictly necessary, its beauty further heightened by this rarity, which showed it off to advantage" (32).

---

[d] Once again *Manhattan Terminus* conforms to the rule, only here the "library" contains more bottles than books. The 3 Ws Bar: ". . . a veritable library of fermentation, displaying on its shelves an encyclopedia of alcohol . . . [and] hundreds of leather-bound reference books, the encyclopedia organized according to geographical and alphabetical order. This library-like atmosphere. . . ." (*MT*, 17) This "library" is pictured on the book's cover in the original French edition. On the significance of libraries in Rio's first six novels, see Arent Safir.

[e] As far as space and emptiness also the 3 Ws is decorated in "Rio style": "The immense space that the four walls delimited was furnished with no more than thirty round tables . . . where one could easily have placed three times as many . . . and this disposition left each table with a 'zone of isolation' approaching a hundred square meters" (*MT*, 22–23). One thinks of Pastoureau's reference in his essay to Rio as "Breton and misanthrope." Nonetheless, while retaining the physical characteristics of the earlier novels that Swenson describes, *Manhattan Terminus* escapes his general conclusion. The 3 Ws is a very personal projection, the direct materialization of the mind, philosophy, and likes and dislikes of its owner, Hugo Usher.

6. The construction is old and of the highest quality, of a sort no longer to be found. The walls are thick, the windows numerous and well-disposed. The "magnificent" interior woodwork "in heart of oak" is "a true masterpiece of craftsmanship distinguished by the richness and finish of the material" (30). Generally, one can say that it is an ideal house, in two senses. First, it is the most beautiful and most comfortable of houses; simultaneously luxurious and discrete, the house gives a rational organization to space and thereby to daily life, allowing one to live life as it should be lived. But for Rio there is also a Platonic ideal of the house: the model, the blueprint from which he constructs all his houses. The elements enumerated here could all be equally well applied to the house of Alexandra Hamilton in *Archipelago* or that inhabited by Pierre Brémont in *Faux Pas*.

We have here a series of elements common to all of Rio's architectural descriptions. An examination of their signification, and above all of the signification of their quasi-impersonal precision, must begin with the question of the relations they entertain with the novels' characters. Can they be interpreted in characterological terms? Is this precision a reflection of, or a commentary upon, a character? Up to this point I have emphasized the gap that exists between Harrison, who is both the proprietor of the domain and the focus of the narration,[6] and the descriptive discourse itself. These are the two positions to which a metaphorical meaning of the description could be most easily referred, and it seems to me that it is because Harrison occupies them both that the description becomes even more impersonal than usual and maintains a particularly marked distance with respect to him. The discourse does not in any way follow his thought, and thus does not reveal his psychology. But this is not always the case. The two other novels by Rio that I am considering here, *Faux Pas* and *Archipelago*, stage their houses through the device of an inquisitive character who explores them for the first time. This procedure produces an effect of indecision as to the metaphorical force of the description. What in *The Uncertainty Principle* was located firmly on the side of the object of the description, in this case vacillates between the explorer and the house itself, or even slides entirely over to the side of subjectivity.

Faux Pas begins with the minute examination of a house in the suburbs by an unknown man. Toward the end of this long description, the

---

[6] On the concept of focalization, see Genette, *Narrative Discourse: A Study in Method*, trans. Jane E. Lewin (Ithaca: Cornell University Press, 1980), 189–94.

man finds a photograph of a woman and a little girl that he "observed . . . for a time, with the analytical and cold eye he had had until then" (*FP*, 13). This sentence has a retroactive effect on everything that has preceded it, which thereby becomes a sort of free indirect discourse (*discours indirect libre*), translating the thoughts or at least the mode of thought of the unknown man:

> He stopped in front of a residence, the courtyard of which was separated from the street by a thick hedge. He went through the white gate and began a tour of the house from the left, advancing slowly and steadily. It was a squat building, solid and graceless. The facade was composed of a massive central door, atop a low perron, flanked by four large windows. . . . Following the gravel path that went around the building, the unknown man walked along the western gable wall. . . . This wall had two openings per story. . . . The back of the house offered the same arrangement as the facade. . . . The garden, very deep, hardly wider than the house, consisted of a simple lawn studded with flowered banks and conifers. The unknown man passed in front of the eastern gable and came back into the courtyard. Once at the gate, he began watching the street. (8–9)

The description is studded with verbs in the *passé simple*, integrating it into the temporality of the narrative. Rio alternates verbs of movement introducing a new portion of the space with predicative verbs in the imperfect. One could not find a better example of what Mieke Bal calls the "motivation" of descriptions, which consists in their integration into narrative time and thus their naturalization in the discourse of the story.[7] The description of the house *is* the story of its observation by the unknown man, who has strong reasons (even though we do not yet know them) for examining it so minutely. This integration of descriptive space into narrative time is echoed by the possibility of a psychological understanding of style. In fact, the question immediately raised by the appellation "the unknown man" (*l'inconnu*)—who is he?—is principally determined by his examination of the house. Why is he exploring it? Why does he put the pistol back in the drawer? Why is he so interested in the

---

[7] Mieke Bal, "On Meaning and Descriptions," *Studies in Twentieth-Century Literature* 6 (fall 1981–spring 1982): 108.

books? The description not only sets the stage in its physical topography; it also characterizes the protagonist and prepares the objects that will play a role in the plot. This characterization occurs primarily at the level of style: until the confrontation between the killer and his victim Brémont, there is nothing but the dry, cold, and austere style of the description to guide us.

And nonetheless a moment does arrive at which the alternation of movements and descriptions is broken. When the man enters the house, Rio presents an overview, which corresponds trait for trait with what we saw in *The Uncertainty Principle*. The house has the same size, construction, and layout. Above all it is described with the same precisions (facades and gables, figures of volume, etc.):

> The layout of the house was very simple. The twenty meters of facade and fifteen meters of gable made for an interior ground surface of slightly less than three hundred square meters, divided into five equal parts: the entrance hall and four rooms, each part thus measuring more than fifty square meters. This economical arrangement, ruled by the strictly utilitarian from the point of view of usage, but generous to excess from the point of view of space, gave an impression of size that could not have been suspected from the outside view of the building. The western part of the ground floor consisted of a dining room to the south, next to the courtyard and the street, and a kitchen of unusual size to the north, next to the garden. The eastern part, a living room and a library. Each room was abundantly lighted by three windows, two in the facade and one in the gable. (*FP*, 10)

Until this point the precision of the discourse seems to express the meticulous character of the unknown man. But this overview cannot represent the retrospective reconstruction of the house he has just seen; in fact, it precedes the examination of the rooms. The text continues: "The unknown man rapidly visited the kitchen, the dining room and the living room. He lingered for a moment in the library" (10–11). Technically, this is only a slight fault with respect to the rule of alternation. But in the absence of other marks, this rule alone maintains the logic of a *discours indirect libre* in which the precision of the discourse represents or signifies the psychology of the focalizing character. The blueprint does not merely present itself here as it appears within the logical breakdown of space under the cold and analytical gaze of the killer. It steps forth as an organization of space independent of the protagonist's perspective, an organization of space that precedes and perhaps even renders that perspective possible. But if the appellation "the unknown man" calls forth a series of questions to which the style, at a certain moment, might seem to respond, it also implies the presence in the enunciation of a third party for whom he would be unknown. There will always remain this element of the discourse that he cannot assume, which implies that the precision of the discourse will always retain an irreducible element of autonomy.

In *Archipelago*, the house occupied by Alexandra Hamilton on the grounds of the school that bears her name shares the same fundamental layout. This time the situation is complicated not only by the presence of upper levels, but even more so by the fact that the young narrator does not discover it all at once. His first visit shows him the hall, the stairway, and the library; his return visit the guest quarters; the lunch with Hamilton the dining room and the living room. It is only the later scene in which he surprises the librarian Leonard Wilde spying on Hamilton in her bath that will give the narrator a confirmation of the placement of the rooms of Hamilton and her maid. The layout is thus given as a mental reconstruction (partially anticipated) on the part of the narrator:

> I began to picture for myself the general layout of the house. Its architecture was simple, and the owner had taken comfortable advantage of it, harmonizing the public space for guests, visitors, or servants with the private space she needed for her own independence and solitude. This layout exactly reflected the spirit that had inspired the division of the general property. On the first floor, on one side of the entrance hall, were the drawing room and the dining room; on the other, the kitchen and pantries. On the second floor, the library and no doubt Alexandra Hamilton's chambers. On the third, the guest rooms and the chambers of the governess. (*Ar*, 53)

The combination of first-person narration with the procedure of posterior reconstruction marks the description as entirely the production of the narrator.^ʄ There is no element of the discourse that cannot be attributed

---

ʄ The narrator in question is the same that we find appearing and reappearing, and to whom we owe the descriptions in fully half of Rio's novels. He is the solitary navigator in

to him: not only is the expression his, but even more importantly there is an exact correspondence between his knowledge of the diegetic space and that of the reader. But the precision of the discourse (which is, in this case, a little less pronounced) is nonetheless entirely objectified. It has nothing to do with the amorous confusion that overtakes the narrator, preventing him from reading and generally making him act like the dizzy teenager he is. The precision of the discourse finds its metaphorical reference and justification in the object described and, in the end, in the constructive will of Alexandra Hamilton. Even though the house dates to the eighteenth century it displays "all the signs of a perfect restoration" (*Ar*, 10). "The spirit that had inspired the division of the general property" signifies above all a desire for solitude and withdrawal, given that the proprietress

> at least while school was in session, never stepped beyond the limits of territory reserved for the institution: a strict and immutable boundary she had drawn between the public life of her establishment and her own discretion, perhaps indifference. (2)

But this division also creates a "kind of *hortus conclusus*" that reproduces in miniature the preexisting division of the domain between lawn and trees:

> Lawns, bounded by the alleys, surrounded the building and occupied nearly a third of the grounds. The remaining portion, planted with oaks, offered a mirror image of the larger park to which it had belonged before construction of the interior wall. (10)

We will later return to the description of the garden. For the moment we should notice above all that if the property informs us about the proprietress, what we learn is quite precisely *schematic*, that is, it is communicated at the level of the *schema*, the map. Alexandra Hamilton has drawn a dividing line. In doing this she has reproduced—or displaced—a dividing line that was already drawn. It is the fact and above all the clarity

---

Melancholy North, the castaway on Sailaway Island in *Trade Winds*; he takes Alan Stewart's yacht to rescue Leonard Wilde, held prisoner on the island-brothel of Ecstasy in *Tlacuilo*; and, thirty years after his adolescent passion for Alexandra Hamilton at the boarding school in *Archipelago* where he first encounters Alan and the then-librarian Wilde, he meets up with the two men in *Manhattan Terminus*, at the 3 Ws Bar in New York. On first-person narration and description, true and false *I*'s, in Rio's work, see Metz.

of the division and not the detail of its placement that expresses the will that determines it and thus reveals the personality of Alexandra Hamilton.

Rio's details in fact express nothing other than the precision of the discourse that names them. The exactitude of the vocabulary used by Rio might tend to hide it, but what is missing in his work is realist detail.[8] It is in fact very difficult to imagine visually what he describes. Rio does not paint; he delimits. This is the opposite of the situation in the realist novel in which the detail (when it does not simply signify "realism")[8] has the primary function of situating a character with respect to social differentiations, to reveal his or her belonging to a particular region, class, or mentality. Whether they are presented pell-mell or in order, the details add up to form a *milieu*. The theory of the *milieu* dominates the aesthetics of the novel in France from Balzac to Zola, in whose work it finds its most complete flowering. Zola defines description as "a state of the environment [*milieu*] that determines and completes man," a concept of determination that presents itself as scientific:

> Description is no longer our aim; we wish simply to complete and to determine. For example, the zoologist who, speaking of a particular insect, finds himself obliged to study at length the plant upon which this insect lives, from which he draws his being, even his form and his color, would indeed be describing; but this description would in fact be part of the analysis of the insect itself. It would respond to a scholarly necessity rather than being a painterly exercise. . . . It is our position that man cannot be separated from his environment [*milieu*], that he is completed by his clothing, his house, his city, his province; and that we will

---

[8] On the precision of this discourse and on specialized vocabularies and realism, see Metz. On historical detail in Rio's work, see Pastoureau.

[8] See the famous article by Roland Barthes, "The Reality Effect," in *The Rustle of Language*, trans. Richard Howard (Berkeley and Los Angeles: University of California Press, 1989), 141–48. Barthes's analysis emphasizes what we have called "the autonomy of descriptions" by attributing an *aesthetic* function to them (an aesthetics of "the real" rather than an aesthetics of the beautiful, and that does not acknowledge itself as such). "Description has long had an aesthetic function. . . . Although the description of Rouen is quite irrelevant to the narrative structure of *Madame Bovary* (we can attach it to no functional sequence nor to any characterial, atmospheric, or sapiential signified), it is not in the least scandalous, it is justified, if not by the work's logic, at least by the laws of literature. . . ." (143–45).

therefore not describe a single mental or emotional phenomenon without seeking the causes or the repercussions in his environment. Whence come what are called our endless descriptions.[9]

The idea of the *milieu* fundamentally rests on a simultaneity of character and decor that assures the possibility of a reciprocal influence between the two, which Zola expresses by situating the notions of cause and repercussion on the same level. If the character expresses himself in the objects that surround him—in his clothing, his furniture, his street, and his neighborhood—they on the other hand have made him become what he is. The causality here is both expressive and reciprocal. This is true of the entire realist tradition, in which, in Genette's words, "physical portraits and descriptions of clothing and furnishings tend to reveal and at the same time to justify the psychology of the characters, of which they are at once sign, cause, and effect."[10] An expression from *Le Père Goriot*, linking Madame Vauquer to her pension, summarizes the theory and technique of Balzac: "her entire person, in short, explains the pension, as the pension implies her person" (*enfin toute sa personne explique la pension, comme la pension implique sa personne*).[11][h] The pension has an unhealthy and stingy "atmosphere" that insinuates itself into every detail. Character and decor are "in harmony."

Now, in Rio's work characters and the decor in which they live and move are never entirely contemporaneous with one another. Both large

---

[9] Emile Zola, "De la description," from *Le Roman expérimental*, in *Oeuvres complètes* (Paris: Cercle du livre précieux, 1966–1970), 10:1299–1300 (my translation). The sociobiological alibi takes up the terms used by Balzac in the Avant-propos of *La Comédie humaine* ([Paris: Gallimard, Bibliothèque de la Pléiade, 1951], 1:4, my translation): "The animal is a principle whose external form, or more precisely the differences in his external form, are derived from the *milieux* in which he is called upon to develop. . . . Does not Society make of man, according to all the different *milieux* in which his action unfolds, as many different sorts of men as there are varieties in zoology?"

[10] Genette, "Boundaries," 6.

[11] Balzac, *Le Père Goriot*, in *La Comédie humaine*, 2:852 (my translation). This passage has been the object of an important analysis by Erich Auerbach, in *Mimesis: The Representation of Reality in Western Literature*, trans. Willard R. Trask (Princeton: Princeton University Press, 1968), 468–74.

[h] Realism, naturalism, and ideality in literature, discussed in terms of "Hugo against Balzac and Flaubert against himself" (*MT*, 51) form part of a conversation among the narrator, Leonard Wilde, and "Roger Rabbit," a thinly disguised John Updike, in *Manhattan Terminus*. Neither Swenson nor Rio, obviously, was aware of the other's work when he was writing, but both were familiar with the enlightening list of books read by the

houses in *Faux Pas*, for example, belong to never-named friends, whence they draw a strong tint of anonymity. The cottage in which the unknown man camps suits him perfectly, but it does so because it expresses nothing more than work well done. The school library in *Archipelago* must be apprehended through a historical development; its current configuration being due to the superimposition of rapid growth upon Tudor magnificence (*Ar*, 56–57). *Rio always conceives of buildings on the basis of their construction.* If the description of Harrison's house teaches us something about his character, it is that he is rich and has good taste (a combination that is by no means self-evident). He has chosen this house on account of its agreement with his aesthetic sensibility, but he is not the one who built it: it is distinguished precisely on account of its age. In this respect, the keystone of the passage cited at the beginning is the following sentence: "The interior architecture was magnificent, and its framework in heart of oak, a true masterpiece of craftsmanship distinguished by the richness and finish of the material, . . . recalled the most beautiful ribs of ancient naval construction" (*UP*, 30). We have already seen how the relation of Alexandra Hamilton to her house is situated in a similar gesture of construction. But this gesture is always situated in a past whose access is difficult, breaking the simultaneity and reciprocal causality (what Hegel calls *Wechselwirkung*) necessary to the functioning of the *milieu*.

This emphasis on the construction of the objects described allows us to see the kinship that exists between the terrestrial topographies discussed here and certain passages in more maritime novels such as *Trade Winds* and *Tlacuilo*.[i] If the *Lady Mary*, Alan Stewart's boat in *Tlacuilo*, exemplifies "ancient naval construction" joined to the latest technology (*Tl*, 27–33), even more revealing is the story of the makeshift construction of *Rêve de Suzanne* (Suzanne's Dream) in *Trade Winds*, which, granting the same place to the precision of the discourse and particularly to technical vocabulary, can be considered as a canonical example of Homeric description as theorized by Lessing (*TW*, 100–112). The insistent utilization, in *Melancholy North*,[j] *Trade Winds*, *Archipelago*, and *Tlacuilo*, of the vocabulary of sailing in many properly narrative passages doubtless responds to a similar intention; this discourse is descriptive insofar as it

---

narrator and commented on by Wilde in *Archipelago* (67). On Flaubert, see Rabaté; on Balzac's realism, see also Metz.

[i] On *Trade Winds*, see Arent Safir and Metz. On *Tlacuilo*, see Galarza and Metz.

[j] On *Melancholy North*, see Arent Safir, Rabaté, and Metz.

displays a certain knowledge that is expressed both in a technical vocabulary and in the fabrication of a material object.[12][k] This way of emphasizing the construction of the objects described also recalls to us that Homeric description, description in the form of a narrated fabrication, is always *ekphrasis*, that is, the literary description of a work of art. As such it always has an eminently aesthetic function: the poet competes with painters and other artists.[13] What Rio describes is always, at least to some extent, a work of art.

This is even—or perhaps particularly—true of descriptions of nature. The question of the relation between art and nature in description indicates the exemplary importance of gardens, which are always the work of art and nature at the same time. Rio's gardens resemble one another as much as the houses they surround do. They stem from a well-established but often-forgotten tradition, the pleasance or *locus amoenus*. As Ernst Robert Curtius describes it in his seminal study, this topos depicts:

> a beautiful, shaded natural site. Its minimum ingredients comprise a tree (or several trees), a meadow, and a spring or brook. Birdsong and flowers may be added. The most elaborate examples also add a breeze.[14]

This minimum decor (the spring having been transmuted into the ocean) forms a trinity dominating the grounds of the Hamilton School. The scene is divided into three regions (right, left, and opposite, which are echoed by supplementary compass-point determinations) in order to clearly separate forest, lawn, and water, each in its place:

> On my right, covering the entire eastern part of the property, the park's large, century-old oaks . . . were planted with perfect regu-

---

[12] On the importance of lexical development in description, see Philippe Hamon, "What Is a Description?" in *French Literary Theory Today: A Reader*, ed. Tzvetan Todorov (Cambridge: Cambridge University Press and Paris: Editions de la Maison des Sciences de l'Homme, 1982), 147–78.

[k] On shipbuilding and technical vocabulary, see Metz.

[13] See the examples given by Raymonde Debray-Genette, "La pierre descriptive," *Poétique* 43 (1980): 293–304.

[14] Ernst Robert Curtius, *European Literature and the Latin Middle Ages*, trans. Willard R. Trask (Princeton: Princeton University Press, 1990), 195.

larity, in such a way that each tree had space and light sufficient
to enable it to develop without obstacle. . . . On my left, immense
lawns, representing an ideal of an English turf, extended over the
western half of the property. . . . Opposite me, in the continuation
of the central alley that crossed the north wall and joined up with
the road descending to the village of Rozel, the gigantic open
gates framed a narrow perspective over the eastern part of Bouley
Bay. . . . (*Ar*, 8–9)

Rio always combines these elements within an enclosure (here a wall
three meters high that surrounds the entire grounds) with the "perfect
regularity" that guarantees nature the opportunity to incorporate art and
thereby to surpass itself: these products of a skillful and learned arbori-
culture grow "in size and splendor to dimensions rarely attained" (20).
The same combination can be found around the large country house in
Faux Pas: "vast lawns, well maintained," "trees judiciously spread out,"
limits marked by a "system of sloped, planted earth banks. . . ." (*FP*, 54).
The Provençal garden of *The Uncertainty Principle* also comprises "thick
lawns, perfectly maintained, ornamental trees where diverse species of
palm dominated," the sea of course, and a series of "terraces . . . rigorously
horizontal" (*UP*, 11).

Cultivated nature is subject to the same concern with order and the
same intellectual geometry as interior space.[1] It too is taken to an ideal
scale of grandeur and discretion; it too is measured and revealed by the
map; it too is a construction employing skill and knowledge, a work of
art. From Longus to Rousseau, the *locus amoenus* has always been a site of
beauty in which the contributions of nature and culture are impossible to
discern.[15] Since these descriptions are eulogies of the beauty of the site, it
is precisely nature's art—that is, nature as a production combining skill and

---

[1] On Rio's concern with order, or the relation order-disorder, see Pastoureau, Ritter,
Galarza, and Metz. This aesthetic, systematically combining natural chance and human
intervention, is evident on a different level in Rio's assessment that behavior depends both
on heredity (genetic chance) and learning. See Gould.

[15] In Longus's walled garden, a high point of the topos that has many structural affinities
with Rio's, what "had happened naturally . . . gave the impression of having been done on
purpose" (*Daphnis and Chloe*, trans. Paul Turner [Harmondsworth: Penguin, 1989], 96). In
Rousseau's Elyseum on the other hand it is art that is hidden under the appearance of
uncultivated nature. See *La Nouvelle Héloïse*, in *Oeuvres complètes*, ed. Bernard Gagnebin
and Marcel Raymond (Paris: Gallimard, Bibliothèque de la Pléiade, 1964), 2:472.

knowledge—that is to be praised.[16] This imbrication of nature and art is also expressed in the continuity between the garden and the landscape. The garden always opens upon the perspective of a landscape that is exterior to it but that gives it its raison d'être. For Rio's landscape is "ordered like a painting" (*FP*, 55–56), comprising both perspective and composition. But the perspective is incorporated by the composition; point of view is part of the skillful disposition of elements.[17][m] The composition of this perspective is fundamentally defined as the unity of opposites.[n] The moment when this view is most precious is thus twilight, a moment of melancholy but also of peace and harmony, which is always a balancing of contraries. In its ephemerality twilight participates in the composition of the scene by uniting day and night. The perspective of Dan Harrison's garden is a perfect tableau that offers a veritable catalog of united opposites:

> The uniformity and the chaos, the hot and the cold, the shadow and the radiance, the opaque and the diaphanous, everything allied itself to constitute the perfection of an inextricable landscape, pictorial and natural, an infinite interweaving of nuances that observation seemed unable to exhaust, and that nonetheless at first glance offered a clear composition, outlined by the simplifying effect of a harsh light. (*UP*, 13)

This alliance is itself made possible by an identically inextricable construction. There is a stone bench "placed at the exact middle" of the southern wall, giving it a "perspective ideally premeditated. . . ." (12). But this constructive will is by itself impotent; only when it is conjoined with chance can it produce such a marvel:

---

[16] On the relation between *ekphrasis* and epideictic rhetoric, see Curtius, *European Literature and the Latin Middle Ages*, 193–94.

[17] Pictorial composition in Rio in terms of windows and frames would reward a more extensive study. See the scenes of voyeurism through the framing of windows in *Faux Pas* and *Archipelago*, as well as the initial framing of the landscape by the window in *Parrot's Perch*. The frames of Dan Harrison's paintings play an indispensable role of conferring value.

[m] On Rio's early interest in these questions of frame and visual composition, see the introduction in this volume and Galarza.

[n] On the unity of opposites in Rio's aesthetic and thought, see, for example, the description of the jungle in Gould's essay; also, in Arent Safir, the descriptions of the jungle, of the mother, and of Jane Sheldon, the dreamer-logician relation, and Alan Stewart's discourse on the "meeting of extremes."

Set in this natural masterpiece, the enclosed garden, born of the
calculations of the mind, was an ultimate counterpoint giving
the whole that absolute harmony attained only by the felicitous
joint work of chance and thought. . . . (13)

The landscape is perfect precisely insofar as the portion due to nature
and the portion due to art, the pictorial and the natural, chance and calculation are inextricable.[o] On the level of discourse, this inextricability can
only be expressed by the rhetorical figure of oxymoron. One of the twilight landscapes of *Faux Pas* presents "an absolute beauty composed by
meticulous chance" (*FP*, 70), while another balances "the absolute lim-
pidity of the sky" with "the calculated jungle of greenery" (9). Each of
these expressions conjoins art—production of skill and knowledge, the
domain of mind, exactitude, and premeditation—with the raw, wild, and
indifferent existence of nature. It is precisely this conjunction that is signified by the adjective par excellence, "absolute," which inevitably appears
linked to these expressions. The landscape inserts the character in the
mystic experience of participation in the impersonality of nature, that is, of
the absolute. At the end of *Faux Pas*, before as well as after the death of the
protagonist, "nature left to itself in the gentleness of the twilight showed
the secret splendors of the law" (122). This law, "the only one . . . natural
law," (92) is splendid precisely in that it is absolutely indifferent to us.[p]
Nature and her law display their splendors even when there is no one to
see them. The beauty of nature is another name for this indifference, for
this law.

Our "description of description" in Michel Rio's work, following a
trajectory from architecture to landscapes, has revealed two sensitive points
of every descriptive discourse: the integration of descriptive space in narrative temporality, and the insertion of the character in the decor, on the
level of signification as well as on that of representation. In many respects

---

[o] On poetry born of mathematics, a variation on this aesthetic, see the introduction in this
volume.
[p] Nature's indifference, present anew in *Manhattan Terminus*, as before in so many of Rio's
novels, is evoked with eloquent simplicity in the last words of *Merlin*: "I look at Bois-en-
Val, the palace on the Lake of Diane, Trebes, Avalon, the sky and the sea. And I can see
nothing but the death of man, thrice-laid in the tomb, and the triumph of summer" (*M*,
152). On natural law and nature's indifference, see Gould and Ritter.

these problems are in fact the same; Rio's topographies, in any case, propose a single solution: the refusal of any psychological interpretation of the
relation between the character and the decor in favor of an objective
aesthetics. Temporal integration is often accomplished through the exploration of space by a character, but because this space is always a product of
art, integration is accompanied by a projection into the past of the internal
temporality of the object in the form of the (often inaccessible) story of its
fabrication. The consequence of this projection into the past is to break
any psychological link of the realist type between character and *milieu*.^{q} If
the decor is a work of art, the character is not the artist. As works of art,
the house and the landscape indeed express a creative intention and a
knowledge. But it is an intention that is fundamentally foreign to the
character, and a knowledge that speaks of his inconsequentiality. The
beauty of this decor—of the houses as well as of the landscapes—depends
upon this impersonality. Rio's characters find themselves in these immense
spaces as the spectators of a drama that is indifferent to their presence, and
that draws its splendor from that indifference.

We have also seen that the precision of the descriptive discourse can
never be entirely reduced to a psychological effect, even when the narrative is told in the first person. If this precision expresses an aesthetics, it is
an objective aesthetics. This precision corresponds to the knowledge that
is concretized in the fabrication of the object. Style for Michel Rio is "a
personal object," as Maxime Lesourd calls the cabin he has built. "I built
it entirely by myself," he says (*FP*, 59–60). The only knowledge absolutely
proper to the writer is lexical, the employment of the entire wealth of the
vocabulary of a language. Gautier, Hugo, and Flaubert—Rio's favorite
writers—all, as if by chance, have in common the use of a dispropor-
tionately large vocabulary. "[W]hich prompts the thought," concludes
Rio ironically, "that knowledge is no stranger to poetics" (*DL*, 76).^{r}

---

^{q} While also arriving at the total absence of conventional realism in Rio's work, Metz puts
forth a different hypothesis as to the subjectivity and objectivity of its aesthetic. See Metz.
^{r} Rio again expresses his views on this subject in *Manhattan Terminus*: "This is translated
also stylistically by the search for an ideal musicality, the musicality of poetry in the service
of that explosion of meaning, and facilitated by the considerable stock of sounds supplied
by these [specialized] vocabularies.... It's a question of precision and of music. One cannot
describe the universe with the usual two thousand words and their disco music.... Rigor
does not mean poverty, nor abundance wasteful preciosity" (*MT*, 54).

6

The Temptation of the Last Man

Jean-Michel Rabaté

The Son's Misstep or *Faux Pas*

Through their lurid stories, Christian martyrologists have shaped the Western imagination, managing to spread their cruel fantasies even to distant climes, as in the well-known case of that recidivist voluntary martyr Saint Sebastian who so fascinated Mishima among others.[1] Jacobus de Voragine's *Legenda aurea* (Golden Legend) is teeming with horrendous details intended to teach by example. Let me give just one example, the death of Saint James Intercisus ("cut to pieces"). If it is told with such precision, this is perhaps because he had the same name as the author of this exhaustive chronicle of "witness" saints. Saint James, whose parents and wife were Christian, succumbs to the idolatrous cults of Persia and is converted, and when his family learns this it flees from him. The prince has him summoned and demands an explanation, whereupon James professes his faith, adding that he does not fear death, assured as he is that soon he will gain eternal life. Sentence is pronounced: "In order to imprint terror in the hearts of others," James is to be cut up into pieces.[2] There

---

[1] See Yukio Mishima, *Confession d'un masque* (Paris: Gallimard, Folio, 1971), 42–50.

[2] My references throughout are to the French edition: Jacques de Voragine, *La Légende Dorée*, trans. J.-B. Roze (Paris: Flammarion, GF, 1967), 2:396 (my translations from the French). The link between de Voragine's work and the catalogs of tortures in Sade's *One Hundred and Twenty Days of Sodom* is striking.

follows a quite extraordinary dialogue between the saint and his tortured
body: each part that is cut off, finger by finger, limb by limb, is given the
benefit of lighthearted commentary full of biblical metaphors and glad-
ness in a suffering accepted and sublimated (his limbs are thus like vine-
shoots to be pruned so that the sap become more vigorous, or like olive
branches to be planted in fertile soil). His mutilated and dismembered
body becomes a literal allegory of Christ's passion (so, when the big toe
of his right foot is cut off, he says: "The foot of Christ was pierced, and
blood flowed out" [397]). It is not until his torturers are visibly exhausted
(they "sweated in cutting him" from the first hour of the day to the
ninth) that they finally set to the "major work" of sawing off his right leg
at the groin. At this point, James feels—something exceptional in *Legenda
aurea*—an "inexpressible pain," and calls out, "Help me, Lord Jesus Christ,
for the moanings of death have surrounded me" (398). When the turn
comes for the left leg, the man-trunk that remains finds the strength to
count up his missing limbs and to note that there is not a single one he
can move in praise of God; and he asks for the grace of a quick death,
which is accorded him when finally his head is cut off. It is a cheering
version of torment: the torturers worn out before the martyr, who makes
the most of each torture so as to bring out, whether through example,
parable, or metaphor, the depth of his resolution. Today, admittedly, such
piety tinged with sadism is liable to raise a smile, especially when the glib
style of the Archbishop of Genoa falls, as it often does, into the blood-
and-thunder of folklore. It is even somewhat embarrassing to hold up
these catalogs of cruelty against the appalling testimonials of the torture
that is frequently practiced today, which has become a political force
worldwide and that is denounced daily by Amnesty International.

Saint James Intercisus is mentioned as a typical example in the
middle of the long litany of Christian martyrs run off by Joachim, the
priest who has escaped from the prisons of Latin America at the start of
Michel Rio's novel *Parrot's Perch*.[a] In an eloquent Sunday sermon that
culminates in a profession of doubt, this priest, with whose suicide the
book will end, begins by denouncing in front of the monks of the abbey
who have received him, the close complicity between the Catholic religion and the cult of suffering. The relevance of this historical reminder
derives from the split between the very real torture that has been inflicted
upon him in his country in order that he denounce some of his fellow

---

[a] On *Parrot's Perch*, see Arent Safir, Ritter, and Metz.

rebels, and the imagination at work in books on martyrs. For in such books torture is credited as being transfigured into a proof of faith that frees the body of the sinner, and the greater the pain the better it is, since the various torments invented by man's fertile fancy become worthy when they are offered up to God. The redemptive force of suffering is supposed to show, in a paradoxical way, the closeness between infinite love and pain—a pain that is unprecedented, intolerable, incredible even (credibility is ignored from the outset in *Legenda aurea*), and that cannot be evoked without serious disturbance for the imagination and even for the body of the listener. This disturbance is sign of an illicit, dangerous pleasure that may be tasted only insofar as it retains its theological sense, and hence its moral justification. Michel Rio's novel spells out logically and implacably the set of reasons that make Joachim gradually deaf to every justification that might be offered to suffering and absolute evil.

We are therefore not dealing in this intense and captivating novel with Joachim as a sort of *intercisus*, who is cut up and tortured piece by piece. Nor are we dealing with a militant ex-priest who has lost his conviction, a former insurgent who has given up on everything, even on Liberation Theology, who is thus hesitant or at war with himself. We are dealing rather with a lost "son" who has survived the torture of the "parrot's perch" only the better to be completely divided by clamorous internal debate, and who rushes toward death through a final gesture that frees him:

> He woke at dawn, knowing precisely who he was where he was, what had become of him. Again he felt the scorching of memory. He rose and faced the abyss, and, with slow steps and firm, walked forth into peace. (*PP*, 88)

In order to understand the nature of this nihilism, which is at once scandalous, ineluctable, and placed as the horizon in a frightening "end of story," we should first retrace the steps of Joachim's plunge toward nothingness.

It is worth noting initially that the intertextuality that is at first preponderant in Joachim's thoughts becomes progressively less during the course of the novel.[b] As we have seen, his farewell "sermon" to the monks

---

[b] On intertextuality in Rio's work, see Arent Safir (note 19, p. 71), Pastoureau, Galarza, and Metz.

and to his faith alludes to the martyrological tradition; and when he
withdraws into his cell, the few books that are there, in addition to the
handful of religious and theological works (among which some volumes of Saint Thomas Aquinas's *Summa Theologiae*), are the *Divine Comedy*,
Paradise Lost, and *Portrait of the Artist as a Young Man*, which constitute a
trilogy emblematizing the crisis of faith. The third text in particular is
summoned by the famous "sermon on Hell that had terrified Joyce, and
the narration of which had so struck Joachim's imagination" (*PP*, 15).
In his way, Joachim too is an "artist," one who has chosen to be silent,
since he has burned all the notes he has edited. The homily on Hell,
which is so bulky it almost makes chapter 3 of *Portrait* disproportionate,[3]
follows strictly the type of terrifying sermons on "The Hell open to
Christians" that Jesuits were refining ever since the sixteenth century,
aiming directly at the listener's imagination, using a technique inspired
directly by Ignatius de Loyola's *Spiritual Exercises*. Thus the "composition of the place" that the preacher establishes, aims to re-create in the
mind of each person on retreat a very precise image of Hell ("We en-
deavored, that is, to imagine with the senses of the mind, in our imagination, the material character of that awful place and of the physical
torments which all who are in hell endure"[Joyce, 127]). The terrifying
nature of Hell derives not only from the torments of the body, but even
more from those of the mind. The damned suffer doubly: in the flesh
that is preserved postmortem and is thus subject to eternal pain, and in
the imagination that adds to the shame of sin the knowledge of the
endlessness of the sentence:

> In hell on the contrary one torment, instead of counteracting
> another, lends it still greater force: and moreover as the internal
> faculties are more perfect than the external senses, so are they
> more capable of suffering. Just as every sense is afflicted with a
> fitting torment so is every spiritual faculty; the fancy with hor-
> rible images, the sensitive faculty with alternate longing and
> rage, the mind and understanding with an interior darkness more
> terrible even than the exterior darkness which reigns in that
> dreadful prison. (130)

---

[3] See James Joyce, *A Portrait of the Artist as a Young Man* (New York: Viking, Compass,
1967), 102–46.

Joyce dismantles the mechanism by which the preacher manages to play upon the susceptible minds of the young boys listening to him, obliging them to imagine tortures that draw above all upon the *imagining* of torture. . . . A dizzying and implacable circularity of internal imagining is established, by which the excited listener becomes virtually damned, since his mind has to project itself into a world of suffering that subsequently of course will have to be exactly what is shunned.

This sort of play upon the imagining and memory of torture provides the raw material for Michel Rio's novel, which offers an original slant upon just how pain is processed in the overly regulated psychic stage-show of Catholicism. What is more, if there is a further Joycean allusion, it is in the dialogue between Joachim and the abbot. The latter, apparently so as to save Joachim from a fatal swithering, sets out very honestly his own doubts in a version of faith that could be qualified as modern or even "modernist" (e.g., the abbot does not believe in Revelation or in redemption through suffering). At the end of this conversation (to which I will return) Joachim asks: "Are you in the process of damning yourself in order to save me?" (*PP*, 36). This is a question that sounds a distant echo of Stephen Dedalus's question to his Catholic friend Cranly— Cranly who, pushing Stephen toward a final retrenchment, even if it means shocking him (he goes so far as blasphemy when he suggests that Jesus hardly notices hypocrites or rogues), tries to have him swear to a remnant of faith in God. Stephen asks: "But I am curious to know are you trying to make a convert of me or a pervert of yourself" (Joyce, 242). Joachim is no more convinced than is Stephen by the arguments of a crafty casuistry that dresses up like cynicism and scientism only to end up by affirming the divine in nature. Stephen chooses solitude and the rejection of all authority—"I will not serve," he proudly asserts (239). Likewise Joachim, although the abbot repeats to him, "You aren't alone" (*PP*, 35, 36), and warns him against despair, claiming that "utter abjection doesn't kill a man; nor does it, by some anthropocentric contagion, kill God" (34–35). Like Stephen, Joachim remains revolted by the "pain in matter," and claims that he prefers nothingness to eternity (35).

There is something less than convincing in Joachim's final arguments, a hint of paralogism, such as when he refuses both time and eternity in favor of morality. But this hint disappears when it becomes clear that his nihilistic endeavor is not targeting the great instances of metaphysics, merely a particular sort of imagining: "It seems to me that nothingness offers no basis for doubt, for criticism, for suspicion, for the inventive agony of the imagination" (ibid.). The master-word is out, which already served as the guiding concept for the critique contained in his "sermon." The meeting point between Joachim and the abbot is a common refusal of anthropomorphism, of human "projection" by which belief would seem to be reduced to original sin. In his peroration Joachim says:

> "Hell is something that says: Don't shrink from the transitory pain of the here and now, and you will escape absolute torture and absolute despair in the absolute of eternity. Suffer in order not to suffer. This frightful idea, this madman's fantasy, has inspired the greatest preachers. . . ." (9–10)

To which he adds:

> "I reject that religion, a religion in which love has mixed with too much blood. I reject in it what is despicable, and so must also reject its sublimity. It reeks of human cunning, of the didactic imagination. For me God is other, or He doesn't exist." (10)

According to Joachim's skeptical catechism, God really is made in man's image, since he is a hyperbolic hypostasis of his own cruelty and perversions. The only God he could accept would be a figure of absolute otherness (e.g., such a figure as is developed by Emmanuel Levinas).

This critique is subsequently taken up and developed during discussion by the abbot, who thus deprives Joachim of his initial target: naive faith and its crude imagery of suffering. The abbot confides in him, saying:

> "How can you expect our collected doubts to becomes truths— our mistakes and wanderings of our imaginations, the things suggested by our own anxieties, our concessions to the evolution of ideas, to become truths?" (30)

The abbot's credo is such as to recall Teilhard de Chardin, postulating a matter-God in motion: ". . . and this includes Hell and Paradise, stage sets adapted to matter and intended to perpetuate its values" (33). But Joachim remains unconvinced, and refuses even to continue theological debate: he has made his choice (chosen his heresy), and persists in his melancholy opting for death and solitude. Doing so, he becomes like the symbolic "father," Olaf Borgström, chosen by the narrator of *Melancholy*

North, who ushers in a sweet and solitary death through alcohol, even while he regrets not keeping the assignation with his young friend and disciple.[c] He explains his intention so:

> The extreme solitude felt at the very moment when affection, understanding, and solidarity should be more than ever present, is painful but logical. It's melancholic, the vision of death close-up, melancholy in the full meaning of the term, when melancholy is always solitude's big sister. (*MN*, 124)

Melancholy versus Hysteria[d]

If nothingness appears therefore as the only alternative to the subtle yet tyrannical power of the imagination in *Parrot's Perch*, this is because Joachim needs always to fear that the speeches of the abbot, which mold themselves so skillfully to his doubt, may mask a still more subtle manipulation. The assent that for a moment he thinks he has found in such an "enlightened" understanding of his metaphysical anguish reminds him too strongly of the position of the "benevolent torturer" striving to save him from torture. Like the abbot, an officer once said he wanted to save him: it was of course a matter of getting him to talk, and in that way putting an end to torture. This senior officer, "young . . . charming, understanding, eloquent," who seems to be "an island of humanity in the midst of savagery" (*PP*, 37), comforts him after the torture of the "parrot's perch," but only so as to persuade him further, through a "reversal" of the position of victim and through a fundamentally nihilistic logic. His position is simple, and is even commonsensical enough: "Personally, I think no moral conviction justifies a scream of pain" (38). The appeal to cynical realism and overriding self-interest (very close to the position of the unstoppable killer who is the hero of *Faux Pas*, "the unknown man" who starts by murdering an idealistic journalist) amounts to the most tempting and persuasive offer of betrayal.[e]

---

[c] On *Melancholy North*, see Arent Safir and Metz. On the death of this mentor, see note *l*, p. 142.

[d] On melancholy in Rio's work, see the introduction in this volume, Arent Safir, Pastoureau, Ritter, and Metz.

[e] On *Faux Pas*, see Ritter, Swenson, and Metz.

Joachim's precise response to this all-too-seductive offer remains obscure, though his attempted suicide in order to avoid having to respond did constitute his personal way of resisting. He will re-enact this radical refusal at the end of the novel when he relives a doubt so radical that language itself is attacked. But ever since he has listened to the honeyed tongue of his tormentor, words have been infected with perversity and serve only to lie (PP, 39–40). This is why, equally, when Joachim understands that the abbot intends to deal with his worrying mutism by giving him the chance to express himself, and invites him to read his "sermon," he fears another rhetorical trap. His launch into utterance, what is more, anticipates minimally, and may even precipitate, the final fall. The single resting point, and the final dialogic stage, is the conversation with the woman, who, humble and dumb as she is, excluded from the escape-routes and trapdoors of speech, hesitates between compassion and erotic attraction. These are both refused by Joachim, however, even while he uses this pause in his descent toward nothingness to speak superbly about the din of torture victims that he still hears across the world. As he explains, the torturer also still hears this din and is led by it to a parallel impasse, his very own hell that he can never escape. The torturer's only way out of his painful lucidity and an awareness of his abjection—as well as an abjection that can become general at any moment—is by going recklessly on. "Torture is his life" (61), Joachim comments, no longer certain which is preferable, his own hopelessness or that which he ascribes to torturers.

What is the origin of Joachim's "misstep" or *faux pas*? The intelligence officer wished to have him abjure his faith in man and thereby in the liberation of the oppressed, in the name of a false "realism" that states that only the current state of things matters, a state that must not be changed. But this position serves merely to mask hypocritically the abjection of the victims' bodies, minds, and words. Joachim has already explained that he cannot be a mystic since he cannot adopt the position of the hysteric. This "hysteria" would amount to "an idea that mobilizes the spirit and the body totally and purposefully . . . [and] so much more . . . because the idea is of the realm of faith alone. . . ." (8). He is unable to give his support to a cause both transcendental and totalitarian. The term *hysteria* points toward Barthes more than toward Freud here (and one is reminded of the way in which Barthes kept a distance that was at once respectful, anxious, and ironic, between himself and the "hysterias" of hardened militants). What is fundamentally at issue is faith in the value attributed to speech, and this is why imagination remains so powerful, since it takes over when speech fails. Right from when the famous frescoes of hell in San Gimignano are evoked, "such a hallowed debauchery of the imagination, in which the greatest perversity became a servant to the highest morality" (45–46), Joachim recognizes the existence of a "perversion principle." When he returns through further meditative spirals to the question of eternity and nothingness, it appears that he is indeed being driven by something new, an imagined loss of desire or of being:

> The prospect of approximate nothingness terrified him; it gener-
> ated monstrous, chaotic images. He saw in it the return to a dead
> mother's cold womb. . . . Nouns came to him in swarms—
> twilight, sickliness, stench, must, humidity, whisper, viscosity—
> and their attributes—pallid, mawkish, furtive, sticky. . . . (76–77)

He is correct to discern in these symptoms an "ultimate melancholy" (77) that is probably incurable. He postulates an ultimate act of faith: "And in violation of everything he had been taught of the spirit, he came to that ultimate profession of faith: death would have to kill memory" (ibid.).*f* Suffering through his memory that is wrecked by a melancholy that prevents any hagiographic recuperation of his experience, as well as any hysterical justification through the idea of a gift or sacrifice for a good cause, there remains a single way out: this "witness" of past suffering, this survivor of torture that has become universal and almost mundane, this true martyr and this unspeakable martyrdom, must all disappear. Joachim discovers his utter superfluity; for, if God exists, then he created the continuum of matter-into-mind as necessarily painful. The whole of lan-guage is still resonant with sinister echoes made audible by the anaphoric "parrot's perch": it is therefore obligatory to eliminate the "father," by means of a veritable *unmaking*.

Torture and Unmaking

Rio carries out a radical concentration in his meditation upon tor-ture: not only is humanity reduced to "meat that speaks" (the great lyrical

---

f On Joachim's struggle leading to this conclusion, viewed in terms of the dreamer and the logician, see Arent Safir.

theme exploited in virtuoso manner by Valère Novarina), but more appallingly to "meat" that stutters, stammers, cries tears, and squirms in pain (*PP*, 58). The mere fact that torture is universal obliges the subject to question the Other, and leads to a radical condemnation of language, rendered suspect through the generalized perversion established. Joachim says:

> I say again that matter has done nothing but scream and writhe, from the beginning, before there were words and since, and that they haven't changed that. That's a fact. The rest is trickling from the beak of the parrot, seated on its perch. Below the perch, a bound man is screaming and writhing; and above it, the same man is drivelling. (59–60)

Such remarks can give onto only a parodic conclusion, of the kind which so beautifully marks the climax of Flaubert's "A Simple Heart," when Félicité in her agony believes she is glimpsing the apotheosis of Loulou, her stuffed parrot that is transfigured by her delirium into the Holy Ghost: "And as she breathed her last, she thought she could see, in the opening heavens, a gigantic parrot hovering above her head."[4] To be true to the spirit of Rio's novel, this famous ending would have to be combined with the barely less famous one that concludes *The Temptation of St. Anthony*. Anthony, who at long last is no longer afraid of the creatures born either of his own imagination or of whatever religion or heresy, is led to a general dissolution that has him hoping to become one with the world in all its aspects:

> Would that I had wings, a carapace, a shell,—that I could breathe out smoke, wield a trunk,—make my body writhe,—divide myself everywhere,—be in everything,—emanate with odors,— develop myself like the plants,—flow like water,—vibrate like sound—shine like light, squatting upon all forms—penetrate each atom—descend to the very bottom of matter,—be matter itself![5]

---

[4] Gustave Flaubert, *Three Tales*, trans. Robert Baldick (London: Penguin, 1961), 56.
[5] Flaubert, *The Temptation of St. Anthony*, trans. Lafcadio Hearn (New York: Grosset, The Universal Library, n.d.), 163–64.

By a customary irony, Flaubert, in a final vignette, shows the saint getting back to his prayers in the middle of the desert. Similar ironies eat into the very fabric of Rio's fiction,[g] yet in each work an urgent and vital question does get asked. The "question" in *Parrot's Perch* is, through a further echo effect, the question-of-the-question, since here it is a question of contemplating torture and drawing a fiction from it that manages to stay with all that is serious in the theme, as well as with the possibilities for parody that are offered.[h]

In her book on pain and torture, *The Body in Pain*,[6] Elaine Scarry describes the way in which violence inflicted upon torture victims destroys and undoes their whole world, as a result of a veritable process of unmaking. Scarry's analysis of the "unmaking of the world" can be aligned with the principal narrative structures in *Parrot's Perch*. Scarry shows how torture exploits and amplifies the consequences of the perception of pain. Torture fetishizes the main characteristics of pain, laying bare its fundamental properties. Pain is first an attack by dis-pleasure, and manifests itself by instant aversion. This physical experience of pure negation constitutes an invasion from outside that must be stopped at any price. This foreign guest intruding violently into the self but that is non-self produces a first splitting between self and non-self. This splitting is found in the dialectical structure of torture, for torture demands a response by dint of the fact that as victim one is also the enemy; one is a powerless adversary, captured, brutalized, accused, and obliged to reply on one's own subversive behalf to a kangaroo court, in the name of rules of entirely doubtful legitimacy. This becomes more complex when the ambivalence of the act of torture itself is considered, giving a second clear characteristic of the structure. For the pain is indeed simultaneously internal and external: I do not feel the knife that wounds me as foreign steel penetrating my body, rather I feel my body that hurts at the moment of violation. Next, though I can name with either surprise or amazement the object as separate, I nonetheless can describe my pain only through metaphors whose terms invoke external objects (I speak of a

---

[g] On Rio and Flaubert, see *Manhattan Terminus*, 51–54; also, Swenson, note *h*, p. 121, and Metz.

[h] On the mixture of seriousness and parody, see Metz.

[6] Elaine Scarry, "The Structure of Torture: The Conversion of Real Pain into the Fiction of Power," in *The Body in Pain. The Making and Unmaking of the World* (Oxford: Oxford University Press, 1985).

pain that is burning, sharp, dull, stunning, electric, etc.). Torture reifies this characteristic by playing on the victim's self-destructive action, forcing him to accuse, denounce, and wear himself out in absurd and terrifying rituals.

A further characteristic of pain results from this same dissolving of limits between internal and external: the physical pain destroys the border dividing public from private. As in paintings by Francis Bacon or in Sophocles' *Philoctetes*, the body prey to suffering is at once both emphatically exhibited and severed from all communication: its obscene and laughable gesticulations recall a Freudian "other scene," whose grotesque staging renders visible what is usually private and hidden. What is more, torture destroys the normal places of refuge, by employing the most everyday objects such as tables, chairs, bathtubs, taps, and toilets, so as to inflict pain and to ultimately compound the human with the animal or excremental. The body is thrown back on the absurd materiality of its blood-streaked gasping flesh. The whole world becomes a source of pain: walls, ceiling, floor, electric light bulbs; all contribute to the persecution. And sleep will often be made impossible, the entire body being tirelessly press-ganged until gradually the realms of consciousness, privacy, dream, and humanity are all abolished.

This perversion of the world's immediate data is so systematic that it ends up dragging language into its spiral of negations. Pain itself is first to monopolize the victim's linguistic capacities in a repeated verbal plaint, which rapidly turns into pure instinctive pre-verbal cries. The voice of the victim is controlled, regimented, and interrupted in an arbitrary way; the forced confessions are never sufficient, and language has to turn against and obliterate itself, extinguishing any ethical strongholds that might offer possibilities of resistance. The final aspect of pain that becomes reified in torture is what is totalizing and totalitarian in it. For as long as pain can be localized in a part of the body, it can be resisted for a while. But as it spreads it invades the whole of both body and mind, ruining everything beyond it. Pain thereby progressively wins over the world and over language, and, despite its derisory initial limitedness, wolfs down everything in its path. Just as neurologists are unable to localize a point in the brain that corresponds to the center of pain, since pain can always overflow and ramify, so the torturer multiplies his resources, enabling every perception—visual, auditory, tactile, gustatory—to become in turn the source of pain. The "Theater of Cruelty," by which Antonin Artaud yearned to retrieve a lost intensity by limiting life's potentialities, expands its borders here to the limits of the universe, a universe that does not much need to be re-created since it is subject to constant unmaking.

It is a risky business, generalizing about Michel Rio's novels. There are themes common to them all, such as encyclopedias, paradises lost, solitude, the exact sciences faced with a world of uncertainty, islands, voyages, the fragility of feelings.[i] But a more latent point they have in common involves what I would like to call the "imagination of the survivor," of the one who is there at the end of a reign or rule, and who thus puts imagination itself into question, the imagining of the making and unmaking of a world.[j] As in the poems of Ted Hughes, the witness of modern times becomes a fatalistic *trickster*, similar to the sarcastic crow in *Crow*, which embodies a resistance to everything that normally destroys the human.[7] Creation contains unmaking in its heart, in its very seed,[k] which turns fiction into the testimony of a post-survivor (and even when developed out of true-life drama, it does not leave the realm of fiction). But, while Crow outlives every snub and finds his energy thereby multiplied, a whole series of Rio's characters opt for death. This death, the account of which will be given by others (e.g., by the narrator of *Melancholy North*), will be melancholic, but not absurd. It signals not only the triumph of entropy in a universe ruled by the thermodynamic laws of forbidden passions, it signals a veritable end to History. The death of Olaf Borgström brings him back to his real size, which is not insignificant, but cleared of the illusion of time with its inevitable teleology. When close to death, the philosopher, while noting that despite it all he *is* writing to his young friend, admits that his "death without perspective" (and thus "two-dimensional") affirms his freedom nonetheless:

> It's a freedom no longer coming from the desire for compromise, or from limiting compromise to suit other people's reasoning, but rather born of the absolute-to-come: nothing henceforth.

---

[i] On these themes, see especially Gould, Arent Safir, and Ritter.

[j] On the making and unmaking of a world, the survivor's view, see especially *Merlin*: ". . . I created a world, and it is dead. . . . Whatever is godlike in that claim is tempered by its outcome, which is a corpse. . . ." (*M*, 9).

[7] Ted Hughes, *Crow* (London: Faber and Faber, 1972).

[k] On this question, see Arent Safir and the perversity of doing and undoing.

It's a freedom, without overplaying with terms, *ex nihilo*, which goes against the grain and contaminates History, both my own and that of my era, through some sort of convulsion of memory. (*MN*, 125–26)[l]

What remains is the question of how to conceptualize the relation between what could be called "Rio melancholy" and the grand chronicle of universal History.[m]

The End of the Story or the End of History?

As we have seen, Rio's fictions treat, rework, and sound out in an original and imaginative way those problems that philosophy and science approach in their own different processes and languages.[n] This is why it is unsurprising to find, under the cover of the classic detective novel, a meditation upon historiography. I am speaking, of course, of *Faux Pas*. The first thing to note is the curious parallel between the endings of *Parrot's Perch* and *Faux Pas*: in both novels the protagonist's suicide forms a surprising episode, an unexpected denouement, and a nevertheless satisfying conclusion. The unstoppable killer embodies solitude and absolute rationality until he finds himself overwhelmed by feelings. The "fatherless" killer, or "father to himself" (and as Beckett and Robbe-Grillet noted in relation to *Gommes*, all detective novels retell the Oedipus myth), aims to establish a world that he has to imagine in its every detail, by tireless mental exertion, before concluding that all that remains is for him to remove himself from it.

---

[l] The death of Olaf Borgström in Rio's first novel anticipates that of Leonard Wilde in *Manhattan Terminus*, his tenth: a mentor, a final dialogue, a conversation with young interlocutors (the narrator and Alan Stewart from *Archipelago* and *Tlacuilo*), a freely taken decision to put an end to one's story, one's own history, all the while reflecting on the history of the universe, and, as in the case of Borgström, a gentle death, the instrument of which is alcohol. On Borgström, see Arent Safir and Metz.

[m] On Rio's relation to history, see Gould, Pastoureau, and Galarza. On the melancholy of the individual in the face of the history of mankind or of the universe, see Arent Safir (on *Dreaming Jungles* and *Merlin*) and Ritter.

[n] On questions of philosophical and scientific discourse as central to Rio's work, see the introduction in this volume, Gould, Pastoureau, Ritter, and Galarza.

The "hero" of *Faux Pas*—a novel symptomatically written in the third person—is never named other than as "the unknown man."[o] He is indeed a curious sort of contract killer, who starts by murdering Brémont, a courageous journalist who has put together a compromising dossier on a Mafia boss named Alberti. The unknown man first murders more or less in self-defense, though he intends to kill Brémont anyway; but when he guesses that he will be eliminated in turn once he has committed the assassination, he decides to turn the contract against the one who has ordered it, whom he then cold-bloodedly murders. The plot develops not only within the detective genre (reminiscent of the elliptic style of thrillers by Manchette), for the unknown man is driven mad with desire for Brémont's wife Marie. He finds her hideaway, saves her from a second gang of killers sent after her, and gets her daughter Julie to trust in him, after saving her from drowning. As a lover, he reveals to Marie a pleasure of exceptional intensity because free of all sentiment. At the end of the novel the unknown man decides to do away with himself, apparently unsure of how to integrate the new element of love revealed to him by this woman. This is an element that contradicts the entire logic of the rational killer who has reduced the world to pure instrumentality—an instrumentality mapped by the abrupt and taut language in which the story is told.

One of the keys to the novel, which certainly opens the secret of the title, is introduced at the outset, when the unknown man flicks through a book while waiting for the journalist to arrive: this book being *Apologie pour l'histoire ou Métier d'historien* (The Historian's Craft) by Marc Bloch. He takes the book from Brémont's library, and has it with him during his wait in front of the home of Marie and Julie. The final chapter, prelude to the killer's suicide, quotes from Bloch's unfinished work, omitting a few sentences. Here is the quotation in full:

Let us suppose that a man is walking along a mountain path. He trips and falls off a precipice. For this accident to happen, the combination of a great number of determining elements was necessary, such as, among others, the existence of gravity;

---

[o] Indeed, *Faux Pas*, like *Parrot's Perch* written in the third person, is an exception to the first-person narrative rule of Rio's fiction; in both cases first-person narration is necessarily excluded by reason of the suicide of the protagonist. On first- and third-person narration in Rio, see Metz.

a terrain resulting from protracted geological changes; the laying out of a path for the purpose, let us say, of connecting a village with its summer pastures. It would, therefore, be perfectly legitimate to say that, were the laws of celestial mechanics different, had the evolution of the earth been otherwise, were alpine economy not founded upon the seasonal migration of flocks, the fall would not have happened. Nevertheless, should we inquire as to the cause, everyone would answer: "A misstep."[8][p]

Marc Bloch's meditation on the "causes" of history seeks on the one hand to dissociate the principle of causality from inquiry into individual "motives," and on the other hand to reveal how causes should be sought for and not just assumed, and this according to an explicative hierarchy. The clumsy gesture of the walker who falls will certainly not be "explained" tautologically by the "misstep" (or *faux pas*), though this remains the best description of what happened:

> From the viewpoint of common sense, which has always been reluctant to rid itself of a certain anthropomorphism in speaking of cause, this last-minute component, this specific and unexpected component, is a little like the artist who gives form to plastic material which is already completely prepared. (Bloch, 191)[q]

Though Bloch, the celebrated founder of the *Annales* school, states that historical facts are first and foremost of a psychological order (188), he immediately qualifies this idea by adding that human beings cannot

---

[8] Marc Bloch, *The Historian's Craft*, trans. Peter Putnam (New York: Knopf, 1954), 190–91.

[p] Like Bloch, both Gould and Rio have a keen awareness of all of the contingencies, the mixture of accident and cause, which go into the evolution not only of a species but of an event. See Gould; also, one of Gould's most famous essays, written in collaboration with Richard C. Lewontin, "The spandrels of San Marco and the Panglossian paradigm: A critique of the adaptationist programme," *Proceedings of the Royal Society of London Series B* (1979), 205: 581–98. It is this essay that is the object of rhetorical analysis by Selzer et al. in *Understanding Scientific Prose*.

[q] That "certain anthropomorphism" to which Bloch refers, and that is evoked earlier by Rabaté, raises once more the question of the singularity, or nonsingularity, of man's evolution. See Gould.

be supposed to have a clear consciousness of their actions. What is more, this is the very passage quoted in the same chapter of *Faux Pas*:

Psychology goes beyond what's clear and conscious. Reading certain history books, one could believe humanity to be composed exclusively of the will of logicians, for whom their motivations for acting would never contain the slightest secret. (*FP*, 122)

In its context in *Faux Pas*, the relation becomes clearer between Brémont, who thought he was improving the world by sending a crook to prison, and Marc Bloch, a Jewish member of the Resistance shot by the Germans in June 1944 after being tortured by Klaus Barbie's men. Both "die for an idea" (123),' an idea that the novel's unknown man is apparently unable to grasp. The stranger tries to reduce Brémont's efforts to nothing when he says to him:

But the truth about Alberti is worthless anecdote. There's always an Alberti and there always will be. They're nothing but a miserable symptom of the general wickedness of the species, which for its part is a widespread reality. Destroying Alberti means nothing. It's as if you were trying to destroy the very concept of counting by eliminating the number eight thousand four hundred and twenty-six. . . . Is that worth your life? (*FP*, 21)

The killer therefore embodies the "logician's determination," and he is strong enough in dialectics to be able to foresee the exact order of subsequent events. But, despite the series of "good deeds" he commits during the novel (the countless gangsters and stooges he eliminates), he still has to expiate his first murder, that of Brémont.

' Bloch's book is necessarily added to the question of intertextuality that Rabaté touches on earlier. On this subject, see also Arent Safir (note 19, p. 71), Pastoureau, and Galarza. In an essay dealing with *Parrot's Perch* and *Faux Pas*, one can also see a parallel here with the other fictional character that Rabaté discusses, Joachim, who was tortured because of his convictions (to use Rabaté's term, "the son's misstep"). The distinction that Rabaté introduces regarding the unknown man, however, is important: the protagonist of *Faux Pas* is not a torturer, neither in his ends nor his means, like those that Joachim or Marc Bloch himself faced.

It is in the name of a logic rather similar to that of Joachim that the nameless killer of *Faux Pas* governs his behavior: he strictly opposes "natural law," defined as predation, domination, and survival of the fittest, to what he names the "codes," which encompass law, morality, philosophy, and religion.[5] As he recognizes, faced with Alberti who believes everything can be reduced to selfishness and that he can still buy him off (the unknown man kills him directly afterward): "Brémont disturbed me. He escaped my logic. Whereas you, you are reassuring" (*FP*, 45). Love certainly sits awkwardly with such a radical dichotomy: the killer's Occam's razor turns against him; he cannot accept to submit to the law of this "anomaly," and so has to do away with himself. He has achieved the speed and precision that mark his "faultless course" as a fighter by transforming himself into a killing machine, through a sort of ataraxy (he does not care if he lives or dies [27]). As a pitiless "cleaner" he knows that no weakness is allowed him: he is less of a Barbie than a *terminator* who terminates himself (for his own reasons, not because of other people, as in the film *Terminator II*). He has become a superman at the cost of his humanity; and, although he occupies the overarching place of absolute Hegelian knowledge, he has not yet learned to take into account the negativity of death or the ethical power of emotions. With his death he ushers in the end of the novel, showing himself to be less a superman than a Nietzschean "last man."[9]

It is not love that could be seen to have got in like a "grain of sand" and spoiled the perfect killer's well-oiled mechanism, since he makes the fully conscious choice not so much of taking a "misstep" (a *faux pas*) as of "sidestepping" the simplicity of the rule. He writes to Marie in a final farewell:

> Yet perhaps matter, life, rules, and even chance find a meaning, which is to say a prior plan and a subsequent excuse, in the

---

[5] On natural law, see Gould.

[9] Friedrich Nietzsche, *Thus Spake Zarathustra*, in *The Complete Works*, trans. and ed. Oscar Levy (Edinburgh and London: T. N. Foulis, 1911), 11: 12. See how these themes are taken up by Francis Fukuyama who gives a "liberal" reading of Kojève and Nietzsche in *La Fin de l'histoire et le Dernier Homme* (Paris: Flammarion, Champs, 1992). And for a critique of the religious and political presuppositions of Fukuyama's thesis, see Jacques Derrida's entralling plea for a contemporary (but also messianic) reading of Marx in *Specters of Marx: The State of the Debt, the Work of Mourning and the New International*, trans. Peggy Kamuf (New York and London: Routledge, 1994), 56–94.

achievement of the double and futureless anomaly that consists in a love story. . . . And that absurd finality which my state, my reality, and my gestures prevent me from even pretending to live, and which blocks my path to any return to the law, has for me the other meaning of the word "end." (*FP*, 123–24)

Nothingness remains Joachim's only weapon against the proliferation of a radically distorted imagination perverted by torture that has contaminated even language. Similarly, the unknown man of *Faux Pas*, whose specialty is hunting predators, and who implicitly wants to be the king of creation, a creation whose coordinates he has to simplify outrageously so as to survive according to his own rules, has no recourse but annihilation if he is to remain faithful to himself. This could count as the main effect of Rio's stories: purifying the imagination that first they have summoned. It is an imagination that at times does not stop at adolescent poor taste. For it so relishes its stories told in the first person with an end to offering the reader the waking dream of the archaic omnipotence of "his majesty the baby," as Freud said of novels (and in this respect the novel *Archipelago* is symptomatic, deploying as it does this type of unbridled fantasy).[t] Though even here there is something of the outline, the nervous quickness of a story that is titillating, admittedly, but only so as to flit quickly on toward other horizons. Fiction, which is, according to a phrase Rio likes to cite, "the last discourse of disorder" (*MN*, 128), allows not only a return to knowledge (either historical or encyclopedic), but also a shift toward the ethical. Whether through the suicides of Joachim and the killer in *Faux Pas*, or through the quest of the narrator of *Melancholy North* that is frustrated at the last moment, it becomes clear how a central image, teetering on the edge of allegory, manages to make the imaginary consistency of the novels tremble.[u] Just such a capacity is attributed by Lacan to the tragedy of *Antigone*, which mixes up the aesthetic and ethical categories, purging its readers, spectators, or listeners, of their own imagination—and this through an image that is not so much fascinating as

---

[t] On this type of adolescent or juvenile fantasy, see Metz.

[u] It is hard to avoid the question of suicide in Rio. To the two suicides that Rabaté cites here, and the death of Olaf Borgström to which he makes reference, are added Leonard Wilde's attempted suicide in *Archipelago*, Vivian's suicide in *Merlin*, and Wilde's successful suicide in *Manhattan Terminus*.

sublime.[10] The piercing brightness of these brief lightning images left to us by Rio's novels can be painful, yet the memory of them is liable to be enduring, not to say unforgettable.

TRANSLATED FROM THE FRENCH BY DANIEL GUNN.

---

[10] Jacques Lacan, *The Ethics of Psychoanalysis, 1959–1960*, trans. Dennis Porter, The Seminar of Jacques Lacan, bk. 7 (New York: Norton, 1992), 247–48.

7

The Aztec *tlacuilo* and the Other

Joaquín Galarza

It is thanks to image and text (image-text and text-image) that I came to know Michel Rio, through Abraham Zemsz, the distinguished semiologist and art historian, in the early 1970s.[a] We were working, the latter and I, on the *Codex Tovar*, an Aztec-Nahuatl pictographic manuscript with a historical theme. From a detailed analysis of its graphic and plastic elements we were trying to derive laws and rules for the Aztec form-sound system, which I believe to be a genuine script. Zemsz used to enjoy passing on to Rio the most minute details of our research, which seemed interesting to him. Rio always had questions to put to me, through Zemsz, which I would try to answer. I had the feeling that we were arousing his curiosity. His comments always took us on to basic features that we had still not resolved, or still had to find. He seemed to have such an eye for our weak points that I pictured him physically as a mature, even an elderly man. Which is why I had such a surprise when I did finally meet him. By then, our exchanges, although indirect and

---

[a] Abraham Zemsz, like Galarza himself, appears by name in *Melancholy North* and *Tlacuilo*. These novels, like *Archipelago* and *Manhattan Terminus*, include in their list of characters older men who to some extent play the part of intellectual guide for the young narrator. Christian Metz, with whom Rio also worked, argues that the only autobiographical features worth noting are those that Rio clearly puts into his work. I share this view completely, and Galarza's appraisal of the scholarly work carried out by the young Rio with Zemsz and him is particularly intriguing in this context, as is the essay by Metz himself. See Metz.

distant, had already been very fruitful for me, for they set up doubts in my mind; and that encouraged me to scrutinize more closely the Aztec image, the Aztec drawings. It was only because of needs arising during the preparation of a text purporting to explain our work, and that Rio was helping to get published, that I found it necessary in my turn to ask certain questions that brought me to see Rio personally.

At that time he was editing a collective publication on "The Image,"[b] and he had asked us to contribute by presenting the Aztecs. I wanted to know certain details concerning the plates that would illustrate our text; and it is by way of the drawings (which at that time I felt I had to produce myself) that dialogue with Rio became less difficult for me, for, like Zemsz, he had a gift for "foreign languages," which is how I saw the diverse terminologies of the various disciplines with which they were familiar, and with which they made such effortless play.[c] Black lines, forms, and colors helped me to explain to him the aspects that I thought I already knew; but more important still, all those that I did not yet know, and toward which I was pushing my analyses.

At that time also I was still unaware of Rio's literary qualities, and I saw him as a highly intelligent young man, with a gift for research, from art to linguistics and philosophy. I had immediately compared him to a very brilliant Mexican writer whom I had met during my childhood, and who was then labeled an *ensayista,* "essayist." Much later, my second surprise was receiving in the mail part of his work; a considerable number of novels that I there and then, I would not say read, rather fell upon. At that moment I knew only *Dreams of Logic,* a book that had confirmed my earliest impressions.[d] From the outset I felt a need to tell him directly about my projects, to talk to him in my own voice about my research. I had confidence in him straightaway, for I felt that there really was an interest there, something I seldom if ever found in my dealings with my fellows and colleagues in linguistics, art history, and anthropology.

Rio's critical essays, in his *Dreams of Logic,* play in depth with image and word by way of their relationship in different civilizations. These writings, or essays, led me from the "pretext image" of the comic strip, compared to painting and cinema, located within frames and lengths of

---

[b] The issue of *Communications* to which Galarza later refers.

[c] On the diverse disciplines and their terminologies, as well as the use that Rio makes of them, see the introduction in this volume, Gould, Pastoureau, Ritter, Swenson, and Metz.

[d] On *Dreams of Logic,* see the introduction in this volume and Metz.

shot, by way of "image and text," the said and the seen, from the story of the image in Western painting all the way to the "text-image" of my own research:[e] sign and figure, where I found in Rio the basic elements of the writing system of Meso-America, especially those designed to transcribe and represent the Nahuatl language of the Aztec civilization of Mexico. These elements had appeared at very remote periods, and had even been preserved in the form of spuriously European drawings, in the much later documents called "codex," or "codices," up to the eighteenth century.

By 1978 (*Communications*), already Rio is very much aware of the methodological problem in his study of the image in Mexico, previously judged only on the basis of the European image, and seen through Western ethnocentrism.[f] This last came to dominate because of the setting-up of a model of analysis and interpretation derived from European iconography (the Italian Renaissance). Michel Rio observes and points out its inadequacy for the analysis of a pictorial, sound-and-image-based system such as that of the Aztecs, starting out from the confusion of the two phenomena of "translation" and "phonetization" that is part of the whole, intercultural problem of the sign. In word-image relationships, Rio concludes that there has been a significant pulling apart, where one extreme might be the European image, the other, that of Meso-America. His interest, affective and intellectual, requires us to turn now to the Mexican image-text in anything bearing on the origins of writing. By the clarity of his argument, he got me to understand his position. It delighted me and won me over at once, at two levels; for it is very rare to hear, from a European, a language that shows understanding of the systems of drawn-written expression. This was acceptance of the image of the Other, of the other image.

---

[e] See *Dreams of Logic*, 7–65. Already in these essays, as later in his novels, Rio is examining the relation of frame to image. See Swenson (note 17, p. 125). As for the said and the seen, one thinks in particular of *Parrot's Perch*, and the remarkable description there of an image, the fresco by Taddeo di Bartolo (*PP*, 61–68), a "translation" that seems to me wholly linked to the work described here by Galarza. See the introduction in this volume and Rabaté.

[f] Galarza's reference is to the original publication of Rio's essays, later reprinted in *Dreams of Logic*: "Cadre, plan, lecture" (Frame, Shot, Reading), *Communications* 24, EHESS (1976): 94–107; "Signe et figure" (Sign and Figure) and "Le dit et le vu" (The Said and the Seen), *Communications* 29, EHESS (1978): 5–12 and 57–70. In this same issue, see Galarza, "Lire l'image aztèque," 15–42. On Rio's work of this period, see the introduction in this volume and Metz.

Whole years went by, for me, in ever shorter, ever more frequent journeys between Europe and America. My professional and personal life was running its course between France, the United States, Italy, and Mexico, in two-month bouts. I lost sight of Michel Rio for I do not know how long. The sessions in which we exchanged ideas on the Aztec image had never grown dim in my memory. I know that he seemed to me the most positive and open of the Europeans I knew on the subject of the Meso-American "text-image," which I was trying to decipher and read in Nahuatl. I remembered that his comments and questions, even when difficult, or perhaps because difficult, were solid and constructive. But the curiosity and the interest that Rio showed at that time were bound, it seemed to me, not to last. That is, the theme of Aztec writing would be only one among many interesting subjects that occupied and drew his attention. I did not doubt that he would carry on down the intersecting paths of image and imaginary, text and drawing. But I thought that the Aztecs would not reappear in his writings (still less in those in novel form). I had not yet read his novels. Only a few of his essays, some of them rather hard for my little world, all full of Aztec lines, figures, colors, and sounds. That is why I was so pleasantly surprised all over again when I learned from the press, in 1992, that a certain *Tlacuilo* had won the *Prix Médicis* (Medicis Prize).[g] And I felt doubly happy when I saw the author's name. This meant that Rio had not only not forgotten ancient Mexico, but had kept enough of it for it to become, by way of an important character, the center of his novel.

But who was this *tlacuilo*? A genuine creature, from the real Mexican past, or simply the fruit of a rich European imagination? These were the questions that kept going around in my head. I was thinking of going in search of Michel Rio himself, finding out where he now lived, when *Tlacuilo* itself came my way. I received through the mail a copy signed by the author, with an indication of the pages where he talks of the results of my research.[h] *Tlacuilo*, that Nahuatl word (from the Nahuatl verb *tlacuiloa*, to write by painting) that indicates and names the Aztec writer-painter, painter-writer, was turning into a myth. Now it is the name of a Mexican cartoon-film, a medium-length film which, together with the drawings from the *Codex Mendoza* itself, introduces to a wide audience my thirty years of work on Aztec script by taking as an example the Nahuatl reading

---

[g] One of France's major literary prizes. On *Tlacuilo*, see Metz.
[h] See *Tlacuilo*, 40–41 and the final chapter, especially 194–200.

that I gave of the opening page. It is also the name of a fine book in Spanish, in which the film director Enrique Escalona shows, with the aid of color images, the applying of my method, and the history of the making of his film. Then, in Italy, *Tlacuilo* became another small, copiously illustrated book, in colors, written in Italian by myself and a journalist, its cover announcing to all and sundry the discovery of the Aztec writing system and its decipherment, by a "Mexican Champollion."[i] And finally, with Rio, *tlacuilo* becomes the central character of a French novel.

The story is built up around a codex, a precious pictographic Aztec-Nahuatl manuscript of the colonial period, from Central Mexico, and a scholarly decipherer who manages to give us his reading, translated into French (or English).[j] By explaining to us the personality and the thoughts of the *tlacuilo*, Rio acquaints us with the data that allowed him, on the basis of substantiated historical sources, to bring to life, or rather back to life, this noble, cultured Mexican Aztec Indian, Nahuatl-speaking, but also knowing Spanish, French, and Latin. We can finally picture him, pulsatingly real, in the seventeenth century, living in a fine colonial house, in a suburb of Mexico City-Tenochtitlán, capital of New Spain. Tezozomoc and Chimalpahin, Indian chroniclers of the New Spain of the sixteenth and seventeenth centuries, writing in Nahuatl and Spanish, helped Rio to understand the life and thought of his character, who, without ever appearing directly in the action, fills story and scenes with his hidden presence. Through him and his codex, the researcher in the novel realizes and explains that the Aztec's is a genuine writing system. That what has been said over and over again from the nineteenth century on can only come from the same prejudices: negative, ethnocentric, European, anti-native. And he can conclude "that Aztec pictography has the status, without any reservations or qualifications, of a writing system; a status founded on systematization and recurrence in the relation of graphic to phonetic" (*Tl*, 196). And that "it is truly an open system, capable of formulating new

---

[i] Galarza (with Albert Siliotti), *Tlacuilo: il segreto svelato della scrittura azteca*, (Florence: Giunti, 1992). Once more we encounter Rio's rewriting of legends or of other texts. On rewriting and intertextuality, see Arent Safir (note 19, p. 71), Pastoureau especially, Rabaté, and Metz. *Manhattan Terminus*, which revives characters from *Archipelago* and *Tlacuilo* and even recovers certain discourses (on ugliness, e.g.), continues the pattern.

[j] The scholar is, once again, Leonard Wilde (*Archipelago* and *Manhattan Terminus*), like Galarza himself scholar and sometime librarian. The codex in question will be given his name and be known as the *Wilde Codex*.

concepts" (ibid.). In this way we are brought up against the fact that the scholarly character in the novel, along with its author, have grasped, better than most of the research workers commonly referred to as "specialists on the codex," the complexity and refinement of the Aztec text-image.[k]

This *tlacuilo* was, then, as we have seen, the anonymous author of a codex that has disappeared and been rediscovered; ancient by its traditional, native writing; modern by the period in which it was put together;[l] and eternal by the idea of surviving death. Without actually mentioning the working methods of certain contemporary research workers, Michel Rio realizes the difficulty, not to say impossibility of rediscovering and elucidating the plastic writing system of ancient Meso-American civilizations if one uses only European parameters. His position, to my mind so positive, is virtually unique among those who study the cultures and ancient civilizations of America. I have the feeling that his qualities as Breton in Madagascar and Paris naturally give him another way of seeing, based on another way of feeling and seeking out the Other.[m] For Rio, the point is to get to know him properly, for what he is, without seeing him through the prejudices that have settled in advance what he must be.

---

[k] On fiction as a vehicle to specialized knowledge often ignored by specialists, see Gould especially, and Pastoureau.

[l] Rio's interest in the *tlacuilo* as a figure seems to connect with the concept of "out of time" and "out of place" that Gould elucidates in his analysis of *Dreaming Jungles* (seen as well in the marine crocodile of that novel). The *tlacuilo*, in the novel that bears his name, is displaced in time and space, the product of a world that no longer exists and of the culture that destroyed it: "I feel I have sprung from two worlds, a hybrid *tlacuilo*. . . . No longer clearly aware of where I come from, not aware at all of where I am going, and so ultimately ignorant of who I am: what bearings, what points of reference shall I give for access to my wisdom?" (*TI*, 200).

[m] On these biographical details—Rio the Breton, Rio in Madagascar—see Pastoureau and Metz. The notion of "the Other" that Galarza brings up occurs in numerous forms in Rio's work, for instance, the clash of cultures in *Trade Winds*; in *Dreaming Jungles* (metropolis and colony, or man and chimpanzee, or even the question of who or which is "the Other" [see Gould]); in *Archipelago* the Franco-British Hamilton School, situated on the isle of Jersey, between two countries and cultures; the collision of alien worlds in *Faux Pas*; and of course *Tlacuilo*. Moreover, Rio's protagonists themselves tend to be "the Other": women and men of solitude, cut off and different from the culture in which they are steeped. This "otherness" may be a matter of birth, of intellect, or of temperament, but it is a constant (e.g., *Trade Winds*, *Merlin*, Alexandra Hamilton in *Archipelago*, and the unknown man in *Faux Pas*). See also Arent Safir on "difference" in personal relationships, a possible variation on the theme.

Anyone who makes an a priori assessment of the Meso-American, in this case the Aztec-Nahuatl, without trying to rediscover him, and does it through the European eyes of Spanish conquest and colonization, in the conviction that what comes from Europe is superior, will never come to know him; above all, will locate him in an inferior position. This, more or less overtly, is what we have always sought to do; and our "curiosity" has not been disinterested.

For a start, we know that we shall not be able to follow or to find, in the Meso-American past, the paths taken by Mediterranean aesthetic development (before the 1492 "discovery" and during the Conquest), and that our native pre-Hispanic ancestors have no logical reason to follow artistic rules born of conventions they do not yet know, deriving from the Italian Renaissance (the Quattrocento). And yet, art historians do make comparisons between this European movement and all the graphic and plastic forms of expression of Meso-America. The results, we know from the outset, can only be negative. "They had no . . . ." or "They were unaware of . . . ." are expressions prefacing comparative judgments, to be followed by the terms *perspective, golden/gilded zone, Leonardo's human proportions, horizon line, land line, volume,* and so forth. As the negative judgments pile up, the art historians "specializing in the codex" come up eventually with the conclusion that "the Meso-American Indians were ignorant of drawing." They ought to add: "drawing like Renaissance Italians, like the Europeans of their time. . . ."

I used to talk about all this, first of all with Zemsz, then with Rio, in order to explain my despair at finding myself up against a solid wall of prejudices taken for scientific statements. I would explain to them how I had started out on my research, since it was only after reading everything that had been said and written up to the 1960s by the specialists, above all art historians, that I began to take an interest in the Aztec image, to try to find out what it really was. At least to try to get a sense of what was left after so many negations, in order perhaps to get as far as defining what would *not* fit with all these things that were being so confidently said. I told them that what interested me above all in the Aztec image was what it contained once one had eliminated everything that people had said about what it was not. I was continually surprised to find that it was even possible for certain specialists to apply Panofsky's[n] method (some are still

---

[n] Erwin Panofsky, the art historian, is cited in *Melancholy North* and *Trade Winds.*

using it) to analyze and compare the pre-Hispanic Meso-American artistic periods. Although it is highly effective for the Middle Ages and the Italian Renaissance, the periods for which it was designed and tested, there is no reason to apply it in America, where the series of cultural origins that runs Egypt-Greece-Rome does not exist as an evolutionary base either for traditional native art or for Meso-American artistic thought.

Michel Rio is familiar with the work of Eduard Seler.[o] He cannot accept his idea of the "nonexistence" of writing in Meso-America before the Latin ABC, and endorses the results of my own research, which he has followed at different stages, especially in collaboration with Zemsz. Eduard Seler, a great nineteenth-century Austrian scholar, is a true pioneer of Americanist research, especially on ancient Mexico. What he wrote, now almost entirely translated into English, continues to be followed blindly, even today, by certain specialists and enthusiasts. He is still quoted and taken as a model, usually without analysis or discussion. And yet scholarly work in the field of writing systems now moves along different lines, above all the line made possible by the working out and applying of a proper, systematic, scientific method, tested across more than thirty years of research, individual and collective (teams and groups from CISI-NAH-CIESAS, MH, AGN, University of Mexico [UNAM], La Sapienza, from Mexico City, Paris, Rome, Bologna, etc.) on all the types of manuscripts called "pictographic." The results obtained by myself, my pupils, and international disciples, with the direct involvement in our interdisciplinary research groups of at least one painter and one *nahuatlato* (someone who thinks and speaks in Nahuatl, the language of the Aztecs), allow me to state that the system affixed to the Aztec-Nahuatl codices is a genuine writing system that must be phonetized in Nahuatl before it can be interpreted by way of its content: plastic, thematic, symbolic, and so forth. One must decipher the basic graphic and plastic elements in order to recover the minimal sound and semantic elements of the original spoken language, in this case Nahuatl.

The blind repetition of the contents of Seler's many research findings and publications, without critical appraisal or new findings, or even, no

---

[o] The anthropologist Eduard Seler is cited in *Tlacuilo*. Among his works, see, for example, "The Venus Period, in the Borgian Codex Group," Bureau of American Ethnology, *Bulletin* 28 (1904): 353–92, or "Der Charakter der aztekischen und der Maya Hands-chriften," *Zeitschrift für Ethnologie* 20 (1888).

doubt, new reflections, has crippled research into native writing. Rio, for his part, realized the necessity to strike out in a new direction of research and thought, one that started out from a hypothesis alternative to the negative one of the impossibility of the Amerindians having any means other than the Latin alphabet of transmitting their ideas. That is, a non-alphabetic script; a codified image. His writer's sensibility allowed him to recognize, to feel the existence of this text-image of the Aztecs. This is what explains how he came to accept the hypotheses that have guided my research, and that are still being followed today by a third generation of young researchers who, applying my methods, have been studying the different types of traditional native Mexican manuscripts. Many features of Seler's work are still valid, within the perspective of his interpretation of the image that is not read. But scholarly studies of these documents from the pre-Hispanic period up to the sixteenth and seventeenth centuries, on all themes, require a systematic, exhaustive approach: a scientific method.[p] Mine is the only one that really exists. I have followed the example of Professor André Leroi-Gourhan, for whom the methodological problem is essential.[q] The method has been tested on at least one example from each group: Lienzo, Mapa, Plano, Tira, Panel, Hoja, and so forth, on the basis of the whole typology established as an initial stage in order to obtain first of all a reading, in the original spoken language, of the glyphs (Nahuatl in the case of the Aztec-Nahuatl manuscripts), before being in possession of the elements necessary to proceed to interpretation, which is then complete and valid, since it rests on a genuine reading of the text-images, written and painted at the same time.

In his *Tlacuilo*, Rio recognizes unambiguously that he is in agreement with my research, showing as it does that the Aztec system is a complete and genuine writing system. For the creation, gestation, and construction of his principal character, the *tlacuilo* evoked and described as the anonymous author of the codex forged by him, which becomes the center of his novel, Rio had to read and document himself in the

---

[p] The methodology and hypotheses to which Galarza refers might be seen in relation to the structuralist experiment (see the introduction in this volume); also, to the precision of language commented on by Swenson and Metz. The integrating of a hypothesis and a research project within a work of fiction, present as a corollary in *Tlacuilo*, is central in *Dreaming Jungles*. See Gould.

[q] André Leroi-Gourhan, the celebrated French anthropologist, is cited in *Trade Winds* and *Faux Pas*.

historical Mexican sources. Thus the reader finds references to Indian authors who have written in Nahuatl and Spanish historical chronicles of Indian and European life in New Spain in the sixteenth and seventeenth centuries. In this way we may come across the names of Tezozomoc and Chimalpahin, among others, in the novel. The latter author seems to have been his favorite. It is possible that it is his complex personality and his human and intellectual situation that drew Rio's interest. Chimalpahin is noble, refined, of great breadth of culture, knowing several languages: Nahuatl, Spanish, French, and Latin. Traditional Indian lore and accomplished European culture: these are the main qualities of Don Francisco de San Anton Muñon Chimalpahin Quauhtlehuanitzin, which make of him a man worth admiring, even in our own time. Rio finds him so interesting that he takes inspiration from him for his *tlacuilo*-character. But in the end, he does not quite seem to Rio to combine all the necessary conditions for becoming the genuine writer-painter character that he had conceived.

Michel Rio's knowledge of ancient Mexico comes by way of the *Codex Mendoza* (our basic model for constructing the *Dictionary of Aztec Glyphs*), in the extremely rare 1938 English edition by James Cooper Clark,[r] most of the volumes of which were destroyed in the Second World War, during the German bombing of London. Around the themes of the Mexican codices and Aztec writing, Rio quotes names known to the specialist, such as Bernardino de Sahagún, P. F. Velásquez, Angel María Garibay, Alfonso Caso, Robert Barlow, scholars from the sixteenth, nineteenth, and twentieth centuries. He also refers to the international academic institutions that now hold the best-known codices, such as the Bodleian Library in Oxford, the British Museum in London, the Bibliothèque Nationale in Paris, the Library of Congress in Washington, and the Museo Nacional in Mexico City. Among the great codices, he does not fail to name the *Florence Codex*, the *Mendoza Codex*, the *Lienzos de Chiepetlan*, and the *Doctrina christiana*, and even gives passages from Aztec poems translated into French, such as the *Chant de Huitzilopochtli* (Song of Huitzilopochtli), the hummingbird god of the Aztecs; all the while evoking the traditional musical instruments, the horizontal drum or *teponaztli*, and the stick-cowbell or *chicahuaztli*, both of which might find a place (why not?) in a mixed European band. And later on, speaking of

---

[r] James Cooper Clark, the anthropologist and author of *The Mexican Manuscript known as the Collection of Mendoza preserved in the Bodleian Library Oxford* (London: Waterloo & Sons, 1938), is cited in *Tlacuilo*.

the research carried out by Abraham Zemsz and myself, he explains my earliest attempts to draw up a method first, and a theory afterward, for Aztec writing as an open system, capable of transcribing any utterance in the Nahuatl language.[5] This is totally contrary to the ideas of Eduard Seler, who saw it as a set of academic rebuses that work to finite, nonproductive codes. Still more, Rio claims that he has seen in this an ideal ground for reflection on emergent iconology, particularly the free-ranging passages on semiotics, on the relation of word to image within the meaning of art; or, more generally, on the genesis of the transcription of thought.

Reading his sprightly, firsthand prose twenty years on, I find myself thinking that Michel Rio very nearly opted for the "image," before embarking on his brilliant career as a writer. And I wonder, might he have become a true "knower": a totally competent, systematic interpreter of the *tlacuilo*, and an outstanding teacher of the Aztec script?

And his research in this area: Could it be that research in such a field put off and delayed his literary output? It is not for me to say. But personally, without brushing aside his dream of logic, I prefer it when he transforms it into the anonymous *tlacuilo*, hidden, merely suggested, but so much there and alive through his personality, his work, and his thought; the whole transcribed thanks to a codex created by Rio himself.[†] His *Tlacuilo* has taken me on a long journey, on a refined and beautiful boat, toward a distant country that is my own. Irish music, which is a character on the journey far more than a part of the background, has flooded me with another reality-dream, and led me, by the presence of the Other, still more intensely toward the codices and the writing of the Aztecs, toward myself and my own native roots.

TRANSLATED FROM THE FRENCH BY GEORGE CRAIG.

---

[5] See Galarza, *Lienzos de Chiepetlan* (Mexico City: French Archaeological and Ethnological Mission in Mexico, Meso-American Studies, 1972); *Doctrina christiana*, with Aurore Monod Becquelin (Paris: Société d'Ethnographie, 1980); also, "Glyphes et attributs chrétiens dans les manuscrits pictographiques du seizième siècle," *Journal de la Société des américanistes*, new series 55, no. 1 (1966): 7–32, and "Prénoms et noms des lieux dans les manuscrits pictographiques mexicains," *Journal de la Société des américanistes*, new series 56, no. 2 (1967): 533–84.

[†] This codex created by Rio is in fact a perfect example of the intersection of knowledge and the imaginative, his dream of logic. On the dreamer and the logician in Rio, see the introduction in this volume and Arent Safir.

8

The Mind's I^a

Christian Metz

Nine novels to date.^{b} On each of their covers, underneath the title: "novel," an ancient, proud designation, now being revived. Three of them without narrator: *Parrot's Perch*, *Faux Pas*, and *The Uncertainty Principle*. A fourth, *Merlin*,^{c} presided over by an *I* (Merlin himself), but a historical *I*, safe behind a thousand distances; a Merovingian *I*, if history will allow me this incongruous mixture of Celt and Frank, in short an objectified *I*, far removed, it would seem, from that other world, oceanic and argumentative, which, taken together with various seductions and the splendor of the writing, has made me into a devotee, feverish and probably foolish, of the narratives of Michel Rio. But I come back for a moment to Merlin, for, of the Rio coloring, he does have the melancholy, so essential.^{d} The fineness of the writing, its natural and thoroughgoing distinction, show perhaps more clearly in him than anywhere else. Thus when King Arthur and Morgan, his baleful half sister, stand face-to-face:

---

^{a} Christian Metz's original essay was untitled. I have drawn this title from the substance and temper of his text. M.A.S.

^{b} On Rio's subsequent novels, see the editor's note and bibliography in this volume.

^{c} On *Parrot's Perch*, see Arent Safir, Ritter, and Rabaté. On *Faux Pas*, see Swenson and Rabaté. On *The Uncertainty Principle*, see the introduction in this volume, Ritter, and Swenson. On *Merlin*, see Arent Safir, Pastoureau, and Ritter.

^{d} On melancholy in Rio, see the introduction in this volume, Arent Safir, Pastoureau, Ritter, and Rabaté.

They gazed at each other. They were like day and night appearing together, and the splendor of the night cast in shadow that of the day. Morgan was smiling, but in the green gleam of her eyes I caught sight of something icy and deliberate, like the outward manifestation of an intelligence fallen prey to calculation. And I said to myself, looking at these two children of my mind, that God himself, in creating man, had not been exempt from lack of foresight. (*M*, 84–85)

Among the three works without narrator, *Faux Pas* is (arguably) an exception, for the character of the "unknown man" displays a number of features—natural elegance of body, courage, haughty moral tone—which, at some remove, and in a different light, might recall the "true narrators" (those who, unlike Merlin, are identificatory) who guide our steps through the five remaining novels; that is, in chronological order, *Melancholy North, Trade Winds, Dreaming Jungles, Archipelago*, and *Tlacuilo*.[e]

Total: five true *I*'s, one third-person *I* (Merlin), one *non-I* that perhaps flirts with *I* (*Faux Pas*), and two true *non-I*'s (*Parrot's Perch* and *The Uncertainty Principle*). Must I still, in 1993, forestall a possible (I hope impossible) misunderstanding over my "true *I*'s"? Well, they are those of the narrators, but they tell us nothing of the character and life of Michel Rio. I would not wish, lacking the talent, to do another *Against Sainte-Beuve*. But by making the move from an *I* who lives in a paper world to a Rio who (happily) is alive, we compound indiscretion with a strong dose of rashness, for we can never truly know a human being, so that the gangplanks we throw out, secured at one end only, are always fragile, even for someone who has more or less frequent dealings with the author from one day to the next. I shall not be venturing into the little game of allusions and other keys, even though the accident of a brief and cordial collaboration with Rio, some time ago, supplied me with certain pieces of information, which have nothing intimate about them, and which I am not going to discuss. The difficulty, in this matter, is always the same: it often happens that the narrator is a reflection, from certain angles, of the author; but one never knows which, nor how much, short of a detailed personal investigation that no talk of Lanson will rid of its nasty, police-inquiry smell.

---

[e] On *Melancholy North*, see Arent Safir and Rabaté. On *Trade Winds*, see Arent Safir. On *Dreaming Jungles*, see Gould and Arent Safir. On *Archipelago*, see Arent Safir and Swenson. On *Tlacuilo*, see Galarza.

On the other hand there is the information that the author himself gives us, of his own accord, through the play of connections and comparisons. Michel Rio's Breton origins, several times mentioned in blurbs, is referred to in passing in *Melancholy North*, in a few elegant and cautious words: "a land where a few roots of childhood still lay embedded" (*MN*, 41; see also 75).[f] In *Trade Winds* another childhood moment, in Madagascar, is evoked, very discreetly (three lines in all), and we know from the cover that on this point author and narrator are one (*TW*, 54). (But let us go no further: having a good knowledge of the Indian Ocean will not allow us to write *Trade Winds*, which is part of literature, not part of the Indian Ocean.) I continue. The narrator of *Tlacuilo* has a "literary vocation" (*Tl*, 87; see also 119), and has written three stories and five essays; one thinks, inevitably, of the stories published by Rio, and the five essays in iconological anthropology that he brought out in the 1992 volume *Dreams of Logic*.[g] The essays, among other things, bear on the status of pictographic writing systems, the relationship between image and writing, writing and language; and the whole plot of *Tlacuilo* turns on an Aztec codex (and its translator) that have to be saved. For these works, Rio was closely involved with Joaquín Galarza and Abraham Zemsz, particularly over the course of the journal *Communications*, and the names of these scholars appear at least twice in *Tlacuilo* (*Tl*, 40, 196) in support of an idea that runs right through the novel, the conception of Aztec writing as an open system, capable of recording anything, and even of inventing.[h] No need to stretch the list further. I merely wanted to show that the only indications about the life and person of Rio that can be found in his work are those that he himself supplies in published form, in one passage or in the relation between two passages. The rest—in this case the temptation to describe a Michel Rio modeled on his narrators—is mere color-supplement psychology.[i]

---

[f] On Rio's Breton origins, see Pastoureau and Galarza.

[g] On the stories, see the bibliography in this volume. On the essays and on *Dreams of Logic*, see the introduction in this volume and Galarza.

[h] On Aztec writing and on Rio's association with Galarza and Zemsz, see Galarza. See also, *Communications* 29, EHESS (1978).

[i] Pastoureau and Galarza both refer to details of Rio's life in their essays, but, like Metz, confine their comments to references brought into his works by the author himself. See Pastoureau and Galarza.

For some time now, these novels have been referring to each other, "reclaiming" characters, even lining up to form the makings of a chronology.[j] The great-uncle of the narrator of *Trade Winds* (1984), a rich eccentric who had put up the money for a twenty-volume bilingual encyclopedia that sold at twenty-five million for the set—there is, in Michel Rio, a near-permanent vein of humor: derisive, poker-faced, grandiloquent, schoolboyish, regal; this great-uncle, then, is the same who, in *Archipelago* (1987), finances, or, if we go back to the order of the fiction, had financed the highly expensive studies of the same narrator, then an adolescent, at the private Alexandra Hamilton establishment on the isle of Jersey. But it is not until 1992, with *Tlacuilo*, that the reappearances proliferate and ramify. They do not do so in the manner of Balzac (always mentioned in this connection), the hallmark of which is its creation of a world-effect. They remain, for all their now considerable number, separate, all length and no width, unconnected. As far as plot goes, this tale can be seen as the direct "sequel" of *Trade Winds*; it catches up word for word, as its first paragraph, the final paragraph of the earlier novel: not changing a single comma—a way of "saying" the connection without saying that it is one—but adding to the date ("5 August") one extra detail, "1980," the bearing and importance of which it is too early to measure, in an author still in full creative flow (*Tl*, 7). Whatever these may be, on 5 August 1980, the seafaring narrator returns from Sailaway Island, touches Rodriguez, in the Mascarene Islands, at Port-Mathurin, and from there sets out again, on a friend's boat, for the coast of Mexico via the Cape of Good Hope. But *Tlacuilo* is just as much a sequel to *Archipelago*, whose main characters it redeploys: the narrator (he is indeed the same again, the text says so); the boyhood friend from Hamilton School, Alan Stewart, now leader of the expedition; Leonard Wilde, ex-librarian of the school, misshapen, with touches of genius, whose love of knowledge has put him in jeopardy, and whom the two friends plan to save by their raid; and even the lovely Alexandra Hamilton herself (50), who, for the narrator at school, was lover for one day and mother for rather more than that.[k] Still in *Tlacuilo*, Alan's cousin, a figure of some magic, is called Laura Savile, like the Jane Savile of *Dreaming Jungles*, who led the English scientific research expedition to the African jungle; both are genuine "ladies" from Great Britain,

---

[j] See Arent Safir, note 19, p. 71.

[k] On Alexandra Hamilton and other women who are lovers and mothers or mother substitutes in Rio, see Arent Safir.

intelligent and calm, perfect in body, wholly untouched by the overlarded language of morality or feeling, but ready to give themselves boldly and generously, taking at need all the initiatives that will force matters to the next stage.[1] *Tlacuilo* also contains allusions of less import: mere touches. The Atlantic escapade in *Melancholy North* is mentioned in passing (*Tl*, 26), as is the character Brieuc de Goulven (50), the narrator's friend who had spoken out against this carefully planned piece of madness, while helping with the preparations for it as soon as he was convinced that his exhortations would be fruitless. Elsewhere, the crux of *Parrot's Perch*, the dangerous confusion of torture and rapture in the Catholic idea of redemption, makes a brief but unmistakable appearance in the course of a conversation (180). Alan, the school-friend, who is a British peer, is Duke of Camlann; Camlann, in *Merlin*, is the site of the decisive battle in which Mordred's treachery brings about the ruin of Logres and the Round Table. For that matter, the names of Guinevere (154) and Merlin himself (112) turn up in the novel in reference to something else, outside their context; mere reminders, minimal and taciturn. (But it is also the inclusive, unabridged utterance of the author, which, by its radical refusal of triviality, its unfailing nobility, sets off a kind of vibrant, highly worked silence.) To come back to *Tlacuilo*, one can make out in it something like a retrospective attempt, on the part of the author, at pulling together his entire work. But there is nothing very systematic about the venture; the touch is light, and the pulling together, no more than partial. We must await the future.[m] Meanwhile, this lack of forcefulness has its charms.

---

[1] On Jane Savile, see Gould and Arent Safir; for a different view of Laura Savile, see Arent Safir.

[m] To the list of names drawn up by Metz may be added that of Jérôme Avalon from *The Uncertainty Principle*, Jérôme being the first name of the aspiring young writer in Rio's play *Hound's-tooth Whale*, and Avalon the island exile of Morgan in *Merlin*. As to the "future," it is already on us with *Manhattan Terminus*, where the pattern Metz describes is carried further. *Manhattan Terminus* brings back the narrator of *Melancholy North*, *Trade Winds*, *Archipelago*, and *Tlacuilo*, as well as two figures central to *Archipelago* and *Tlacuilo*, Alan Stewart and Leonard Wilde. They reappear in New York, thirty years after their adventures at Hamilton School; the themes of *Merlin* centering on melancholy and death also recur here. On Rio rewriting Rio, see Arent Safir (note 19, p. 71); on rewriting in a wider sense, see Pastoureau, Rabaté, and Galarza. On *Manhattan Terminus*, see the introduction and editor's note in this volume.

Michel Rio has written stories for children.[n] And his novels—at any rate the five with narrator, as well as *Faux Pas*—have something childlike, adolescent about them. "Childlike" is not the same thing as "childish," almost its opposite, rather. In his stories, the unfailing firmness of style, and the permanent distance kept up by a highly distinctive kind of humor succeed in preserving, and passing on to the adult those blossomings of infancy and childhood, more or less discreetly advantageous, which as a rule do not survive changes of genre (*DJ*, 32, 61–62, 83–84; *Ar*, 7, 29–30; *Tl*, 17, 81, 100; the whole of *MN*, etc.); we might, reading hastily, find ourselves smiling at this *I* who makes sure we know all about his powerful frame, his great height, his outstanding gifts as a seaman, his sporting and intellectual feats, his daring, his charm, his quickness in battles of wits: the list is endless.[o] And then, with the exception of *Parrot's Perch* and *The Uncertainty Principle*, Rio's stories are all to some extent adventure stories. I shall not attempt a detailed count of all the features in them that seem to fit with a juvenile and stereotypical fantasy.[p]

For this fantasy is not what makes the novel. It is, true enough, like a lump of childhood that comes along and splashes the whole text, giving it the type of joy that is the mark of early life. (Michel Rio is extraordinarily invigorating, as if he were more alive than other people.) But this fantasy combines subtly with other elements—and it is the result that "is" at work—with a working on and in language that holds off immediate, naive appearances, and with a very odd kind of humor, an original variant of the deadpan the most certain effect of which is to throw the reader, who wonders if he is being gently mocked (not entirely false), or if he is being treated to the loftiest thoughts (that too) on facing death, on the desire for incest, the roots of morals or of writing, or even the "Big

---

[n] See the bibliography in this volume.

[o] Nor does *Manhattan Terminus* disappoint in this respect. The splendid Mary-Olivia Milton Ambrose, eyed hungrily by all the men in the 3 Ws Bar, sets her cap for the narrator. After a fistfight (during which the latter is complimented on his performance, "quite creditable for a writer"), Miss Milton Ambrose, the woman lusted after by everyone, calls the narrator, with gentle irony, her "hero," and says of her striptease act in which words and gestures were intensely alluring: ". . . I was thinking of you. I was doing it for you" (*MT*, 96, 98–99). The character Roger Rabbit, New York writer, critic, and guru, sums it up thus: "Your characters all have in common a certain elitism, mentally and very often physically, in no way sharing in the common human condition, which they ignore with superb nonchalance" (46).

[p] On Rio's juvenile fantasies, see Rabaté.

Bang" and the galaxies.[q] In *The Uncertainty Principle*, the astrophysical and interstellar pessimism that underlies the whole text is continually tempered by a sort of proper and unbending drollness, only ever expressed in the noblest of words, the most commendably philosophical of thoughts. In this work, so beautiful in the setting that frames it, in its two panels that fold over on each other like a book, in its contemplative, pagan atmosphere, every, or almost every sentence contains (*is*) its own parody: a tendency already perceptible in most of the earlier novels, and, here, reaching its provisional limit.[r] There is a touch of Brichot in Rio, but a Brichot without the fustian, the obtuseness, the bulk.

I want to take, from *Tlacuilo* (77 et seq.), one of those passages where our man seems to be taking things a little too far. It is a highly intellectual conversation, such as we might find anywhere in the novel, but this time by intercom (!), between Alan Stewart and the narrator, the latter at that same moment at the helm of a great sailing ship in the middle of a colossal storm (!!). Quite. Let us get our breath back. But how could we not see, from this very outrageousness, that the point is not to strip all meaning from what the friends have been saying, but to *stage* an impossible-possible, to squeeze all the pleasure from that, to apply a touch of doubt, gaiety or melancholy, something like a tiny, playful, and dreamy unreality, to the erudite thoughts that the narrator, at the same time, continues to be interested in, and to interest us in. (But I shall leave unexplored in this article the author's theories; my concern is with his art.[s]) Let us come back to the meritorious conversation in the storm: a little after it is over, Laura Savile says to the narrator:

> "I have listened to your whole conversation. . . . I was watching Alan. He was animated, no, more, actively engaged. At the most

---

[q] Metz is holding a master key when he associates, instead of dissociating, humor and knowledge in Rio's work. Indeed, with the notable exception of *Parrot's Perch*, humor has an important part to play in almost all the novels, and *Manhattan Terminus*, which Metz had not read, gives his thesis spectacular retrospective confirmation. A large part of the novel consists, precisely, of a "show" in which philosophy, biology, astrophysics, and metaphysics are illustrated by songs, dances, and striptease: that is, what Metz later calls "these conversations, at once ferociously serious and secretly amused."

[r] On parody—"every, or almost every sentence contains (*is*) its own parody"—and other aspects of this general tendency, see the discussion of doing and undoing in Arent Safir; also, of making and unmaking in Rabaté.

[s] For the author's theories, see the introduction in this volume.

eloquent moments, which were also the most aggressive, he seemed to be experiencing a sort of jubilation, a terrible urge to laugh mixed with the most affectionate expression. . . . It was, behind the disguise of rhetoric, an absolutely genuine exchange. . . ." (*TI*, 97–98)

There it is: I could not improve on that. Except by adding a related point: in Michel Rio, all the characters speak in the same way: cultured, eloquent, ironic, enviably assured. No attempt at realism, at "capturing" the different modes of expression. No question of hiding from us the fact that it is always the work that speaks. Or at least that what is there is a dream model, something made, in the wish that it might be harmonious and intricate, and not a reproduction of reality.[t]

In the course of another of those conversations, at once ferociously serious and secretly amused (this one taking place, just for a change, in the heart of the African jungle), the narrator says, among other things:

"A man who knows nothing is a wretched dreamer. At the very least his dream runs the risk of lacking the material precision necessary for it to become a work of art. . . ." (*DJ*, 51)[u]

Now the laughter has stopped: taken with the rest of the work, it is obvious that this sentence is of far-reaching importance. It is also, to my knowledge, of quite radical originality: everyone and anyone has said that the work of art is something made, a precise construct, and so forth, but I can think of no one who has argued its *material* precision. And it is true that in this respect there is something unique about the novels of Michel Rio: we are informed of the length and the width, to within a centimeter, of the canvas needed, in *Melancholy North*, to cover up and bind in safely

---

[t] The narrator of *Manhattan Terminus* says to Roger Rabbit that he considers realism to be not a mirror "but a decorative screen" (*MT*, 53), while a reflection by Rabbit corresponds to what Metz remarks: "But those dialogues of yours. . . . Nobody talks like that. . . ." (54). On Rio's "no attempt at realism," see the introduction in this volume and Swenson.

[u] *Material exactitude* is the term used in the published translation of *Dreamng Jungles*. For consistency with Metz's essay, I have preferred to use *material precision*.

the splintering hull. We are told, in *Trade Winds*, how Suzanne's house is built, beam by beam, and tenon by mortise; the assembling of the makeshift boat at the end is set out in the smallest detail: amount of zinc, to the nearest square centimeter, needed to make a hull, method of bending bamboo poles in order to give them the right oval curvature for planking, and so forth. In every novel, each time a house has any part to play, we are treated to its measurements, the number of its windows, front and side, the floor space of each of the rooms. All this in the technical terms (i.e., *the exact terms*), the craft terms (*carpenter, stonemason, . . .*), in an orgy of rare words that is nothing other—we forget this when what is at issue is manual labor—than a form of erudition.[v] And I shall say nothing, of course (though this also for want of firsthand knowledge), of the huge presence, in Rio, of the sea and the world of boats, something to which several of his novels owe a radiant beauty that seems to me to be on a par with the Anglo-American classics. The great breaker advancing like a black wall puts one in mind of Conrad, of course (I am baptizing him Anglo-American), but I am thinking of great seafaring literature as a whole, and, for me, Rio has a clear place in that.

I come back once more to material precision. Some, I realize, will wonder what use it is, and why a novel should be inflicting on us a sort of unsolicited specialized course. One example among others: what, in *Tlacuilo*, is the point of telling us in great detail about traditional Irish music and songs? (This time we have gone outside arts and crafts, but the point is that Michel Rio does not make that distinction, and that is something really appealing.) And then, whether we're looking at Gaelic traditions or joinery, nothing is more poetic than extreme precision,[w] and these passages, even for the nonexpert (like me), are as enjoyable as a dip in fresh water, or a brisk walk through changing countryside. The text teaches us a little of what it knows. Above all, obsessive, tireless exactness has something intoxicating about it; it belongs with drunkenness, with intellectual overstimulation; exactness makes you drunk, sets off a sort of merry stagger, an utterly charming tipsiness where the vague and the sharply defined intermingle, a high excitement comparable to that which grips us when lengthy calculations finally "come

---

[v] On all these manifestations of material precision, exact measurements, construction (terrestrial and maritime), and specialized vocabularies in Rio's descriptions, see Swenson.
[w] On poetry and precision and on knowledge as a necessary and constituent part of poetry, see the introduction in this volume and Swenson (especially the final paragraph).

out," and finish on a figure that we had already obtained independently. Precision is strong drink.

There have, of course, already been precise writers. There will be talk of Balzac, with his red Utrecht velvet armchairs and his mantelpieces with decorative wall clock above.[x] I shall be reminded that Proust used to harry his correspondents with questions on the exact shade of a piece of fabric, or the name of a flower. But they, and many others, were concerned with exactness in respect of aesthetic, socially valued objects (or else their opposites, as for example characters dressed in rags), but not when what was in question—what might have been in question—was the way in which one cuts a sheet of zinc if one has no oxyacetylene torch (*TW*, 105). There are, for that matter, exceptions, like the opening of *Lost Illusions* with all the facts about trades in the paper industry. But above all, Michel Rio's precision ("material," I have called it, after him), is not of the same kind as that of his forerunners: it is much more "manual," much closer to the material; a considerable innovation. Take this passage, again from *Trade Winds*, where the narrator, in coastal waters, goes off in search of objects that he had deliberately thrown overboard before his shipwreck:

> The difficulty that I had had in pushing the chests overboard, because of their weight, had made me overlook the question of whether or not they would sink to the bottom. Each chest had an external volume of 190 liters, and therefore, when immersed, displaced 190 kilograms of water. If it was obvious that two of them, containing the encyclopedias, the tinned food, the crockery and the weapons, went beyond that weight (although the difference could not have been more than some twenty kilograms), the third, which held the coils of hawsers and the tools, was much lighter, and the fourth, where I had stowed my papers, clothes and blankets, weighed hardly anything. I worked out that their total weight was 600 kilograms at the most, giving a displacement of 760 kilograms of water. But they were roped together. The whole thing floated. Therefore it was drifting. (59)

It is this "it was drifting" that will allow the narrator to recover, a little later, his four chests. And the distinguishing of these by content, the

---

[x] Indeed there is talk of Balzac. On Balzac, realism, or its absence in Rio, see Swenson; also, note *h*, p. 121 on *Manhattan Terminus*.

figures giving the relation of weight to volume, does not take the form of a disinterested evoking, a "description," but that of the calculations of a man of action wrestling with the physical world, any error in whose reasoning will have serious practical consequences. Some exactnesses are more exact than others, and the narrator (still that of *Trade Winds*) is not wrong to describe his own cast of mind as "a mixture of metaphysics and do-it-yourself handiwork," a temperament that is "contemplative and calculating" (100–01).

I have said nothing of the *metaphysical* and *contemplative side*, to pick up again terms rich in humor and appropriateness. But I shall come at it by talking about feeling. Or rather about one feeling, the one that presides over the whole of Michel Rio's work, and that gave its name to his first book: melancholy.[y] There are melancholic characters: Alan Stewart in *Tlacuilo*, Avalon in *The Uncertainty Principle*, the "unknown man" in *Faux Pas*, Merlin, of course. But not in quite the same way as the narrator, Avalon's melancholy being too purely cerebral, Alan's too Oedipal, and so on. As for the narrator's own, it is unconnected, or has no immediate connection with what the word usually denotes, what has been described (notably) by Melanie Klein, in the area of depression. On the contrary, what is at issue here is a feeling that accompanies violent action or deliberately hazardous ventures: the flarings up of will, alertness, weariness, effort; situations that set up death at their outer edge as a possibility that is both close and constant; or that allow a sense, running through the whole body bristling with fe r and courage, of the crushing power of nature, the inanimate world, faced by a consciousness that can think the All but is crushed by any one of its particles, and which, even without that, lasts infinitely less long than the mineral incapable of thinking it (Rio's ninth novel is entirely about this, by way of scientific notions about the beginning and the end of the world).[z] In *Archipelago*, the librarian says to the

---

[y] On melancholy, see the introduction in this volume, Arent Safir, Pastoureau, Ritter, and especially Rabaté.

[z] On the individual and the indifference of Nature, see Gould, Swenson, and Ritter. It is just this question, with the accompanying melancholy, which pervades *Manhattan Terminus* as well; see the editor's note in this volume. On "scientific notions about the beginning and the end of the world," see Ritter.

narrator: "All of this [i.e., the books that the boy has borrowed from the library] expresses a good deal of irony and pessimism and a melancholy attraction for the solitary freedom of the heights, or the abysses. Dreams of logic and the logic of dreams" (*Ar*, 67).[aa] There is also, then, a touch of misanthropy in the melancholy. (Rio's work contains hardly any ordinary men; it is peopled with exceptional beings.[bb]) In *Tlacuilo*:

> Having myself mildly psychotic tendencies held in check by a rigorous education, a general philosophy inherited more or less from the doctrine of the Porch, an introspective discipline of iron and some solid ruins of humanism, I had at once recognized. . . .
> (*Tl*, 166)

In *Dreaming Jungles*, at the moment when the narrator, a naturalist, having finished the solitary part of his African mission—long weeks in the jungle, amid difficulties and dangers that have tested and stirred him—is preparing to return to the base camp, a luxury hotel by comparison: "And it seemed to me, leaving this place, that I carried away with me, within me, forever, a trace of violence and solitude, the stamp of a permanent melancholy" (*DJ*, 102): the sentence is sumptuous.

As for the philosophical or scientific discussions between characters, which take up an important, an unusual space in the work, they touch on a range of problems, and reveal in the author an intellectual curiosity and a breadth of information that make of him, the author of nine fictional works, the very opposite of many of the defenders of "pure literature."[α] For if humor and a gamesome rhetoric, ironically amplifying these exchanges into versions of the medieval *disputatio*, combine to put into perspective the perorations of these admirably fluent contestants, the substance of the discourse remains, and Michel Rio never embarks on it without a great many weapons; weapons of knowledge, weapons of reflection. The subjects discussed are many, and some are classic: the anthropological prob-

---

[aa] This same quotation opens to a view of the dreamer and the logician in Arent Safir.
[bb] As for Rio's novels being peopled with exceptional beings, Roger Rabbit, speaking of the narrator's works, comments in *Manhattan Terminus*: ". . . these characters that live outside of the norm and beyond class, as one says of some particularly luxurious establishment 'in a class of its own'. . . ." (*MT*, 50). See note *o*, p. 166.
[α] On literature that aims at an intellectual utility (what I have called "elucidating fiction"), and Metz's other concerns in this section, see the introduction in this volume.

lem of intercultural borrowings or natural spread (in the case of disturbing resemblances), relationship between art and scientific truth, between literature and religion, exact nature of nonalphabetic writing, skepticism toward the human sciences and the society of intellectuals, powerlessness of law against crime, love as enigmatic exception to the universal law that might is right, the search for origins and therefore the join between legend and history, equality among men as a principle at once desirable and deceptive, and so forth;[dd] the list is far from complete, for it is obvious that there can be no question here of my going through all these debates by content. It is their status that interests me, since they appear in novels, and not in specialized works; and this highly distinctive status is unfailingly captivating. Basing himself on lines of solid, sometimes "state of the art" theoretical research, without denying himself the pleasure of drawing consequences that they have not yet come up with, combining them among themselves in groups or oppositions that might sometimes astound the researchers;[ee] mixing them in with reminders of the plot in hand, expressing them in relatively simple, sometimes very beautiful terms, Rio sets about making them yield, as one might a fruit for its juice, every last drop that is in them, sometimes unbeknownst even to their authors, of poetic philosophy, of practical philosophy if it comes to that, of fictional speculation held in suspension among the episodes of an invented story. The great discussions are always linked to the action, are always tightly bound up with it; the characters are eloquent soldiers of fortune, armor-plated with knowledge and bare of modesty, who could not endure not to raise to a higher level—that of a theorization that is pompous, amused, and relevant—the invariably very physical events in which they have just taken part. And so these long passages, which can seem caricaturally intellectual (and which, in one direction, do indeed aim at pastiche), are essentially playing the wholly original role of a *transformer*; they transform theory into something that can be consumed then and there, that is, out at sea, or in the tropical forest; into a comestible that fits in surprisingly well with surroundings little used to it, a product that prolongs the actions of the heroes, redoubles them, and finally becomes part of them. The reader, in his turn—at any rate if he likes the Rio manner, for I can sense possible exasperations: there is no avoiding diversity of temperaments, and the price of fraternities is enmities—the reader watches joyfully "coming

---

[dd] On these various subjects, see Gould, Pastoureau, Rabaté, and Galarza.

[ee] See Gould and Pastoureau.

back into life," in a precise situation, notions that he had forgotten or dismissed as unconnected to any particular experience. In a word, these passages transform theory into novelistic matter.[ff]

"The essential information in a real book is its writing, the rhythm of the syntax, and the musical coloring of its vocabulary" (*UP*, 75). This statement is not new or original; has not been so since literature first saw itself as its own domain (since Flaubert, say).[gg] But it is particularly appropriate in a work where the style stands out by its brilliance.[hh] Listen to the narrator of *Melancholy North*, when, finally back on land after long weeks of an unbelievable ordeal, he looks at himself in the mirror for the first time: "Recognizing only the curve of the nose, the height of the forehead, the fullness of the lips, it seemed to me that I was being gazed at from the mirror by a sort of Sea Father, his features painted in hardship, light, and salt" (*MN*, 119). Consider Father Joachim (*Parrot's Perch*), out of the hands of his Latin American torturers but permanently damaged, having lost his faith in God and in the word of Man, now staying in a French monastery:

> The sound of closing doors, of wooden benches that continued their creaking after the occupants had gone, the fading footsteps of a lay brother come to extinguish the tall tapers, the faint resonance of the arches among which the echo of prayers and song still moved—all that murmur of things little by little gave way to silence and conspired to increase Joachim's solitude. He lingered there, in a place abandoned by the spirit, where he

---

[ff] Metz touches here on one of the central preoccupations of the present collection. Gould in particular is responsive to this kind of transformation of theory into novelistic matter. On this subject, see the introduction in this volume and Gould, especially; also, Ritter and Galarza.

[gg] Flaubert is often named as being, after Hugo, one of Rio's favorite writers; see *Archipelago* (*Ar*, 67) and "Le rêveur et le logicien" (The Dreamer and the Logician), in *Dreams of Logic*, 71-72, quoted in the introduction in this volume. In the discussion on realism in *Manhattan Terminus*, both writers are to be found (*MT*, 51). See Swenson; also, note *h*, p. 121 and Rabaté.

[hh] On Rio's style, particularly in descriptions, see Swenson.

found nothing now but the tranquil bitterness, the bland oppression of a lost faith. (*PP*, 13)[ii]

And, from the same book, this astonishing description:

The banks of the waterway were shored up with mortared paving stones through which, here and there, poked a weed—an incomprehensible penetration of the solid by the fragile [these last nine words have Proustian overtones]. The canal had begun to silt up, too, and held a few densely packed beds of duckweed. It had the melancholy quality one associates with recently abandoned structures, straddling the line between the vulgarity of the functional and the nobility of ruin, between the moribund affirmation of its artificial character and its final submersion, by a kind of slow chromatic melding, into its natural surroundings. (47)

A storm, in *Trade Winds*:

A light flurry shook the halyards and made the lackluster water shiver. To the northeast a black wall appeared on the horizon, and came at me like a block of darkness crawling over the sea with I knew not what murderous haste. (*TW*, 37)

Same novel: knowing that the narrator is about to leave the island, Suzanne deliberately avoids showing herself, so as to cut short the tearful huddles of parting, what the novel puts as: "Iron generosity that set right the turmoil of love by the deliberations of dignity" (115); an expression worthy of Radiguet. This other, from *Dreaming Jungles*, also notably elegant, puts one in mind of the penetrating sharpness of the eighteenth-century novelists. Jane Savile is angry at her own fondness for the narrator:

"You make me vulnerable and scattered [*scattered* is admirable]. Every day you are more and more of a burden on my mind. It comes at the wrong time. I would like to free myself of you, in vain. You are an unwelcome emotion for me, a pleasure that drives me to despair." (*DJ*, 83–84)

[ii] On Joachim, his loss of faith and his melancholy, see Rabaté.

In *Archipelago*, Alan Stewart, whose feelings for the narrator are at the outset those of a rather vague and distant friendship, announces to him one fine day that he entertains toward his mother, Lady Stewart, violent feelings of love. Here is the narrator's reaction:

> At the same time, confusedly, I feared that this violent, abrupt discovery of a real being in place of an image, this dawn of a new sharing of mind and sensibility where the stakes were richer and more perilous, might also be an ending. (*Ar*, 50)

Another coloring, taken this time from *Tlacuilo*, when the text details a fashionable reception aboard a luxury yacht, at once pretentious, absurd, and vulgar:

> There were young men crazed by drugs, vacuity or spleen; heedless old men, dawdling bondsmen of the life of pleasure; noisy women. . . . (*Tl*, 116)

But let us come back to greater gravity by listening now to Merlin; Merlin who has outlived the world that he built:

> But I am well aware, I who only a little while ago built the mausoleum where now Arthur and Morgan sleep, brother and sister, at one and at peace after a long passion of love and hate, that it is an empty place, and that the fruit of the countless trees are falling and rotting on a desolate ground enriched in vain. . . . (*M*, 12)

And the same Merlin, in the very moment of the disaster at Camlann:

> When I arrived at Camlann, all was over.
> My horse advanced cautiously, with no small effort avoiding the bodies that lay there, pulling away abruptly when, amid this sea of dead flesh, something stirred, still animated by the last pains of life. This apocalypse, which marked my revisiting [he had retired in the interim] of a world of which I could see only the last remains, took me back to a genesis, another tramping through mounds of corpses, my first contact lost in the night of time with death in the mass [the battle of Isca, a mighty victory of the

Demetae over the Silurii]. I could hear the deep voice that I loved and hated of him whose law had finally prevailed: "There is only war, Merlin" [this was Merlin's grandfather, then king of the Demetae]. And in the bloody light of this dawn and that dusk, identical moments bounding the splendor of the short-lived, brilliant day that was the Round Table, I saw the memory and the harbinger of illimitable night. (132)

The passages of this kind, and there are many of them, have something Parnassian about them, with in addition a sort of intellectual sharpness that saves them from the blandness of decorativism. I draw a line there, since I cannot copy out all of my author's novels, in an act of piety of uncertain social usefulness.

How to define the astonishing power of this writing? In the first place, it is firmly linked to a structure that may be described as classical; never anything trivial, any trace of spoken language; total absence of passing fashions (no point in looking here for "feeling high," or "having a bad trip"), and on the other hand, extensive use (something nowadays out of the ordinary) of long-established terms. For the reader, willy-nilly accustomed to newspapers that talk to him of "delocalizings" or "turnover," a dip into a Michel Rio novel brings the abrupt, unlooked-for joy of hearing French again. Classic too (in a sense) is the loftiness of tone, a loftiness that is sometimes almost disdainful, which never leaves the text, whether in the (many) humorous passages, or, a fortiori, in the moments of high seriousness. Rio's syntax never seeks the deliberately odd; it remains within a scrupulous and permanent correctness. It is, I come back to this, the tone that is the hallmark of our man; a tone that has in it something aristocratic toward people, something modest toward things; ready to enjoy anything, and at the same time assiduous, almost zealous, when it comes to expounding an anthropological theory or explaining how to make a bow and arrows from a hazel branch and a piece of wire. In any event, seldom can refusal of the slovenly have been taken so far.

In another direction, Michel Rio breaks sharply with classical working practices. If the quarrel between Malherbe and Régnier were to start up again today (!), it would be long odds on his being on the side of Régnier, for all that he would deplore his sloppiness. On the side of Régnier, that is, of Desportes, that is, of the Pléiade, which wanted to enrich the French language by systematically bringing in new cohorts of terms, and especially the vernacular of the crafts. And this is exactly what

Rio does with his "material precision" that I have already commented on. We are treated to exhilarating terminological blasts: first and foremost, of course, seagoing terms, particularly copious (in themselves and in the text) and reminiscent of English novels, but also the vocabularies of the master mason or the master carpenter; the language of figures (there are calculations all over the place: it is a delight), of the tropical botanist and his zoologist colleague, of the Americanist-iconologist, and of a number of other little trades that I cannot remember. . . .* jj*

There. I have turned my subject around under several angles, in the vague hope of understanding it better. In doing so I have doubtless gone too fast and too slowly. I have said no more than what I felt. This ingenuous proceeding may perhaps be allowed a simple conclusion, namely, that Michel Rio is, in my view, one of the great writers of today.

TRANSLATED FROM THE FRENCH BY GEORGE CRAIG.

A Postscript to the Essay by Christian Metz

Christian Metz died on 6 September 1993, leaving behind this draft of his essay, written in July–August, untitled; an exceedingly acute view of the work of Michel Rio. He was the first to accept my invitation to take part in this interdisciplinary experiment, and I shall always be grateful to him for his open-mindedness and exceptional graciousness. I want also to express my gratitude to Michèle Lacoste for sending on to me this essay, the last that Christian Metz wrote.

Roland Barthes, who knew Christian Metz well, made him the subject of an essay entitled "To Learn and to Teach":

> There are perhaps two ways of avoiding mastery (is that not the stake today of all teaching, of any intellectual "role"?): either to produce a perforated, elliptical, drifting, skidding discourse; or, conversely, to load knowledge with an excess of clarity. This is the way chosen (savored?) by Metz.

---

jj On these specialized vocabularies, see Swenson especially, and Galarza.

And he goes on:

> Christian Metz is a marvelous didactician; when we read him, we know everything, as if we had learned it ourselves. The secret of this effectiveness is not difficult to find: when Metz teaches a piece of knowledge, a classification, a synthesis, when he explicates certain new concepts, he always demonstrates, by the didactic perfection of his utterance, that *he is teaching himself* what he is supposed to be communicating to others. His discourse—this is his characteristic, his idiolectal virtue—manages to unite two tenses: that of assimilation and that of exposition. Hence, we understand why the transparency of this discourse is not reductive: the (heteroclite) substance of knowledge is clarified before our eyes; what remains is neither a scheme nor a type, but rather a "solution" of the problem, briefly suspended before us solely so that we can traverse and inhabit it ourselves. Metz knows and invents many things, and these things he says very well: not by mastery, . . . but by *talent*: by this old word, I mean not some innate disposition but the artist's or scholar's happy submission to the effect he wants to produce, to the encounter he wants to provoke: even to the *transference* he thus accepts, lucidly, outside any scientific image-repertoire, as the very principle of writing.[1]

Christian Metz was Michel Rio's research director at the Ecole des hautes études en sciences sociales, and very clearly there is a kinship of mind between the two men:

> Anyone who knows Metz . . . is always struck by this paradox, which is merely apparent: a radical demand for precision and clarity generates a free, somehow dreamy tone . . . : here an *enraged* exactitude prevails. (Barthes, 176)

Barthes's words not only make the most eloquent of homages, but also reveal with perfect clarity why Christian Metz was an uncommon reader of Michel Rio, and why Michel Rio chose as research director Christian Metz.

M.A.S.

---

[1] Roland Barthes, "To Learn and to Teach," in *The Rustle of Language*, trans. Richard Howard (Berkeley and Los Angeles: University of California Press, 1989), 177–78.

APPENDICES

BIBLIOGRAPHY: MICHEL RIO

Novels

Mélancolie Nord (Melancholy North). Paris: Editions Balland, 1982.
    Paperback edition: Paris: Editions du Seuil, Points Roman, 1986.
    Athens: Zacharopoulos, 1996.
    Paris: Editions du Seuil, 1997.
    Santiago: Andrés Bello, 1998.
Le Perchoir du perroquet (Parrot's Perch). Paris: Editions Balland, 1983.
    Paperback edition: Paris: Editions du Seuil, Points Roman, 1987.
    New York: Harcourt, 1985.
    London: Dent Publishers, 1986.
    Barcelona: Muchnik Editores, 1988.
    Athens: Zacharopoulos, 1992.
    Paris: Editions du Seuil, 1997.
Alizés (Trade Winds). Paris: Editions Balland, 1984.
    Paperback edition: Paris: Editions Gallimard, Folio, 1987.
    Barcelona: Muchnik Editores, 1988.
    Berlin: Verlag Volk & Welt, 1991.
    Athens: Zacharopoulos, 1992.
    Paris: Editions du Seuil, 1997.
    Santiago: Andrés Bello (forthcoming).
Les Jungles pensives (Dreaming Jungles). Paris: Editions Balland, 1985.
    Paperback edition: Paris: Editions du Seuil, Points Roman, 1989.
    New York: Pantheon Books, 1987.
    Paris: Editions du Seuil, 1997.
Archipel (Archipelago). Paris: Editions du Seuil, 1987.
    Paperback edition: Paris: Editions du Seuil, Points Roman, 1989.
    New York: Pantheon Books, 1989.
    Zurich: Arche Verlag, 1989.
    Athens: Exantas, 1990.
    London: Quartet Books, 1990.

English paperback edition: Quartet Books, 1991.
Lisbon: Editorial Teorema, 1991.
Naples: Guida, 1993.
Rijswijk, Holland: Goosens, 1994.
Moscow: Inostrannaya Literatura, 1996.
Moscow: Vagrius, 1996.
Merlin. Paris: Editions du Seuil, 1989.
Paperback edition: Paris: Editions du Seuil, Points Roman, 1991.
Barcelona: Muchnik Editores, 1990.
Barcelona (Catalan): Editorial Empuries, 1990.
Lisbon: Editorial Teorema, 1990.
Copenhagen: Rosinante, 1990.
São Paulo: Paz e Terra, 1991.
Torino: Instar, 1994.
Athens: Zacharopoulos, 1994.
Madrid: Editorial Debate, 1995.
Moscow: Text, 1995.
Prague: Paseka, 1995.
Mexico City: Mortiz, 1995.
Amsterdam: Aristos, 1998.
Faux Pas. Paris: Editions du Seuil, 1991.
Paperback edition: Paris: Editions du Seuil, Points Roman, 1993.
Rijswijk, Holland: Goosens, 1992.
Lisbon: Editorial Teorema, 1992.
Berlin: Verlag Volk & Welt, 1992.
Tokyo: Hakusuisha, 1994.
Sofia: Atlantida, 1994.
Athens: Zacharopoulos, 1994.
Istanbul: Özgür, 1995.
Moscow: Vagrius, 1996.
Seoul: Book World, 1996.
Berlin: Ullstein, 1997.
Stockholm: Anamma (forthcoming).
Tlacuilo. Paris: Editions du Seuil, 1992.
Paperback edition: Paris: Editions du Seuil, Points Roman, 1994.
Lisbon: Editorial Teorema, 1994.
Seoul: Book World, 1996.
Le Principe d'incertitude (The Uncertainty Principle). Paris: Editions du Seuil, 1993.
Paperback edition: Paris: Editions du Seuil, Points Roman, 1995.
Madrid: Editorial Debate, 1994.
Istanbul: Özgür, 1995.
Seoul: Book World, 1996.

Lisbon: Editorial Teorema, 1997.
Prague: Paseka, 1997.
Santiago: Andrés Bello, 1997.
Manhattan Terminus. Paris: Editions du Seuil, 1995.
Paperback edition: Paris: Editions du Seuil, Points Roman, 1997.
Istanbul: Özgür, 1997.
São Paulo: José Olympio (forthcoming).
La Statue de la liberté (The Statue of Liberty). Paris: Editions du Seuil, 1997.
Madrid: Editorial Debate, 1997.
Athens: Polis (forthcoming).
La Mort (une enquête de Francis Malone) (The Death: An Investigation by Francis Malone). Paris: Editions du Seuil, 1998.
Vilnies: Alma Littera (forthcoming).

Other Publications

Essays

"Images and Words." *New Literary History*. University of Virginia. (1975).
*"Cadre, plan, lecture" (Frame, Shot, Reading). *Communications* 24. Paris: Ecole des hautes études en sciences sociales (1976).
*"Signe et figure" (Sign and Figure). *Communications* 29. Paris: Ecole des hautes études en sciences sociales (1978).
*"Le dit et le vu" (The Said and the Seen). *Communications* 29. Paris: Ecole des hautes études en sciences sociales (1978).
"Images sans Histoire" (Images without History) (with M. Préaud). *History of Art and Computer Sciences*. Proceedings of the International Colloquium at Pisa (1978).
*"L'essentiel et l'accessoire" (The Essential and the Accessory). *Quai Voltaire* 3. Paris: Editions Quai Voltaire (1991).
Rêve de logique: essais critiques (Dreams of Logic: Critical Essays). Paris: Editions du Seuil, 1992.
"Grâce au ciel, à Sokal et à ses pareils" (Thank Heaven, Sokal, and his Like). *Le Monde* (11 February 1997).

Children's Stories

La Petite Tomate (Little Tomato). Paris: Editions Nathan, 1973.
Vienna, Munich, Zurich: Breitschopf, 1974.
Athens: Cruse Penna, 1974.

---

* Reprinted in Michel Rio, *Rêve de logique: essais critiques*.

Les Petits Oeufs (The Little Eggs). Paris: Editions Nathan, 1973.
    Vienna, Munich, Zurich: Breitschopf, 1974.
    Athens: Cruse Penna, 1974.
Les Aventures des oiseaux-fruits (The Adventures of the Fruit-Birds). Paris: Editions
Deux Coqs d'Or, 1978.
    Paris: Editions du Seuil, 1995.
Les Polymorphes (The Polymorphs) (illustrated by the author). Paris: Editions
Polyprint, 1991.
    Rijswijk, Holland: Editions Elmar, 1992.
    Paris: Editions du Seuil, 1994.
Les Oiseaux-Fruits et le serpent de mer (The Fruit-Birds and the Sea Serpent). Paris:
Editions du Seuil, 1995.
Les Oiseaux-Fruits et les oiseaux-ferrailles (The Fruit-Birds and the Scrap-iron
Birds). Paris: Editions du Seuil, 1995.

Theater

l'Ouroboros (The Ouroboros). Paris: Editions Balland, 1985.
    Paris: Editions du Seuil, 1993.
Baleine pied-de-poule (Hound's-tooth Whale). Paris: Editions du Seuil, 1990.

On Michel Rio (selection)

Updike, John. "A Pair of Parrots." *The New Yorker* (22 July 1985): 87–90.
*Nadaud, Alain. "Le rêveur et le logicien" (interview with Michel Rio). *L'Infini*
    19. Paris: Editions Gallimard (summer 1987).
Andrews, Mark W. "Michel Rio: *Mélancolie nord, Le perchoir du perroquet, Alizés, Les
    jungles pensives." Phenomenological Inquiry*, vol. 11. The World Institute for
    Advanced Phenomenological Research and Learning (October 1987):
    157–65.
Schertenleib, Anne-Sylvie, under the direction of Prof. André Wyss. "Michel
    Rio, *Le perchoir du perroquet*: essai d'interprétation." Thesis. Université de
    Lausanne (1989).
Andrews, Mark W. "Nature and Civilization as Metaphor in Michel Rio's
    Dreaming Jungles." Analecta Husserliana, vol. 32. Kluwer Publishers (1990):
    149–56.
Prévost, Claude, and Jean-Claude Lebrun. "Michel Rio ou la leçon d'abîmes," in
    Nouveaux territoires romanesques. Paris: Messidor, Editions Sociales, 1990,
    203–20.
Chatelin, Caroline, under the direction of Prof. E. Baumgartner. "*Merlin* de
    Michel Rio: 'L'appropriation scandaleuse d'une grande légende.'" Thesis,
    Université de Paris III (1992).

Outzen, Vagn. "Rêve et logique dans l'univers romanesque de Michel Rio." University of Arhus. Arhus, Denmark (1993).

Savigneau, Josyane. "Le livre devient l'étouffoir de la littérature" (interview with Michel Rio). "*Le Monde* des livres." *Le Monde* (12 November 1993): 19, 26.

Gillain, Anne, and Martine Loufti. "Entretien avec Michel Rio." *French Review* 67, no. 5 (April 1994): 786-92.

Fricke, Alessandra, under the direction of Prof. M. A. Mingelgrun. "Michel Rio, écrivain de la mélancolie." Thesis, Université Libre de Bruxelles (1994).

International Colloquium: Literature and Philosophy in the Works of Michel Rio and J.M.G. Le Clézio. Paris: Université de Paris III (1995).

International Colloquium: "*Rémanences*": On the Reception of the Medieval Poetic Heritage in Contemporary Fiction (from Apollinaire to Michel Rio) and in Film. Paris: Ecole Normale Supérieure (1996).

INDEX OF PROPER NAMES
BY DISCIPLINE AND
BY NOVEL

The following is a list of proper names by discipline appearing by reference in Michel Rio's novels. Names are listed in alphabetical order, with first names being given only where they are needed for unambiguous identification; historical figures (kings, presidents, saints, etc.) and fictional characters are not listed. Brackets signal that the name is also listed under another discipline. The italicized initials following the name indicate in abbreviated form and in order of publication the novel(s) in which the name appears.

Natural Sciences/Mathematics

1. *mathematics*: d'Alembert *TW, MT*. Bernoulli *UP*. [Descartes *UP, MT*]. [Laplace *UP, MT*]. [Newton *TW, UP, MT*]. Poincaré *UP*. [Pythagoras *UP*]. Riemann *MT*.

2. *physics/astrophysics, astronomy, cosmology, chemistry*: Alfvén *UP*. Arnold *UP*. Carter *MT*. Chandrasekhar *MT*. Copernicus *TW*. [Democritus *TW, MT*]. Dirac *MT*. Dyson *TW, MT*. Einstein *TW, UP, MT*. Everett *MT*. Feynman *MT*. Galileo *TW, UP*. Hawking *UP, MT*. Heisenberg *UP, MT*. Hoyle *TW*. Hubble *TW*. Kepler *TW*. Kolmogorov *UP*. [Laplace *UP, MT*]. Lerner *UP*. [Lucretius *TW*]. Moser *UP*. [Newton *TW, UP, MT*]. Peratt *UP*. Planck *TW, MT*. Prigogine *UP, MT*. [Ptolemy *TW, M*]. Schrödinger *UP, MT*. Weinberg *MT*. Wheeler *MT*.

3. *naturalism, paleontology, biology, botany, medicine, cognitive sciences*: Bolk *MT*. Buffon *DJ*. Changeux *MT*. Darwin *DJ, UP, MT*. Dreyfus *MT*. Eccles

MT. S. J. Gould *MT*. Haeckel *MT*. Hippocrates *MT*. François Jacob *TW*. Johansen *DJ*. Lamarck *DJ*. La Mettrie *MT*. Mendel *DJ*. Monod *MT*. Weismann *DJ*.Winograd *MT*.
4. *geography*: Arago *DJ*. Clozel *DJ*. Marchand *DJ*. Monnier *DJ*. Monteil *DJ*. Palierne *TW*. [Ptolemy *TW, M*]. Quiquerez *DJ*. Segonzac *DJ*. Tavernost *DJ*.

Social Sciences/Philosophy

1. *history, archeology, history of art*: Alcock *FP*. Ata-Malik Juvaini *FP*. Bloch *Ar, FP*. Braudel *FP*. Chang *FP*. Chimalpahin *Tl*. Robert de Clari *FP*. Clarke *FP*. Dumézil *TW*. Gallay *FP*. Garibay *Tl*. Herckmans *Tl*. Josephus Flavius *FP*. Francastel *TW*. Leroi-Gourhan *TW, FP*. Panofsky *MN, TW*. Paszkiewicz *MN*. Préaud *MN, TW*. Ruskin *MT*. Sahagún *Tl*. Schapiro *TW*. Tezozomoc *Tl*. Veyne *FP*. Xenophon *M*. [Zemsz *MN, Tl*].
2. *anthropology, ethnology, sociology*: Barlow *Tl*. Caso *Tl*. Cooper Clark *Tl*. Galarza *MN, Tl*. Lévi-Strauss *TW*. Merleau-Ponty *MT*. Seler *Tl*. P.F. Velázquez *Tl*. [Zemsz *MN, Tl*].
3. *linguistics*: Benveniste *TW*. Chomsky *TW, MT*. Guillaume *TW*. Jacobson *MT*. Saussure *TW*.
4. *economy*: Keynes *TW*. [Marx *TW, UP*]. Ricardo *TW*. Samuelson *MT*. Say *TW*. Smith *TW*.
5. *philosophy, theology*: Alcmaeon *MT*. Anaxagoras *MT*. Aristotle *UP, MT*. Augustine *PP*. Bergson *MT*. Berkeley *Tl*. Davidson *MT*. [Descartes *UP, MT*]. [Democritus *TW, MT*]. [Diderot *MT*]. Diogenes *MT*. [Erasmus *Tl*]. Hegel *MT*. Heidegger *UP, MT*. Heraclitus *MT*. Holbach *MT*. Husserl *MT*. Jankélévitch *MT*. Kant *DJ, MT*. Machiavelli *Tl*. Malebranche *MT*. [Marx *TW, UP*]. Plato *MT*. [Pythagoras *UP*]. Rancé *PP*. Sartre *TW, MT*. Scheurer *TW*. Socrates *MT*. Spinoza *MT*.Thomas of Aquinas *PP*.Voragine *PP*.

Arts and Letters

1. *literature*: Anderson *TW*. d'Avenant *TW*. Apuleius *Ar*. Asturias *Tl*. Balzac *MT*. Borges *Tl*. Breton *MT*. Carroll *UP*. Cervantes *Ar, Tl*. Conrad *DJ, Ar*. Dante *PP*. de Quincey *Ar*. Déroulède *Tl*. [Diderot *Ar, MT*]. T.S. Eliot *MN*. [Erasmus *Tl*]. Fielding *DJ*. Flaubert *Ar, MT*. Gautier *Ar, Tl, MT*.

Goethe *MT*. Guillevic *MN*. Homer *Tl*. Horace *Tl*. Hugo *MN*, *DJ*, *Ar*, *Tl*, *MT*. Joyce *PP*, *Ar*. London *MN*, *DJ*, *Tl*. Lucan *M*. [Lucretius *TW*]. Benoit de Maillet a.k.a. Telliamed *DJ*. Malet *Ar*. Henry Miller *TW*. Milton *PP*. Gabriela Mistral *PP*. Molière *Tl*. Montherlant *MT*. Neruda *Tl*. Nerval *MN*. O'Casey *Tl*. Paz *Tl*. Poe *Ar*, *Tl*, *MT*. Rabelais *Tl*. Reyes *Tl*. Richardson *DJ*. Rousseau *Tl*. Sainte-Beuve *MT*. Shakespeare *Ar*, *Tl*. Simenon *UP*. Steinbeck *TW*. Sterne *DJ*, *Ar*. Stevenson *DJ*. Valle-Inclán *Tl*. Vasconcelos *Tl*. Voltaire *DJ*, *MT*. Wilde *MT*. Yourcenar *MN*.

2. *visual and plastic arts, architecture*: Taddeo di Bartolo *PP*. Bassano *Tl*. Baumgarten *MT*. Beuys *MT*. Blomaert *Tl*. Braque *TW*. Bruegel the Elder *PP*. Calder *TW*. Cézanne *Tl*. Chagall *TW*. Chirico *TW*. Dalí *TW*, *MT*. Duchamp *TW*. Feininger *TW*. Fujita *TW*. Gauguin *MT*. Gellée a.k.a. le Lorrain *Tl*. Giacometti *TW*. Guas *Tl*. Jordaens *Tl*. Kline *TW*. Lawrie *MT*. Lescot *Tl*: LeWitt *MT*. Magritte *TW*, *MT*. Manship *MT*. Mantegna *Tl*. Marcon *MT*. Marini *TW*. Michelangelo *Tl*. Moore *TW*. Palma the Younger *Tl*. Phidias *Tl*. Picasso *TW*, *MT*. Poliakoff *TW*. Pollock *TW*. Polyclitus *Tl*. Porcellis *Tl*. Praxiteles *Tl*. Philippe Rebuffet *TW*. Rembrandt *TW*, *Tl*. Riccio *Tl*. Rivera *MT*. Sansovino *Tl*. Sert *MT*. Sluter *Tl*. Soulages *TW*. Nicolas de Staël *TW*. Stoss *Tl*. Tintoretto *Tl*. Turner *Tl*. Van Bakel *MT*. Van Dongen *TW*. Van Ostade *Tl*. Veronese *Tl*. da Vinci *DJ*, *Ar*.

3. *music, choreography*:* Bach *MT*. Bartok *MT*. Beethoven *UP*. Bolden *MT*. Cage *MT*. Coleman *MT*. Coltrane *MT*. Davis *MT*. Ellington *MT*. Martha Graham *MT*. Hopkins *MT*. Andy (Irvine) *Tl*. John Lewis *MT*. Donal (Lunny) *Tl*. Monteverdi *MT*. Christy (Moore) *Tl*. John (Moynihan) *Tl*. Mozart *Tl*, *MT*. O'Carolan *Tl*. O'Cathain *Tl*. Liam (O'Flynn) *Tl*. de Pablo *MT*. Charlie Parker *MT*. Purcell *MT*. Rameau *Tl*, *MT*. Rousseau *Tl*. Salieri *Tl*. Schönberg *MT*. Shepp *MT*. Bessie Smith *MT*. Stockhausen *MT*. Mary-Lou Williams *MT*.

4. *cinema (directors), photography*: Aldrich *UP*. Capra *MT*. Cartier-Bresson *TW*. Chaplin *UP*. Curtiz *UP*. Disney *Ar*, *Tl*. Dmytryk *UP*. John Ford *MT*. Hawks *UP*. Terry Jones *MT*. Kazan *UP*. Keaton *UP*. Kubrick *UP*. Kurosawa *MT*. Fritz Lang *MT*. Mankiewicz *UP*, *MT*. Minelli *UP*. King Vidor *UP*. Wilder *UP*.

---

* The names in parentheses are those of the five members of the Irish music group Planxty. In Tlacuilo they appear as five musician brothers; their real first names are given but with the last name of "O'Casey."

CONTRIBUTORS

(Listed in the order of the essays)

STEPHEN JAY GOULD, Alexander Agassiz Professor of Zoology and Professor of Geology at Harvard University and Curator for Invertebrate Paleontology at Harvard's Museum of Comparative Zoology. Translated into all major languages, familiar to readers and television audiences around the globe, he is today's best-known author on paleontology, considered by many the successor to Thomas Huxley, the great nineteenth-century science writer. His books range from scholarly research in the field of evolutionary biology to volumes of essays taken from his column in *Natural History* magazine, "This View of Life." Among his major works for the general public are *Ever Since Darwin*; *The Panda's Thumb* (National Book Award); *The Mismeasure of Man*; *The Flamingo's Smile*; the international best-sellers *Wonderful Life* (Rhone Poulenc Science Book Prize) and *Bully for Brontosaurus*; the illustrated *Book of Life* (general editor); *Eight Little Piggies*; *Dinosaur in a Haystack*; and, most recently, *Full House* and *Questioning the Millennium*.

MARGERY ARENT SAFIR, Professor of Comparative Literature at The American University of Paris and senior member of the Sorbonne's Centre de Recherches Interuniversitaire sur les Champs Culturels en Amérique Latine (CRICCAL, Université de Paris III); Associate Director of the International School of Theory in the Humanities at Santiago de Compostela, Spain. Coauthor of *Earth Tones: The Poetry of Pablo Neruda* (with Manuel Durán); author of *A Woman of Letters*; general editor of the French edition of this collection, *Mélancolies du savoir*; translator from the

Spanish of Julio Cortázar's *Black the Ten* and from the French of Michel Rio's *Archipelago.* She is the author of articles in English, Spanish, and French on Latin American and general contemporary fiction and on literature and science in nineteenth- and twentieth-century Europe and the Americas.

MICHEL PASTOUREAU, Professor, Chair of History of Western Symbolics and Director of Studies at the Ecole pratique des hautes études (IVth section). A paleographic archivist, he is the author of more than twenty books and numerous articles. His early work focuses on the history of coats of arms, emblems, and related disciplines (heraldry, sigillography, numismatics, iconography), while his current research concerns the history of the relation between man and color, as well as the history of zoology and botany. Among his major books are *La vie quotidienne en France et en Angleterre du temps des chevaliers de la Table Ronde* (Daily Life in France and England at the Time of the Knights of the Round Table); *Traité d'héraldique* (A Study of Heraldry); *Armorial des chevaliers de la Table Ronde* (Heraldry of the Knights of the Round Table); *La France des Capétiens (987–1328)* (The France of the Capetians) and *La guerre de Cent ans (1328–1453)* (The Hundred Years War); *Figures et couleurs* (Forms and Colors); *L'étoffe du Diable* (The Devil's Fabric); and *The Bible and the Saints* (with Gaston Duchet-Suchaux).

JAMES RITTER, Director of History and Philosophy of Science, Department of Mathematics, Université de Paris VIII. Codirector of the collection *Histoires de science* (Histories of Science), published by Presses Universitaires de Vincennes. He is the translator of *Elie Cartan, Albert Einstein: Letters on Absolute Parallelism*, and the commentator for the unified theories, vol. 3, of *Albert Einstein: Oeuvres choisies* (Selected Works). He contributed two chapters to *Eléments d'histoire des sciences*, ed. Michel Serres (A History of Scientific Thought: Elements of a History of Science), and was coeditor and contributor to *Histoire des fractions* (History of Fractions) and coeditor of *Mathematical Europe*. He is the coauthor, with Bernard Vitrac, of "La pensée grecque et la pensée orientale" (Greek Thought and Oriental Thought) in *Les textes philosophiques*, vol. 4 of *l'Encyclopédie philosophique* (Encyclopedia of Philosophy). He is the author of articles on the history of relativity theory and cosmology, and the history of science in ancient Mesopotamia and Egypt. A member of the Organizing Committee for the Fourth International Conference on the

History of General Relativity (Berlin 1995), he is an editor of the proceedings (forthcoming 1998).

JAMES SWENSON, Assistant Professor of French, Rutgers University. After doctoral studies at Yale University, he taught at both The Johns Hopkins University and the University of California at Berkeley. He has translated several important works, among them Etienne Balibar's *Masses, Classes, Ideas* and Jacques Lacan's "Kant with Sade," published with his article "Annotations to 'Kant with Sade'" (*October*). He has recently completed a book entitled *On Jean-Jacques Rousseau as One of the First Authors of the French Revolution.*

JEAN-MICHEL RABATÉ, Marjorie Ernest Professor of English Literature at the University of Pennsylvania and Program Director at the Collège International de Philosophie in Paris. A renown expert on the works of James Joyce, among his major books are: *Joyce: Portrait de l'auteur en autre lecteur* (Joyce: Portrait of the Author as Another Reader); *James Joyce*; *Joyce Upon the Void*; and *James Joyce: Authorized Reader*. Other publications include *Language, Sexuality and Ideology in Ezra Pound's Cantos* and *Thomas Bernhard*. He has written as well on the aesthetics of modernism in *La Beauté amère* (The Bitter Beauty) and *La Pénultième est morte* (published in English as *Ghosts of Modernity*). He is editor of *Samuel Beckett: intertextualités et psychoanalyse* (Intertextualities and Psychoanalysis) and of *Beckett avant Beckett* (Beckett before Beckett), and translator from English into French of critical works by Gabriel Josipovici, Beryle Schlossman, Daniel Gunn, and Malcolm Bowie.

JOAQUÍN GALARZA, Director of Research at France's Centre National de la Recherche Scientifique (CNRS), and scientific consultant to the Department of American Studies and the laboratory of ethnology at the Musée de l'Homme. In his native Mexico, he is a member of the Centro de Investigaciones de Estudios Superiores de Antropología, the Archivo General de la Nación, and the Escuela Nacional de Antropología e Historia. He has also taught at the University of Chicago. One of the most distinguished living Americanists, dubbed the "Mexican Champollion," he has devoted his entire life to the study of Aztec writing and is the founder of the theory of Aztec pictograms as an open system of writing. Among his major publications: "Glyphes et attributs chrétiens dans les manuscrits pictographiques du XVIème siècle" (Glyphs and

Christian Attributes in the Pictographic Manuscripts of the XVIth Century), *Journal de la Société des Américanistes*; *Lienzos de* [of] *Chiepetlan*; *Héraldique européenne et manuscrits pictographiques mexicains* (European Heraldry and Mexican Pictographic Manuscripts); *Doctrina christiana* (with A. Monod Becquelin); *Códices mexicanos de la Biblioteca Nacional de París* (Mexican Codices of the National Library in Paris); and *Tlacuilo*.

CHRISTIAN METZ, (deceased). Director of Studies, Ecole des hautes études en sciences sociales. Secretary General of the Department of Semio-linguistics at the Collège de France (Claude Levi-Strauss's laboratory of social anthropology). He was the inventor of a new theory of signification in film, the principle of which he defines in "Le cinéma, langue ou language?" (The Cinema: Language or Language System?), *Communications* 4, and the founder of the semiology of cinema as a discipline. Known and studied worldwide as the author of books on semantics, semiology, theory of cinematographic language, and the relation between image and the written word, his field, Gérard Genette holds, was "an anthropology of language, in the largest possible sense." Among his major books and articles, translated into some twenty languages, are *Essais sur la signification au cinéma*, 2 vols. (Film Language: A Semiotics of the Cinema); *Langage et cinéma* (Language and Cinema); *Essais sémiotiques* (Semiological Essays); *Le Signifiant imaginaire. Psychanalyse et cinéma* (The Imaginary Signifier: Psychoanalysis and the Cinema); and *L'énonciation impersonnelle ou le site du film* (The Impersonal Enunciation, or the Site of Film). Professor Metz left a completed essay for this collection before his unexpected death in 1993. Published posthumously, it is his last known work.

TRANSLATORS: George Craig, Honorary Research Fellow, School of European Studies, University of Sussex, England; English translator of Christiane Olivier's *Jocasta's Children*; regular reviewer for *TLS* (*The Times Literary Supplement*). Daniel Gunn, Associate Professor, The American University of Paris; English translator of Daniel Pennac's *Reads Like a Novel*; author of *Psychoanalysis and Fiction* and of the novel *Almost You*.

INDEX

Action, 48; consciousness of, 145; consequences of, 110; and cosmology, 90; defining, 57; difference as, 68; and the dreamer/logician, 23, 24, 25, 47–48, 53–54, 69, 145; nature of, 48, 57; pedagogical, 51; as personal bond, 69; privileged sites of, 114; representation of, 110; subjects of, 112

Adaptation, 41, 42; and biological determinism, 43. *See also* Evolutionary theory

Aesthetics, 109–27

d'Alembert, Jean Le Rond, 94, 94*f*

Alfvén, Hannes, 14

Alterations, 1–4; affective position, 1; intellectual position, 1; physical, 1; of self, 2; in universe, 2

Altruism, 34, 36–40, 59, 68; and anthropomorphism, 36–37, 40; and culture, 36; and Darwinian theory, 39–42; and egoism, 40, 59, 68; as war, 68. *See also* Kin relation theory

Anachronism, 31, 34, 104*p*; and incongruity, 35–36; as literary device, 33, 41; themes of, 36

Anthropology, 14, 21, 36, 149–59; laws of transformation in, 5; literary perspectives, 149–59; mathematization of, 4–5; "sciencing" of, 4–5; social, 4

Anthropomorphism, 40*f*, 144*q*; psychological, 30, 129–48; refusal of, 43–44, 134

Apollinaire, Guillaume, 83, 83n10

Architecture, 109, 122; description of, 112, 115, 117, 118, 168–69; Platonic ideal of, 115; specialized vocabulary of, 113, 120

Aristotle, 14, 85

Arnold, Harold, 14

Art: and nature, 123–27; and science, 31, 44*h*, 45, _ 106, 173. *See also* Iconography; Image(s)

Artaud, Antonin, 140

Arthurian cycle, 53, 71, 77–87; Arthur (King) in, 78, 84, 86, 87, 103, 161, 176; and Bohort, 53; and Gaiwan, 80; and Guinevere, 53, 71, 80, 165; and history, 77–87; and incest, 53, 70, 71; and Lancelot, 53, 71, 80; and Lionel, 53; and Merlin, 24, 53, 70, 73–74, 77–87, 103–05, 161, 162, 165, 176; and Mordred, 53, 74, 84, 165; and Morgan, 24, 53, 71, 74, 85, 86, 103, 104, 105, 161, 162, 165*m*, 176; pedagogy in, 53, 71; and Uther-Pendragon, 80; versions of, 77–87; and Vivian, 53, 71

Asimov, Isaac, 16n35

Aspect, Alain, 1

Astronomy, 12, 103, 104. *See also* Astrophysics; Cosmology

Astrophysics, 15, 99, 101

Athena: as Mentor, 50, 53; as Venus, 53

Attenborough, David, 10

Autobiography, 84, 149, 149*a*,150–52, 163–64

Aztec writing: as form-sound system, 149–59; and *Chant de Huizilopochtli*, 158; and *Codex Mendoza*, 152, 158; and *Codex Tovar*, 149; and *Doctrina christiana*, 158, 159*s*; and *Florence Codex*, 158; images and drawings in, 150, 152, 144; and *Lienzos de Chiepetlan*, 158–59; and *tlacuilo*, 152–55; theories of, 149–59

Bach, Johann Sebastian, 15

Bacon, Francis, 140

Bal, Mieke, 116

Balzac, Honoré de, 111, 120, 121, 121*h*, 164, 170, 170*x*

Banville, John, 15, 15n29

Barlow, Robert, 158

Barrow, John D., 7

197

Barthes, Roland, 5, 22, 120n8, 136, 178, 179
Bartolo, Taddeo di, 22n46, 137, 151*e*
Beckett, Samuel, 142
Behavior: adaptive, 41, 42; altruistic, 37–40; biology of, 36, 37, 38, 39, 40; deterministic, 43; evolution of, 36; genetic sources of, 36, 37, 124*l*; human, 36, 37, 38, 39, 40, 44; and learning, 124*l*; patterning, 60; predispositions for, 41
Bentley, Richard, 93, 94
Bernoulli, Johann, 13–14
"Big Bang" theory, 8, 12, 100, 166–67
Biology, 14, 15, 21, 25; behavioral, 34; determinism in, 41, 43, 44; evolutionary, 37, 39; literary perspectives, 33–45; nature and nurture in, 42; relation to origins, 33–45. *See also* Darwinian theory; Evolutionary theory
Biochemistry, 12
Biophysics, 12
Biotechnology, 3
Blanc, Marcel, 38*e*
Bloch, Marc, 24, 143, 144, 144*g*, 143, 144, 144*q*, 145, 145*r*
Bogdanov, Grichka and Igor Bogdanov, 8n17
Bohm, David, 3n5
Bohr, Niels, 1, 12
Bolk, Louis, 42*g*
Borges, Jorge Luis, 17n36, 18, 18n41, 19, 20
de Boron, Robert, 81
Brentano, Clemens, 83
de Broglie, Louis, 12
il Bronzino, 73
Browning, Robert, 19
Buffon, Georges L.L., comte de, 11

Calvino, Italo, 17, 17n36
Cantor set theory, 18
Capra, Fritsjof, 8n17
Cardenal, Ernesto, 15
Carroll, Lewis, 9, 20
Caso, Alfonso, 158
Catholicism: baptism in, 63–64, 64n13, 67n17; martyrs of, 129–33; processing of pain in, 133; redemption in, 165; symbolism in, 64; visions of, 132, 133, 134
Cause: and accident, 144*p*; and effect, 2; elimination of, 22; in history, 143–44; in quantum theory, 1, 2, 9
Changeux, Jean-Pierre, 7
Chant de Huitzilopochtli. See Aztec writing
Chaos theory, 14, 15, 17n36, 18, 20

Chateaubriand, François, 111
Chimalpahin, Quauhtlehuanitzin (Don Francisco de San Anton Muñon), 153, 158
Chomsky, Noam, 5
Clarke, Samuel, 94
Clausius, Rudolf, 96
Codex Mendoza. See Aztec writing
Codex Tovar. See Aztec writing
Communications, 22n45, 150*b*, 151, 151*f*, 163, 163*h*
Conrad, Joseph, 169
Consciousness: of action, 145; beginning of, 16; imaginary in, 3–4; and morality, 43; and original sin, 69; perversion of, 69
Cooper Clark, James, 158, 158*r*
Copernicus, Nicholas, 3, 24, 74, 103, 104
Cortázar, Julio, 20
Cosmology, 8, 15, 31, 89–107; and action, 90; defining, 90, 91; evidence in, 91; history of, 89–101; as limit case, 90–92; literary perspectives, 89–107; and metaphor, 101–107; nonscientific writing in, 92–93; position within science, 90; relationship to community of physics, 92; relativistic, 100; renewal of interest in, 90–91; standards in, 91
Cousteau, Jacques, 10
Cramer, Peter, 68
Crick, Francis, 12
Culture: and altruism, 36; clash of, 154*m*; and ethnocentrism, 151, 153; general, 34; and nature, 31, 36, 43, 44*h*
Curtius, Ernst Robert, 123, 125n16
Cybernetics, 3

Dante, 17
Darwin, Charles, 14, 15, 36
Darwinian theory, 25, 36–40, 41, 43; and kin relation, 37, 38, 39, 41. *See also* Evolutionary theory
Davies, Paul, 2, 7, 8n17
Dawkins, Richard, 7
Death, 12–13; agents of, 66; and baptism, 63–64, 64n13, 67n17; contemplation of, 53; and cosmos, 90; and dreamer/logician, 48, 67; and freedom, 141; for ideas, 145; inevitability of, 90; killing of memory by, 137; knowledge of, 48, 58, 66, 67; and mother, 50; and natural law, 48, 67; negativity of, 146; opting for, 134, 141; reasons for, 30; and rebirth, 66; surviving, 154; of the universe, 96, 96*i*, 105
Debray-Genette, Raymonde, 123n13

Deconstruction, 5
Derrida, Jacques, 22, 22n44, 146n9
Descartes, René, 14
Description: aesthetic function of, 120n8; architectural, 109–27; autonomy of, 111, 118, 120n8; classical form of, 111; of construction, 113–15, 122, 123, 169; defining, 120; of description, 126; and determination, 120; and dialogue, 25; dimensions in, 113–14; in discourse, 110; endless, 121; exclusion of, 111; of gardens, 123–26; Homeric, 123; of image, 151e; integration into narrative time, 116; literary, 123; material precision in,168–69, 178; metaphorical force of, 115; movement of, 116; naturalization of, 111, 116; of nature, 123; nautical, 113–15, 122–23, 178; orientation of, 113, 114; and perception, 112; perspective of, 112, 113; recounting, 111; repetitive, 109; and representation, 110; specialized/technical vocabulary in, 113
Desportes, Philippe, 177
Determinism, 2; biological, 41–44; and Neo-Darwinism, 42–43; and racism, 41, 42; and sexism, 41, 42
Difference: action as, 68; life as, 68; in pedagogy, 61, 67. See also the Other
DiLillo, Don, 17n36
Dirac, Paul, 14
Discourse: of blasphemy, 69; of criticism, 5; descriptive, 109, 111, 112, 113–15, 115, 122–23, 127; of disorder, 107v, 147; division and narration in, 110; fictional, 110; free indirect, 116, 117; inducto-deductive, 90; intellectual, 22, 59–60; literary, 1, 11–18; and narrator, 118f, 118–19; philosophical, 142n; precision of, 117, 118, 119, 120; scientific, 142n
Doctrina christiana. See Aztec writing
Dreamer/logician, 44h, 58, 66–67, 79, 137f, 159t; and action, 23, 24, 25, 47–48, 53–54, 69, 145; and death, 48–67; and natural law, 48, 67
Ducrot, Oswald, 22
Dyson, Freeman, 7

Economics, 14
Eddington, Sir Arthur, 99
Egoism, 40, 59; and paradox, 68. See also Kin relation theory
Einstein, Albert, 1, 3, 10, 10n20, 12, 14, 98–99, 100, 106
Elijah, 82, 83, 86

Elucidating fiction, 17, 29, 172cc; ancient, 9. See also Literature
Entropy, 20, 96, 107, 141. See also Thermodynamics
Escalona, Enrique, 153
Ethology, 3
Ethnocentrism, 151, 153. See also Difference; the Other
Euclidean geometry, 2
Everett, Hugh, 1
Evolutionary theory, 15, 34, 34n1, 36, 37, 41, 42, 43; and biological determinism, 41–42; and Darwinian theory, 36–40; and neo–Darwinism, 42–43

Faith: and language, 69; loss of, 69; profession of, 69, 133; and torture, 137; ultimate act of, 137
Faye, Hervé, 97–98
Fermi, Enrico, 12
Fiction. See Elucidating fiction; Literature
Flaubert, Gustave, 23, 121h, 127, 138, 139, 174, 174gg
Florence Codex. See Aztec writing
Focalization, 115n6
Fossey, Diane, 36
Fractals, 20
Freud, Sigmund, 136, 147
Fuentes, Carlos, 12, 13, 16n35, 20, 21
Fukuyama, Francis, 146n9

Galarza, Joaquín, 163
Galdikis, Biruté, 36
Galileo, 14, 17, 96
Gamow, George, 100
Gardens, 123–26. See also Landscapes
Gardner, Martin, 7
Garibay, Angel María, 158
Gautier, Théophile, 23, 54n5, 127
Gender: adaptation, 50; confusion, 54, 56, 62; disguises, 72
Genetics, 3, 16, 36, 37, 38, 38e, 41
Genette, Gérard, 22, 110, 115n6, 121
Geocentrism, 24
Goldmann, Lucien, 22
Goodall, Jane, 36, 40, 41, 66m
Gould, Stephen Jay, 6, 7, 10n20, 30, 33a, 154l; rhetorical study of, 7n14,
Greimas, A., 22
Guilbaud, Georges, 5
Guitton, Jean, 8n17
Guinevere, 80, 165

Haeckel, Ernst, 42*g*
Haldane, J.B.S., 37–38, 40, 59, 59n10
Hamilton, W.D., 37, 59n10
Hamon, Philippe, 123n12
Han Yu, 19
Hawking, Stephen W., 7, 10, 14, 100
Hayles, N. Katherine, 18, 18n41, 19
Hegel, G.W.F., 122
Heidegger, Martin, 14
Heine, Heinrich, 83
Heisenberg, Werner, 1, 3, 12, 14, 20. *See also* Uncertainty principle
Heliocentrism, 24, 74, 103, 104
Hell, images of, 132, 133, 134
Helmholz, Hermann, 96
High energies theory, 100
History, 2, 14–15, 21, 23, 25, 30–31, 67, 68; Arthurian cycle and, 77–87; "causes" of, 143–45; of cosmology, 89–101; displacement of, 31; of evolutionary theory, 34; fictionalization of, 78; individual in, 2; intertextual, 31; Latinization of names, 80; legend and, 77–87, 173; literary perspectives, 77–87; and melancholy, 142; of nations, 68; and pedagogy, 30–31; rewriting of, 30, 165*m*; space and time in, 2; and structuralism, 22; teaching of, 15; transience of, 64; of the universe, 96, 100
History and Philosophy of Science, 6–11; relation in, 6, 25; rhetoric and language in, 7; and scientific popularization, 7–8
Hoffman, H., 5
Hoffmann, Roald, 16n35
Hofstadter, Douglas R., 7
Holland, John H., 7
Hoyle, Fred, 16n35
Hughes, Ted, 141
Hugo, Victor, 23, 111n4, 121*b*, 127, 174*gg*
Humanities: boundaries of, 19; language of, 7; "sciencing" of, 4, 5; and structuralism, 4–5
Humor, 167, 167*q*, 168. *See also* Irony; Parody
Hutton, James, 7
Hysteria, 135–37

Iconography, 81, 159; European, 151. *See also* Art; Image(s)
Illness, 62–63; discarding, 65; as equalizer, 62
Image(s): Aztec, 149, 150; baptismal, 64; birth, 57; central, 147; codified, 157; description of, 151*e*; European, 151, 155; of future, 2; God's, 134; of Hell, 132, 133, 134; and imaginary, 152; man's, 134; Meso-American, 151, 155,

156; mirror, 54; of mother, 55–58; of the Other, 151; of pedagogy, 57; pretext, 150; relation of frame to, 151*e*; relation of words to, 151, 159; scientific, 10; sexual, 57; of suffering, 134; text, 149, 151, 152, 154, 157; Western, 151; and writing, 151, 163
Imagination, 9; agony of, 133–34; distorted, 147; and the dreamer, 48; power of, 135, 136; in question, 141; ramblings of, 24; relation to knowledge, 4, 23, 30, 159*t*; of the survivor, 141; and synthetic argumentation, 49; Western, 129
Incest, 30, 47–76, 166; by surrogate, 53; as hubris, 72–75; and knowledge, 50, 51, 52, 53, 71, 72–74; and libraries, 48, 53; and pedagogy, 63, 70, 71; perverseness of, 49; "textual," 71n19, 164–65, 165*m*; variations on, 53
Incongruity, 35–36
Interdisciplinarity, 4, 6, 7, 11, 150, 153*i*; critical methodologies, 18–19, 30; dangers of, 19–20; divergences from, 18–21; expansive nature of, 19; in literary criticism, 18; restrictions in, 19
Intertextuality, 30–31, 71n19, 131, 145*r*, 164–65, 165*m*
Irony, 47, 78, 139, 172

Jacob, François, 5, 7
Jakobson, Roman, 4, 4n9, 5
Jastrow, Robert, 7, 8n17
Jean, Sir James, 99
Johannsen, W.L., 36
Jones, Steve, 7
Joyce, James, 3, 132, 133
Jungle: association with mother, 57n8, 66; extremes of, 44 57, 57n8; images of, 57; as pedagogical encounter, 66; scientific study in, 40–41; silence/solitude of, 66

Kafka, Franz, 3, 19
Kauffman, Stuart A., 7
Keynes, John Maynard, 14
Kierkegaard, Soren, 19
Kin selection theory, 33*a*, 37, 38, 39, 41, 59, 66, 66*n*, 68
Klein, Melanie, 171
Kojéve, Alexander, 146n9
Knowledge: accumulation of, 30; acquired, 65; affective, 66, 67; applied, 17; beyond knowledge, 17; of creation, 75; of death, 48, 58, 66, 67; and desire, 50; of diegetic space, 119; and "doing," 48; effect on individuals, 23;

empirical, 92; environment-shaping, 25; and
evil, 74; evolution of, 66; of foreignness, 68;
geographic, 17; and imagination, 4, 23, 30;
impact of, 105; interdisciplinary, 19;
intersection with imagination, 159*t*; and
isolation, 51, 53, 71; in literature, 23;
movement in, 48–49; mythology of, 9–10,
18–26; and paternity, 73; and poetics, 23,
169*w*; possession of, 49, 51, 53, 105; practical,
66; psychological, 17; relation to imagination,
23, 30; return to, 147; scales of, 66; scientific,
105; and seduction, 49; self, 68; of sex, 51, 58,
59, 75; sociological, 17; and solitude, 50;
specialized, 11, 154*k*; speculative, 17; technical,
17; temptation of, 73; theoretical, 66, 67;
transfer of, 49; and transgression, 72, 74, 75;
universal, 23, 51; use of "later" in literature,
33, 80; worship of, 72, 73

Lacan, Jacques, 147
Landscapes, natural and man-made, 109–27. *See
also* Gardens
Language: artifice in, 66; condemnation of, 138;
of description, 25; evolution, 65; fanciful, 9; of
feeling, 165; interdisciplinary translation of, 7;
and linguistics, 5; loss of faith in, 69; mathematical, 7, 12, 13; of morality, 165; Nahuatl,
151, 152, 153, 156, 157, 159; object, 5;
obliteration of, 140; and pain, 140; precision
of, 31, 157*p*; of reasoning, 25; scientific/
nonscientific, 6, 7; scientific study of, 4n9;
specialized, 31, 178*jj*; unlearning, 66; and
writing, 6, 163. *See also* Vocabulary; Writing
Laplace, Pierre-Simon, marquis de, 2, 14, 95, 95*j*,
97
Lautréamont, called comte de, 20
Law(s): evolution of, 66; natural, 48, 65, 66, 67,
68, 94, 126, 146; of physics, 20; of reason, 48;
societal, 66; state, 66, 68; of thermodynamics,
141; of transformation, 5; universal, 20; of
universal attraction, 93; of war, 68
Lecercle, Jean-Jacques, 20
Leclair, Tom, 15
Leibnitz, Gottfried, 20
Lemaître, Georges, 100
Lenau, Nikolaus, 83
Lerner, 14
Leroi-Gourhan, André, 157, 157*q*
Lessing, G.E., 110, 111, 122
Levi, Primo, 17n36
Lévi-Strauss, Claude, 4, 5

Levinas, Emmanuel, 134
Lewontin, Richard, 38*e*
Libraries, 3, 48, 53, 113–14, 114*d*; and incest, 48,
53
Lienzos de Chiepetlan. See Aztec writing
Lightman, Alan, 7, 16n35
Likeness, 54–57, 67, 67n17; and annihilation, 68;
propagation of, 68; in relations, 68; species, 68;
as stasis, 67; and survival, 68
Linguistics, 4; relation and function in, 4n9;
structuring force in, 5
Literature: anachronism and scientific theory in,
35–45; argumentation in, 17n36; Arthurian,
77–87; belief in, 82; biological perspectives,
33–45; causality in, 22; character introduction
in, 57–58; character reversal in, 62–63; construction of, 17; cosmological perspectives,
89–107; "difference" in, 61, 67; discourse of,
11–18; elucidating fiction, 17, 29, 172*cc*;
explication in, 17n36; exposure to mythologies of knowledge, 21; function subsumed
by science, 9–10; historical perspectives,
77–87; ideality in, 121*h*; incest in, 47–76;
influence of theories on, 21; intellectual utility
of, 17; interdisciplinarity in, 17–18, 18; ironic,
78; and knowledge, 23; knowledge of science
in, 24, 25; language evolution in, 65; militant,
78; as mother, 72; naturalism in, 121*h*; object
and frame in, 22n46; opposites in, 55; realist,
120, 121*h*; and religion, 173; Romantic, 82,
83; "sciencing" of, 5; settings in, 17n36;
specialization of, 19; and structuralism, 23;
style in, 106–07, 111; time in, 22; and
universal laws, 20; use of "later" knowledge
in, 33
Logician/dreamer. *See* Dreamer/logician
Loomis, Roger Sherman, 78n2
Longus, 124, 124n15
Loyola, Ignatius de, 132
Lyell, Charles, 7, 15

McElroy, Joseph, 15, 17n36
Mach, Ernst, 98
Malherbe, François de, 177
Manchette, Jean-Patrick, 143
Martín-Santos, Luis, 17n36
Marx, Karl, 14, 146n9
Material exactitude/precision, 168, 168*u*, 169,
169*v*, 178
Mathematics, 4–5, 14, 17n36, 25, 95, 101–02; as
language, 7, 12, 13

Matter, 3; animate in, 4; homogeneity of, 100; identity of, 105; indifference of, 104, 127; pain in, 133, 138
Meaning: affective, 55; "real," 55; scientific, 55
Mechanics. *See* Quantum theory
Media, popularization of science by, 10–11
Melancholy, 47, 53, 161, 161*d*, 171, 171*y*, 172, 175; as alternative to movement, 68; and hysteria, 135–37; of individuals, 142*m*; permanent, 172; persistent, 134; ultimate, 137
Mentor, 49; Athena disguised as, 50, 53; and Telemachus, 50
Mentors. *See* Pedagogy
Merlin. *See* Arthurian cycle
Metalanguage, 5, 22, 65
Metaphor, 6; and cosmology, 31, 89–107, 101–07; creation of, 102; dangers of, 101; of despair, 105; function of, 14; inexactitude of, 101; in narration, 14; neo-Platonic, 103; for pain, 139; recourse to, 101; reworking of, 102; struggle against, 106
Metaphysics, 10, 30, 102, 133, 171
Metz, Christian, 22, 149*a*, 178–79
Mill, John Stuart, 6
Mishima, Yukio, 129
Monod, Jacques, 7
Molière, 8
Morality, 2, 40, 41, 133, 146. *See also* Altruism; and consciousness, 43; language of, 165
Morazé, Charles, 22
Morgan. *See* Arthurian cycle
Mosley, Nicholas, 14, 14n26
Mother: associations with jungle, 57n8; associations with the sea, 57n8, 63; disguises of, 50, 73; as forbidden woman, 49, 50, 52; images of, 55–58; jungle as, 66; knowledge witheld by, 75; and libraries, 50, 53; links to death, 50; literature as, 72; as *Mater Sapientiae*, 50, 73; and pedagogy, 49; sexual desire for, 51, 52, 53, 70–71; substitutes, 51, 164*k*; as utopia, 75
Murdock, G.P., 4
Murray, Alexander, 64
Mythology: explanatory, 23; of knowledge, 9–10, 18–26; of man and universe, 23; science as, 9

Nahuatl. *See* Language
Narration: in discourse, 110; first–person, 118–19, 119*f*, 127, 143*o*, 161–78; and gender confusion, 54; metaphor in, 14; naturalization of description in, 111, 116; temporal

succession of events in, 110; third-person, 143*o*, 161, 162, 163
Naturalism, 121*h*
Naturalist: and biologist, 59
Natural philosophy. *See* Philosophy
Natural sciences. *See* Science
Natural selection. *See* Darwinian theory
Neo-Darwinism, 42, 43; and "modern synthetic theory," 43. *See also* Evolutionary theory
Newton, Sir Isaac, 2, 3, 14, 93, 94, 95, 96
Nietzsche, Friedrich, 146, 146n9
Nihilism, 131, 133, 135
Nothingness, 131, 133, 135, 136, 137, 147
Novarina, Valère, 138

Obsession, 47, 48; with order, 107*v*
Oppenheimer, J. Robert, 12
Opposition, binary, 22, 23; action in, 48
the Other, 138, 151, 154*m*. *See also* Difference
Order: of interior spaces, 115, 118; and disorder, 107, 107*v*, 124–26; in landscapes, 124–26; obsession with, 107*v*

Pain: external/internal simultaneity, 139, 140; infliction of, 140; and language, 140; in matter, 133, 138; perception of, 139; reification of, 140; resistance to, 140; sources of, 140. *See also* Torture
Paleontology, 12, 15
Panofsky, Erwin, 155–56
Panoramix, 82, 83
Paradox: and egoism, 68; of experimental evidence, 9
Parody, 167, 167*r*
Parra, Nicanor, 17n36
Pauli, Wolfgang, 12
Pauling, Linus, 12
Pedagogy: and action, 51; difference in, 61, 67; dynamic of, 48–49, 51; and history, 30–31; images of, 57; and incest, 63, 70, 71; and lovers, 51–53, 55–61, 70; and mother, 49, 70–71; and personal relationships, 48; possession of, 51–52; and tutors, 50, 51–52, 70–71; schema of, 68; vocabulary of, 57n8
Penrose, Roger, 7
Perversity: "kinetic," 49; creation/"de-creation" (doing/undoing), 49, 69, 141*j*; and unmaking, 137–42, in original sin, 134; principle, 137
Pessimism, 47, 167, 172
Philosophy, 14; moral, 41; natural, vii, 11; poetic, 173; practical, 173

Physics, 14, 21, 25; conceptual changes in, 12;
   metaphor in, 101; new, 1, 2, 4, 12, 91;
   Newtonian, 2, 95, 95j; old, 2; quantum, 1, 2,
   2n2, 8–9, 16; universal laws of, 20. *See also*
   Astrophysics; Cosmology
Piaget, Jean, 5
Pinker, Steven, 7
Planck, Max, 3, 12
Plato, 49
Playfair, John, 7
the Pléiade, 177
Poe, Edgar Allan, 5, 15, 49
Poetics, 23, 24, 110, 111, 169w
Poincaré, Jules Henri, 14
Polkinghorne, John C., 8n17
Poststructuralism, 5
Powers, Richard, 15–16, 19
Predictability, 1, 2; in Newtonian physics, 2; in
   quantum mechanics, 2, 9. *See also* Cause;
   Quantum theory
Prigogine, Ilya, 14
Probability. *See* Predictability; Quantum theory
Prochiantz, Alain, 7
Proust, Marcel, 3, 169, 170
Ptolemy, 103
Pynchon, Thomas, 17n36, 18
Pythagorus, 14

Quantum theory, 1, 2, 2n2, 8–9; measurement
   in, 1, 2; and nonlocality, 1, 14; and uncertainty
   principle, 1, 12–13; in literature, 11–16
Queneau, Raymond, 17n36

Racism, 41, 42, 42g
Rankine, William, 96
Realism, 120, 121, 121h, 168t, 170x; absence of,
   120, 127q, 168; in description, 120, 127; in
   dialogue, 25; false, 136
Reality: influencing, 2; multiple, 1; physical, 2;
   and quantum theory, 2–3
Reductionism, 18, 43
Reeves, Hubert, 7
Régnier, Mathurin, 177
Regnier-Bohler, Danielle, 78n2
Relativity theory, 2, 15, 98, 99, 100
Representation: of action, 110; and description,
   110; support for, 110
Resistance, 136, 140
Rhetoric, 7. *See also* Writing
Rio, Michel: absence of realism in, 127q;
   aesthetic perspectives, 109–27; anachronism

in, 34; anthropological perspective on,
149–59; and *Archipelago* (*Archipel*), 23, 47,
48–49, 49, 51, 53, 70, 72, 96i, 109, 115, 118,
119, 122, 147, 147u, 149a, 153i, 154m, 162,
164, 171–72, 176; autobiographical functions,
84, 85; and binary opposition, 22, 23, 48;
biological perspectives on, 33–45; concern
with order, 107v; cosmological perspectives
on, 89–107; and *The Death: An Investigation by
Francis Malone* (*La Mort: une enquête de Francis
Malone*), 29; descriptive discourse of, 111;
dreamer/ logician pair in, 25, 44h, 47, 48,
53–54, 58, 66, 79, 159t; and *Dreaming Jungles*
(*Les Jungles pensives*), 33a, 34–45, 48–49,
54–69, 72, 104p, 154l, 154m, 162, 172, 175;
and *Dreams of Logic: Critical Essays* (*Rêve de
logique: essais critiques*), 48, 150, 151e, 163; and
Faux Pas, 3, 109, 115–16, 122, 124, 126, 135,
142, 143, 143o, 145r, 146, 147, 154m, 161,
166; historical perspectives on, 77–87; and
Hound's-tooth Whale (*Baleine pied-de-poule*),
70–71, 71n19, 165m; incestual concerns of,
47–76; interdisciplinary criticism of, 21–25;
109–27, 129–48; intertextuality in, 131b;
literary rewriting, 79d, 142, 153i, 165m;
literary style, 106–107, 111, 111n4, 174hh; and
Manhattan Terminus, 25, 33a, 42g, 51f, 52g,
71n19, 71w, 71x, 96i, 113c, 114d, 119f, 121h,
126p, 127q, 142l, 147u, 149a, 153i, 165m,
166o, 168t, 172bb; and *Melancholy North*
(*Mélancolie Nord*), 48–49, 50, 51, 69–70, 72,
103, 113–15, 119f, 122, 134–35, 141, 142,
147, 149a, 162, 163, 165m, 166, 168, 174; and
Merlin, 24, 48–49, 53, 70, 71, 71n19, 72–75,
77–87, 103, 126p, 147u, 161, 165, 165m,
176–77; as methodological test case, 21–25;
novelistic theory of, 23–25; and *The Ouroboros*
(*L'Ouroboros*), 71n19; and *Parrot's Perch* (*Le
Perchoir du perroquet*), 49, 50, 69, 96i, 103, 105,
130, 135, 138, 139, 142, 142o, 145r, 151e, 161,
162, 166, 174; pedagogy in, 47–76; personal
relations in, 48, 55, 69, 75; precision of,
168–70; relation to history, 142m; role of
narrator, 118f, 118–19; structuralism of, 22;
and *The Statue of Liberty* (*La Statue de la
liberté*), 29; and *Tlacuilo*, 47, 52g, 71n19, 71w,
96i, 113–15, 119f, 122, 142l, 149–59, 163,
164, 165m, 167, 169, 171, 172, 176; and *Trade
Winds* (*Alizés*), 47n1, 49, 51, 70, 71n19, 72,
77, 113–15, 119f, 122, 154m, 162, 163, 164,
165m, 169, 170, 175; and *The Uncertainty*

Principle (*Le Principe d'incertitude*), 12–13, 71n19, 96i, 102, 109, 112–14, 117, 122, 124, 161, 162, 165m, 166, 167, 171, 174; use of logic, 22; use of scientific theory, 12–14, 33–45, 59–60, 79–80, 85, 89–90, 95–96, 102–07, 157, 157p, 158, 166

Robbe-Grillet, Alain, 142

Ross, Hugh, 8n17

Roubaud, Jacques, 17n36

Rousseau, Jean-Jacques, 111, 124, 124n15

Russell, Bertrand, 3

Rutherford, Ernest, Lord, 12

Sagan, Carl, 7, 10

Sahagún, Bernardino de, 158

Saint James Intercisus, 129, 130

Saint Sebastian, 129

Saint Thomas Aquinas, 132

Sarduy, Severo, 17n36

Saussure, Ferdinand de, 4, 4n9

Scarry, Elaine, 139

Schlegel, F., 83

Schrödinger, Erwin, 1, 14

Science: and art, 79g, 106; boundary disputes in, 91; commercialization of, 10; in culture, 9–11; and God, 8–9, 12, 13, 100; in literature, 11–17, 29–30; influence on literature, 20, 25–26; and mass media, 10; as mythology of knowledge, 9–10, 18–26; natural, vii, 4, 14, 17; new, 95, 96; objectivity of, 6; paradox in, 9; popularization of, 7–11, 92–93, 95, 97; position of cosmology in, 90; social, vii, 4, 7, 14, 17; social impact of, 89; specialization in, 11; and speculation, 8–9, 11, 13, 17, 29–30, 99; "translation" of, 7, 25–26; truth in, 30; and uniformitarianism debate, 7; writer and, 3; writing in, 7–8. *See also* specific disciplines and theories

Scott, Walter, 83, 83n9

Seler, Eduard, 156, 159

Semiotics, 159, 161–78

Shakespeare, William, 33

Socrates, 49

Sontag, Susan, 62

Sophocles, 140, 147

Space: in cosmology, 8; descriptive, 116, 126; diegetic, 119; elastic, 2; and emptiness, 114, 114e; exploration of, 127; indifference of, 127; interior, 124; knowledge of, 119; organization of, 115, 118; sizes of, 114, 127

Spariosu, Mihai, 18n39

Speculation, 17n36; and scientists 8–9, 11, 13, 17, 29–30, 99

Stendhal, 109

Stengers, Isabelle, 7

Structuralism, 4, 4n9, 6, 7, 17n36, 18, 22, 157p; and Ecole des hautes études en sciences sociales (EHESS), 21–22; history, 22; impact on literature, 23; as method, 4; residue of, 5–8

Style. *See* Writing

Suffering: cult of, 130; redemptive force of, 131

Suicide, 69, 105, 130, 136, 142, 143o, 147u

Swift, Graham, 14–15

Swinburne, Algernon Charles, 98n5

Teilhard de Chardin, Pierre, 134

Telemachus, 49, 50

Tennyson, Alfred Lord, 83

Tezozomoc, 153, 158

Theories. *See* specific name; cosmological consequences of, 94; data in, 91, 102; influence on literature, 21; instability of, 9; revisions of, 34n1; role of language in, 6–7; transformation into novelistic matter, 174ff

Thermodynamics, 15, 20, 95, 96, 100. *See also* Entropy

Tieck, Ludwig, 83

Thrinh, Xuan Thuan, 8n17

Thomas, Lewis, 7

Thomson, William (Lord Kelvin), 96

Time: arrow of, vii, 33; in cosmology, 8; elastic, 2; geological, 64; in literature, 22; narrative, 116; out of, 154l; sense of order in, 33; structure of, 99; universal, 2. *See also* Anachronism; Relativity theory

the *tlacuilo*. *See* Aztec writing

Todorov, Tzvetan, 22, 22n44

Torture, 130, 131, 133, 135, 136, 140, 147, 165; dialectical structure of, 139; and perception of pain, 139; refuge from, 140; universality of, 138; and unmaking, 137–42

Transformation, syntax of, 22

Transgression, 72; cosmological, 93; intellectual, 74; and knowledge, 74, 75; sexual, 74

Troyes, Chrétien de, 78, 79

Tutors. *See* Pedagogy

Uhland, Johann Ludwig, 83

Uncertainty principle, 1, 12–13. *See also* Quantum theory

Universe(s): age of, 96; alterations in, 2; "Big Bang," 100; boundaries of, 98–99;

cosmological study of, 90–91; deuterium in, 100; distribution of matter in, 92; expansion of, 91–92, 99; fate of, 96, 96*i*, 105; galaxies in, 99; history of, 96, 100; infinite size of, 94; justification for, 44; light elements in, 92; limits of, 141; material, 8; measurement in, 92, 100; microwave radiation in, 92, 100; origins of, 30, 98, 100; parallel, 1; rewriting, 31, 89–107; study of, 90; totality of, 44; as a whole, 90, 91, 92, 101. *See also* Cosmology
Updike, John, 11, 12, 12n23, 121*h*
Utopia, 75

Vernant, Jean-Pierre, 22
Velásquez, Primo Feliciano, 158
Vincent, Jean-Didier, 7, 8n15, 9
Vinci, Leonardo da, 9, 155
Voragine, Jacobus de, 129–30
Vocabulary: precision of, 113–17, 120, 127, 168–71; specialized/technical, 23–24, 113, 150, 178. *See also* Writing

Wagner, Richard, 33
War, 68
Weinberg, Steven, 7
Weismann, August, 43
Whewell, William, 6
Wieland, Christoph Martin, 83
Wilson, Edward O., 7
Wittgenstein, Ludwig, 14, 101n7
Writing: and image, 163; and language, 163; mathematical, 7, 12, 12; Meso-American, 149–59, 163; nonalphabetic, 173; nonexistence of, 156; pictographic, 156, 163; research in, 156–57; science, 7–8; style, 174–78; systems, 163

Zemsz, Abraham, 149, 149*a*, 150, 155, 156, 159, 163
Zeno, 19
Zola, Emile, 111, 120, 121, 121n9